Getting
Mentored
in Graduate School

Getting
Mentored
in Graduate School

W. Brad Johnson and Jennifer M. Huwe

American Psychological Association
Washington, DC

Second Printing, August 2014

Published by
American Psychological Association
750 First Street, NE
Washington, DC 20002
www.apa.org

To order
APA Order Department
P.O. Box 92984
Washington, DC 20090-2984
Tel: (800) 374-2721; Direct: (202) 336-5510
Fax: (202) 336-5502; TDD/TTY: (202) 336-6123
Online: www.apa.org/books/
Email: order@apa.org

In the U.K., Europe, Africa, and the Middle East, copies may be ordered from
American Psychological Association
3 Henrietta Street
Covent Garden, London
WC2E 8LU England

Typeset in Meridien by EPS Group Inc., Easton, MD

Printer: Edwards Brothers Malloy
Cover Designer: Naylor Design, Washington, DC
Technical/Production Editor: Jennifer L. Zale

The opinions and statements published are the responsibility of the authors, and such opinions and statements do not necessarily represent the policies of the American Psychological Association.

Library of Congress Cataloging-in-Publication Data
Johnson, W. Brad.
    Getting mentored in graduate school / W. Brad Johnson and Jennifer M. Huwe.—1st ed.
        p. cm.
Includes bibliographical references and index.
    ISBN 1-55798-975-3 (alk. paper)
    1. Graduate students—Handbooks, manuals, etc.   2. Faculty advisors—Handbooks, manuals, etc.   3. Mentoring in education—Handbooks, manuals, etc.   4. Universities and colleges—Graduate work—Handbooks, manuals, etc.   I. Huwe, Jennifer M.   II. Title.
    LB2371 .J62 2003
    378.1'55—dc21
                                                                        2002011470

British Library Cataloguing-in-Publication Data
A CIP record is available from the British Library.

Printed in the United States of America
First Edition

For William L. Johnson—father, mentor, and friend.
—W. Brad Johnson

To Jeremy—for your love, patience, and support.
—Jennifer M. Huwe

Contents

ACKNOWLEDGMENTS   ix

Part I. About Mentoring

1

What Mentoring Is   3

2

What a Mentor Can Do for You   17

3

Who Gets Mentored and Why   39

Part II. How to Find a Mentor

4

What to Look For in a Mentor   63

5

The Intentional Protégé: Initiating a Mentor Relationship   77

Part III. How to Manage the Mentor Relationship

6

Designing the Mentor Relationship   97

7

The Stages of Mentor Relationships (What to Expect)   113

8

Potential Problems (and How to Handle Them)   129

9

On Being an Excellent Protégé   151

10

Mentoring for Women and Minorities   163

11

Some Additional Ways to Get Mentored   177

REFERENCES   191

INDEX   199

ABOUT THE AUTHORS   209

Acknowledgments

A number of people deserve special thanks for helping to bring this work to fruition. First, we are deeply indebted to the members of our mentor relationship research team at George Fox University (1996–1999): Kelley Carmichael, Anne Fallow, Gregg Fallow, Jeff Lucas, and Laura Zorich. We are also indebted to several other excellent doctoral students who committed their dissertations to the topic of mentoring: John Bigelow, Richard Clark, Sherry Harden, Steve Dickinson, Yvette Ward, and Pete Wilson. Their friendship and scholarly contributions formed the inspiration and impetus for the book.

Several colleagues have given us important encouragement and support along the way. We are especially grateful to Marsha Beaugrand, Carol Dell'Oliver, Clark Campbell, Betsy Holmes, Chris Koch, Doug Marlow, Irene Powch, Curtis Kaufmann, and Jim O'Neil. We are also thankful to several pioneers in the field of mentorship for giving us the bedrock on which to stand: Kathy Kram, Daniel Levinson, Jim O'Neil, and Belle Ragins.

The publishing team at APA Books deserves special thanks for a job well done. We are especially grateful to Susan Reynolds for seeing the merit in our idea and urging us on, to Vanessa Downing for managing the revisions so deftly, and to Jennifer Zale for bringing it all together.

Finally, we owe special thanks to our spouses, Laura Johnson and Jeremy Huwe, and our children, Jacob, Daniel, and Stanton Johnson and Maddie Jane Huwe. Your love and support are unsurpassed.

About Mentoring

What Mentoring Is

We begin this guide to *Getting Mentored in Graduate School* with a short imagery exercise. Originally developed by Phillips-Jones (1982), we have adapted it for use in our workshops for graduate students. We think it will help you to better understand how important mentors can be.

Sit back, relax, and think about the important people in your life. In particular, think about the men and women who helped shape your identity. Who were your models? Who encouraged and supported you? Who are your cheerleaders, and who smiles with satisfaction when you do well? Most importantly, who believed in you when you decided to go to graduate school? Now, imagine all of these people together in one room. They are sitting around a conference table, and you are the topic of conversation. Although some seem to know you better than others, each is describing who you are—your talents, accomplishments, and characteristics. These people are enjoying themselves. What exactly are they saying about you? Who is sitting at the head of the table, chairing the meeting? What feelings does this scene evoke in you?

You have just recalled some important developmental relationships. Some are probably mentor relationships. These are the contributors to your story of growth and accomplishment. Each person has played some role in bringing you to the threshold of graduate education. Only you can now step across. For this journey you will need a new guide. Someone seasoned, trustworthy, and familiar with the arduous territory of graduate school—a faculty mentor you can count on.

Why a Guide to Getting Mentored?

Graduate school is difficult. The process of weathering a graduate program is often lengthy, exhausting, and complex. It involves a transformation of identity at both a professional and a personal level (Bruss & Kopala, 1993). There are a number of costs along the way. Some are personal (mental, emotional, and esteem related), some are relational (marriages and friendships may suffer), some are professional, and still others are economic (many graduate students exist near the poverty level). To make matters worse, graduating is not enough. Many professional communities are glutted with MAs, JDs, PhDs, and so on, and good postdoctoral fellowships or entry-level positions are often fiercely competitive. In this trying and competitive landscape, a good predictor of success is the presence of a solid mentor relationship—or what we refer to as a *mentorship*.

Before explaining why having a graduate school mentor is tremendously important, let us first acknowledge an important truth. You do not HAVE to be mentored to succeed in graduate school and beyond. Popular interest in mentoring has led to a sort of *mentor mania* in some quarters. Faddish hype surrounding mentoring leads to the erroneous conclusion that only mentored professionals—including those in graduate school—succeed. This is an oversimplification and a falsehood. Many graduate students are never mentored by a faculty member. In many doctoral programs, roughly half of the students are mentored; in others, the rate is much lower (Clark, Harden, & Johnson, 2000). Some of these nonmentored students go on to be famous contributors to their disciplines. It is clear that many characteristics and opportunities combine to make one successful. Still, research and experience show that those who enjoy strong graduate school mentor relationships are most likely to succeed.

All graduate students can benefit from good mentoring—even those who bring the best "raw" talent to their graduate program. Take, for example, the impressive case of "social heredity" among Nobel Prize laureates in the sciences. In a study of the 92 laureates who did their prize-winning research in the United States by 1972, Zuckerman (1977) found that more than half had been mentored by Nobel laureates themselves—as students, postdoctorates, or junior collaborators. It seems that elite scholars perpetuate their success in junior professionals. Yes, these young scientists were exceptionally gifted, but finding just the right mentor was also important. Across the disciplines and around the world, truly excellent graduate programs are characterized by intense training, demanding requirements, and a faculty serious about supporting and developing graduate students (Ellis, 1992). The primary thesis underlying this book goes something like this: *The probability of your success in graduate school, and beyond, is strongly connected to whether or not you are mentored.*

In the balance of this chapter, we define mentoring and describe what a graduate school mentor is and is not. We summarize what little is known about the prevalence of mentoring in graduate school and offer a sobering analysis of the forces working against good mentoring. Finally, we offer some advice to graduate students on using this guide wisely and to their maximum benefit.

What a Mentor Is

The original "Mentor" was an Ithacan noble in Homer's epic tale, *The Odyssey*. An old and wise friend of Ulysses, Mentor was entrusted with the care and protection of Ulysses' son, Telemachus, while Ulysses was gone fighting the Trojan War. As a figure from Greek mythology, Mentor embodies wisdom. He is a parental archetype with both male and female qualities. Athena later assumed Mentor's form to advise and protect Telemachus during his own journey.

Serious study of mentor relationships did not begin until the publication of two in-depth qualitative studies of normal development in men (Levinson, Darrow, Klein, Levinson, & McKee, 1978; Vaillant, 1977). Levinson studied the adult lives of 40 men and concluded that a mentor relationship with an older man (usually in their field) was the most important relationship these men experienced as young adults. He wrote:

> He [the mentor] may act as a teacher to enhance the young man's skills and intellectual development. Serving as a sponsor, he may use his influence to facilitate the young man's entry and advancement. He may be a host and guide, welcoming the initiate into a new occupational and social world and acquainting him with its values, customs, resources, and cast of characters. Through his own virtues, achievements, and way of living, the mentor may be an exemplar that the protégé can admire and seek to emulate. He may provide counsel and moral support in times of stress. (Levinson et al., 1978, p. 98)

In a longitudinal study of 95 Harvard graduates, Vaillant (1977) found that those with the best life "outcomes" (e.g., coping with major life stressors, giving back to society) were most likely to have enjoyed "sustained relationships with loving people" (p. 337) in both their careers and personal lives.

Various writers offer compelling portraits of the mentor. Most of them are close to what we have in mind. Merriam (1983) wrote, "mentoring is a powerful emotional interaction between an older and younger person, in a relationship in which the older member is trusted, loving, and experienced in the guidance of the younger" (p. 162). Kram (1985) said that the mentor "supports, guides, and counsels a young adult as he or she accomplishes mastery of the adult world or the world of work" (p. 2). Most agree that a mentor is a seasoned and powerful professional in relation to the one being mentored—the protégé.

We use the term *protégé* in this book to refer to one who is mentored. It is not the best word, but we like the alternatives "mentee" and "junior" even less. Protégés are people who are guided and supported in their careers—and in graduate school—by a more powerful person. The French term *protégé* is derived from the Latin word *protegere*, meaning "to protect." We think this works.

In graduate school, a mentor supports, guides, and counsels a student as he or she accomplishes the important life task of successfully navigating a rigorous graduate program and prepares to launch into a new career. The mentor holds power within the graduate school culture. The mentor has transformed himself or herself into a highly achieving and quite visible member of a profession (Corbett, 1995; Wright & Wright, 1987).

In an effort to offer definitional clarity for the remainder of this guide, we recommend the following definition of who a mentor is and what a mentor does in graduate school. It is brief, yet it draws some contours for the boundaries of mentoring.

> Mentoring is a personal relationship in which a more experienced (usually older) faculty member acts as a guide, role model, teacher, and sponsor of a less experienced (usually younger) graduate student. A mentor provides the protégé with knowledge, advice, challenge, counsel, and support in the protégé's pursuit of becoming a full member of a particular profession.

This basic definition has served us well in previous research on the topic (Clark et al., 2000; Dickinson & Johnson, 2000; Johnson, Koch, Fallow, & Huwe, 2000).

Although many graduate students were mentored as undergraduates, there are some important differences between undergraduate and graduate school mentors. College faculty are more likely to serve as advisors, helping students to pick classes, complete degree requirements, and perhaps consider graduate school. In contrast, graduate school faculty specifically and intentionally usher the graduate students into the field and profession they study. Graduate school mentorships are typically longer in duration, more focused on achieving professional competence and identity development, and more likely to yield a collegial friendship at graduation than the typical undergraduate mentorship.

Throughout this book, we refer to mentoring in the classic sense, meaning the traditional or *primary* mentorship (Russell & Adams, 1997). Primary mentorships in graduate school are enduring and somewhat bonded relationships between a single student and professor. The primary mentor will probably be your advisor and ultimately your dissertation chairperson. Graduate school is long and arduous enough that there is ample time for primary mentorships to form if graduate students actively initiate them. In addition to a primary mentor, you may also have one or more *secondary* mentors in graduate school. Secondary mentorships are shorter in duration and less intense. Secondary mentorships may occur with faculty members in your department, faculty members external to your department, supervisors in internship sites away from campus, and so on. Although we strongly endorse secondary mentorships, they will not replace the benefits likely to accrue from a primary mentor relationship.

Finally, it is important to note that no two mentorships will look the same. The unique nature and quality of any mentoring relationship will hinge on several important variables. O'Neil and Wrightsman (2001) articulated several of these, including (a) the role of the mentor; (b) the role of the protégé; (c) the personality, abilities, and needs of the particular persons who fill these roles; and (d) various situational and environmental factors.

What a Mentor Does

Excellent mentors bless their students (Corbett, 1995; Davis, Litle, & Thornton, 1997). By *bless*, we mean that the mentor calls forth and affirms the protégé's life and career aspirations—what Levinson (Levinson et al., 1978) called *the dream*: "The mentor nourishes a dream in the student and sets the student into creative flight, tempering idealism with the wisdom of experience" (Davis et al., 1997, p. 61). A good mentor creates the conditions necessary for your transition from relative immaturity (infancy) in the field to the status of colleague (adulthood). This graduate school transition is often a time of crisis, danger, and vulnerability. A mentor serves as the steady shepherd, guiding you through this transition.

An excellent mentor will *know* you. Absurdly obvious as this may seem, it is a critical point. Many graduate school faculty may know you (e.g., your name, your interests, your main personality features, and your academic potential), but very few faculty will *know* you. The term mentoring signifies a relationship characterized by *knowing*. A faculty mentor will come to *know* you simply by becoming a student of you. He or she will listen to you, tracking what you say and how you feel. A mentor will watch you in different contexts, inquire about your interests and dreams, and pay careful attention to your fears and burdens. When a faculty member commits to *know* you in this way, he or she has begun to mentor.

Outstanding mentors are intentional models (Bolton, 1980; Bruss &

Kopala, 1993; Wright & Wright, 1987). Mentors are aware that protégés need to watch them perform the activities necessary in a particular profession. They also understand that some complex professional behaviors can only be learned by observation (e.g., teaching a course, running a meeting, preparing a brief, or conducting a neuropsychological evaluation). Mentors invite protégés to watch them, to participate in their professional work, and to gradually assume greater responsibility and autonomy. As the protégé demonstrates increasing mastery of the subject matter, the mentor offers a powerful endorsement—they are colleagues. More than technical models, however, mentors show students how to "be" professional. They nurture in their protégés an attitude of personal responsibility for the profession (VanZandt, 1990). A mentor hopes to instill a commitment to behave ethically and morally in protégés, a sense of pride in the profession.

Good mentors are patient. Understanding that graduate school may create in you a range of unpleasant emotions and self-perceptions (e.g., anxiety, confusion, dependency, inadequacy, and incompetence), a mentor works at positively shaping your view of self, your personal and professional self-esteem. True, mentors are not parents or psychotherapists, yet they may be both parental and therapeutic, as student circumstances require. A mentor validates, placing an all-important stamp of "okayness" on the psyche of the sometimes-floundering student. The graduate student, assured of his or her mentor's approval, is heartened and buoyed. He or she risks more, unleashes creative energy, and believes that the *dream* may just be possible. He or she has been *known* and validated.

Mentors do many other things. They create opportunities, promote students for jobs and assistantships, introduce them to important figures in the field, and honestly but gently provide correction when needed. Mentors teach, coach, and challenge their protégés. They teach them to research, write grants, and get articles published. They encourage excellent performance while reinforcing students for maintaining physical, mental, and emotional health. When appropriate, they help protégés become aware of unwritten or implicit rules and politics within the graduate department and the larger professional culture.

What a Mentor Is Not

Although mentors are many things to graduate students, there are some things they are not and some things they should never be. Mentors are caring, protective, and supportive, but they should not be parents. Mentors can be friendly, collegial models, but they should not be siblings or best friends. Mentors are warm and engaged, but they are not psycho-therapists. Finally, mentors may be kind and loving, but they should never be lovers. When a mentor assumes any of these roles with a graduate student, the relationship becomes something other than mentorship, something potentially harmful for both mentor and protégé. Many mentorships are multifaceted—the student and faculty member interact in different settings and different roles (e.g., the mentor may be teacher, clinical supervisor, research advisor, and employer). Furthermore, many (excellent) mentorships are emotionally bonded and long lasting. Nonetheless, both mentor and protégé must intentionally work at honoring the contours that define the relationship; both must prevent the mentorship from becoming something else.

There are other things mentors should not be. Although mentors may at times protect their protégés from toxic departmental politics or unfair evaluations, mentors should never become bullies or assassins on behalf of protégés. A mentor should also never become a religious director or business partner to a protégé. By adding multiple roles to a graduate school mentorship, both parties increase the risk that the relationship will become unproductive, contentious, or exploitive.

The Prevalence of Mentoring in Graduate School

How many graduate students actually get mentored? What program characteristics seem to predict the prevalence of mentoring? Is program prestige correlated with mentoring? Is mentoring more prevalent in certain disciplines and less prevalent in others? Unfortunately, the answer to most of these questions is, we don't know. Good research on the prevalence of mentorships between graduate students and faculty members is sparse. Most graduate programs do not collect data regarding mentoring of their own students. This is problematic for several reasons. First, prospective applicants have difficulty evaluating programs on the basis of quality of mentoring. Second, within specific disciplines (e.g., philosophy, literature, sociology), it is difficult to assess the prevalence of mentoring. Finally, it is nearly impossible to accurately compare prevalence of mentoring across disciplines.

In spite of these difficulties, some scholarly disciplines have accumulated reasonable preliminary data relating to mentoring. The field of psychology is one of them. Here is a brief synopsis of what we know about mentoring in the field of psychology. Three studies of psychology doctoral students found that approximately 50% reported having a mentor (Cronan-Hillix, Gensheimer, Cronan-Hillix, & Davidson, 1986;

Kirchner, 1969; Mintz, Bartels, & Rideout, 1995). Similarly, Atkinson, Casas, and Neville (1994) found that 51% of ethnic minority psychologists had been mentored in graduate school. A new large-scale survey of nearly 800 recent clinical psychology doctorates revealed that 66% were mentored, suggesting that mentoring may be on the rise in psychology (Clark et al., 2000). However, graduates of professional (PsyD) programs were significantly less likely to be mentored than graduates of traditional university-based (PhD) programs (56% vs. 71%). So, programs that admit fewer students and focus more on research and scholarship appear more likely to offer mentorships. Furthermore, within the field of psychology, experimental psychologists are more likely than clinical psychologists to be mentored by faculty (Johnson, Koch, Fallow, & Huwe, 2000). Women are just as likely as men to get mentored in psychology doctoral programs, and the vast majority of mentored graduate students took primary responsibility for initiating the mentorship (Clark et al., 2000; Cronan-Hillix et al., 1986; Johnson, Koch, Fallow, & Huwe, 2000).

This thumbnail sketch gives you a brief picture of what we know about the prevalence of mentoring in the field of psychology. We know less about the prevalence of mentoring in other academic disciplines. Nevertheless, we believe there are some lessons from the psychology literature with relevance for graduate school mentoring overall. First, not all students in doctoral programs get mentored. Second, those who do, work at initiating the mentoring relationship. Third, students in more traditional university-based doctoral programs may be at an advantage compared with students in professional schools or doctoral programs with more students per faculty member and greater emphasis on professional practice than research and teaching.

Finally, although recent research in psychology indicates that women enjoy the same access to mentoring as men, this has not been the case historically and will not be the case in all disciplines or individual departments. In fact, most literature indicates that women are often disadvantaged when it comes to finding a mentor, managing the relationship, and receiving important mentor functions (Bogat & Redner, 1985; Gilbert & Rossman, 1992; Hite, 1985; Richey, Gambrill, & Blythe, 1988). Because most senior graduate school faculty are men, there are also important concerns about access to same-gender mentorships for women (Goldstein, 1979; Richey et al., 1988).

The Imperfect World of Graduate School Mentoring

In many graduate programs, there are significant barriers to finding the right mentor and enjoying the benefits of a good mentor relationship.

These mentoring obstacles prompted us to write this book. Some of these problems are *structural*; they are products of our system of graduate education. Others are *department specific* and reflect problems in a particular faculty culture. Finally, some obstacles are *relational*; these stem from the personality characteristics and behavior patterns of a particular faculty member—a potential mentor—or the interaction of traits in the mentor and protégé.

Structural impediments to getting mentored in graduate school include the following: university accounting systems that give faculty credit exclusively for funded research (not quality of mentoring or teaching), downsizing in the number of tenure-track (full-time) faculty positions, and the growing practice of hiring part-time instructors (Belar, 1998). These systemwide practices communicate clearly that faculty will be evaluated primarily on the basis of research productivity and that quality of relationships with students is a secondary consideration at best. The practice of hiring part-time instructors further dilutes the pool of potential graduate student mentors. Non-tenure-track faculty frequently have less commitment to the department and may be present only for the purpose of teaching classes.

There are also department-specific or cultural hurdles to getting mentored. Among the worst of these local obstacles is departmentally nourished competition among students. For example, some doctoral programs frequently admit more students than they plan to graduate, communicating that the position of all entering students is tenuous at best. In such a culture, students are competitive—as opposed to cooperative—and faculty avoid forging relationships with students until it is clear they will number among the "survivors." This is an indication of either narcissism ("Our program is so good, you'd be lucky just to get an MA here") or sadism ("We like to watch 'em squirm"); neither explanation paints a rosy picture of these departments and we recommend that you avoid them. The best doctoral programs admit excellent students whom the faculty assume will be successful. Students are expected to complete the doctorate, and professors engage prospective protégés early in their training.

Another cultural hurdle to mentoring is evident in large professional programs. Here we refer to graduate programs designed exclusively to train practitioners in a particular field. Professional psychology (PsyD) programs, social work (MSW) programs, and some law (JD) and education (EdD) programs come to mind. Here, the ratios between students and faculty are huge. There is little opportunity for interaction with faculty beyond the classroom. Furthermore, professionally oriented faculty are often engaged in practice outside the department. Although this keeps them on the cutting edge, it naturally decreases time and energy available for student relationships. Of course, we acknowledge that graduate students seek education for a variety of reasons and that students in professional training programs may be willing to sacrifice the benefits of a resident mentor for other benefits, including program "fit," geographic convenience, or quality of applied training. In this case, we highly encourage you to seek external mentors.

Finally, there are personal or relational obstacles to getting mentored in graduate school. At times, faculty mentors may have personal traits that render them corrosive and counterproductive to the development of a student (Bruss & Kopala, 1993). A professor who is rejecting, extremely critical, or, worse, indifferent to the student is unlikely to help the student personally or professionally. Neither are professors who are highly controlling, overprotective, and coercive, perhaps attempting to clone themselves anew in students. Some faculty mentors attempt to meet personal needs in relationships with students, and still others become competitive with or jealous of high-achieving students. Finally, some may have tremendous difficulty allowing a student to transition out of the relationship and move on when the relationship has run its course.

For the most part, graduate programs applaud faculty who actively and successfully mentor students. In general, graduate school faculty members will be bright, successful, and competent when it comes to mentoring. Still, structural, departmental, and relational hurdles make mentoring a challenge for some students.

Prelude to Being a Protégé

We have designed this book as a manual—a strategic guide to understanding what you as a graduate student need from a mentorship, how to intentionally select and connect with the right faculty mentor, and how to shape and manage this mentorship once it begins to take form. To maximize the probability of success, you will need to know yourself, understand the formation and character of mentorships, and then work proactively and diligently to find the right match and keep the relationship healthy and mutually beneficial.

Mentors are naturally drawn to students with talent, drive, and positive attitudes regarding the mentor and the profession (Green & Bauer, 1995). Potential mentors are attracted to graduate students with intelligence, excellent interpersonal skills, self-awareness, and strong interest in the mentor's area of scholarly focus (Johnson, Koch, Fallow, & Huwe, 2000). Among Nobel Prize laureates, Zuckerman (1977) recognized a process of "bilateral assortative selection" (p. 104), meaning that the most promising students tended to choose the most notable masters

BOX 1.1: HOW IT WORKED FOR US

It is important to note that our own interest in and excitement about mentoring is not purely academic. Our experience as a graduate school mentor–protégé pair has affected us—both as people and professionals. We developed a mentor relationship while I (Brad) was a professor and I (Jenny) was a 2nd-year doctoral student at George Fox University. Although I (Brad) have served as a mentor to many graduate students and postdoctoral residents, and although I (Jenny) have had several important mentors, the mentorship we developed was especially productive and enjoyable.

In this guide, we include salient examples and learning experiences from our own mentorship. We highlight aspects of our relationship that were exceptionally beneficial, as well as barriers that were important to address. In most cases, our mistakes or oversights proved instructive, allowing us to make needed adjustments and move ahead. Our relationship shows that graduate school mentorships can be highly rewarding in spite of imperfection.

(mentors) in the field. At the same time, these masters selected the most talented and motivated from among the many gifted students who presented themselves as potential protégés. (See Box 1.1.)

Using This Guide

We divide *Getting Mentored in Graduate School* into three broad sections. We recommend that you read the first two sections—"About Mentoring" and "How to Find a Mentor"—before moving to locate an ideal faculty mentor in your graduate program. If you have only recently been admitted to a graduate program, you have ample time to develop a solid strategy for getting mentored. In this case, you should read the entire book and then return to chapters 4 and 5 to carefully plan your approach. If, on the other hand, you are one of the thousands of graduate students who has completed a year or more of graduate school without any sign of the sort of relationship we discussed earlier in this chapter, you should move quickly to the middle section of this guide and start your search in earnest.

In chapters 2 and 3—the remainder of the "About Mentoring" section—we offer a clear rationale for getting mentored and a summary of the characteristics and behaviors of graduate students most likely to be mentored. In chapter 2, we describe the essential functions of mentors, or the specific ways in which excellent mentors promote both the career and personal development of protégés. This chapter also highlights the main benefits of mentoring for protégés—both during graduate school and later during the professional career. Chapter 3 offers a portrait of the ideal protégé. Titled "Who Gets Mentored and Why," this chapter summarizes the main personality traits and characteristic behaviors of successful protégés. For example, good protégés are often flexible, hard working, and prone to being intentional both in planning and executing projects and in developing a mentorship. Chapter 3 also cautions students by describing the characteristics of students least likely to be mentored.

The second section of this book, "How to Find a Mentor," includes two chapters focused on the actual process of gathering relevant information, assessing the mentoring-relevant traits of prospective faculty mentors, and taking initiative for pursuing and fostering a mentorship. Chapter 4 encourages careful attention to the characteristics of prospective mentors. Salient mentor traits, such as personality, personal health, professional boundaries, attitudes, research interests, and even gender or ethnicity may play an important role in determining the "match" or "fit" between mentor and protégé. We summarize literature bearing on the traits of excellent mentors and encourage students to identify critical matching variables when looking for a mentor.

Chapter 5 will be among the most important for those who have not yet applied to graduate school, as well as those who have only recently been accepted to or begun a graduate program. In this chapter, we offer distinct strategies for collecting data about a program and its approach to mentoring students, collecting data about the mentoring credentials of specific faculty members, and formulating a personal strategy for getting mentored—even in a seemingly unfriendly academic department. Our motto in chapter 5 is "reconnaissance pays."

The final section of this guide, "How to Manage the Mentor Relationship," is designed as a manual for students who have successfully initiated a mentor relationship. In chapter 6, we offer strategies for continuing to intentionally develop the mentorship, with emphasis on clear communication with the mentor around issues such as the anticipated parameters of the relationships (e.g., duration, avenues for interaction, and role expectations for both members). Chapter 7 covers the common stages of mentor relationships and offers graduate students a window into the benefits, characteristics, and challenges that accompany each stage of mentor relationships. We also describe the common phases of graduate student development and how these require mentors to respond with phase-specific functions.

On occasion, problems arise in mentorships. Chapter 8 addresses the common mentoring problems and dilemmas and provides guidance for addressing them clearly and explicitly. Examples include personality conflicts, expectation conflicts, mentor unavailability, boundary violations, and difficulty managing the transitions between relationship stages. Chapter 9, "On Being an Excellent Protégé," shows that excellent protégés tend to keep commitments, meet deadlines, do outstanding work, tolerate the apprentice role, accept increasing responsibility, say yes to new opportunities, and understand their mentor's professional needs and goals. This chapter provides a summary of what makes a student a delight to mentor. Chapter 10 offers important guidance for women and minority group students. Most importantly, we consider the pros and cons of same-gender and cross-gender mentorships, as well as same-race and cross-race mentorships. We conclude this book with a final chapter on alternatives to traditional mentor relationships in graduate school. For example, some students will be well served by peer mentors, external mentors, mentors for hire, and "famous" mentors. Specific mentoring alternatives for students from underrepresented groups are also addressed.

Finally, each chapter in this book begins with two mentor relationship case studies relevant to that chapter. The first case always depicts a successful protégé, whereas the second case offers an unsuccessful protégé scenario. Although these cases are fictitious, they do highlight the common causes of protégé success and failure. We recommend that you pay particular attention to these case studies as salient examples of what to do and what not to do as a protégé.

What a Mentor Can Do for You 2

Case 2.1

Sandy was a 2nd-year counseling psychology doctoral student when her mentor relationship with Dr. Guide began to yield professional and personal benefits. Although Sandy was a talented student, she lacked self-confidence and failed to attract the attention of many professors in the department. Deciding early on that Dr. Guide would be an outstanding mentor, Sandy worked diligently as a volunteer research assistant on one of Dr. Guide's projects. She also took an elective seminar from Dr. Guide and not only produced excellent work but also made a point of talking with Dr. Guide at each opportunity—often highlighting their shared interests. Dr. Guide recognized Sandy's potential and set out to help her develop her skills. He encouraged her to participate in a team research project he was leading with several other key faculty members. When one faculty member expressed doubt that Sandy could creatively contribute to the team, Dr. Guide publicly expressed his confidence in Sandy's abilities. During team meetings, he watched for opportunities to highlight Sandy's contributions and he actively modeled the art of resolving conflict among team members. Dr. Guide frequently provided Sandy with encouragement and affirmation about her professional and research skills. He also went out of his way to schedule biweekly advising meetings with Sandy. During those biweekly meetings, he made suggestions about ways to manage her student responsibilities, various professional relationships, and the stresses inherent in balancing graduate school with other life demands. Eventually, Dr. Guide's endorsement and coaching proved crucial in helping Sandy to network with faculty outside of the university and, ultimately, secure her first academic appointment.

Case 2.2

Kevin was in his 3rd year of graduate training in sociology when he landed his "dream" research position with Dr. Mighty, the department's most famous professor. Kevin knew almost nothing about Dr. Mighty as his international acclaim kept him away from the department much of the time. Kevin never asked fellow students why Dr. Mighty had so few advisees and almost no dissertation students. Undaunted, Kevin set out to make a good impression. Kevin spent extra hours working on projects and frequently requested greater responsibility; however, Dr. Mighty assigned Kevin menial lab tasks that failed to challenge or highlight his skills. Dr. Mighty was also too busy to meet regularly with Kevin and seldom offered him encouragement or advice. When a personality conflict developed between Kevin and an adjunct faculty member, Dr. Mighty responded to Kevin's requests for advice with short remarks such as "you'll figure it out" and "these things have a way of blowing over." While his peers received kudos and coauthorship for their work with other professors, Kevin's talents remained relatively unknown to other faculty, and his professional dreams of landing a research postdoc withered. Although Kevin later received some attention and encouragement from a young faculty member in the department, this relationship only developed in the final semester of his training. Kevin left graduate school feeling that his relationship with Dr. Mighty was unprofitable and unfulfilling. He had a difficult time finding a job in the field and struggled for some time with feelings of professional incompetence.

Although these examples are fictitious, we believe that many graduate students can relate to the disappointment of Kevin and the satisfaction of Sandy in relation to getting mentored in graduate school. Unfortunately, many graduate students fail to secure solid relationships with faculty who understand the art of mentoring. This lack of support and guidance may have both short-term and long-term effects on a student's professional development. Thankfully, many students will enjoy something closer to Sandy's experience—discovering that having an effective mentor can make all the difference in developing self-efficacy, professional networks, and possibly even that first important job. To enhance the probability that you secure a relationship with a faculty mentor who can give you what you need to do well in graduate school, it is essential that you understand the salient components of good mentoring. In this chapter, we highlight the major mentor functions or the primary dimensions of what excellent mentors "do." We then summarize the main benefits enjoyed by well-mentored graduate students.

What Good Graduate School Mentors Do

We have already established that mentors are individuals who provide protégés with knowledge, advice, challenge, and support. However, satisfied protégés know that successful mentors provide a range of specific "mentor functions" at various junctures in the mentor relationship and that the most skilled mentors seem to have an intuitive sense regarding when a protégé is most likely to benefit from each function. In her important book, *Mentoring at Work*, Kram (1985) identified two broad categories of functions that enhance a protégé's personal growth and professional advancement. She labeled these two categories *career functions* and *psychosocial functions* (see Table 2.1). Career functions are those aspects of the relationship that contribute to "learning the ropes and preparing for advancement" (Kram, 1985, p. 22). Graduate school mentors may offer protégés career functions such as sponsorship, exposure and visibility, coaching, protection, and challenging assignments. Mentors who offer these benefits to protégés often possess a good deal

TABLE 2.1

Career and Psychosocial Mentor Functions

Function	Description
Career functions	
Sponsorship	The mentor nominates the protégé for awards, promotes the protégé's work for publication, or recommends the protégé for key positions.
Exposure and visibility	The mentor invites the protégé to participate in research or writing projects and highlights these accomplishments to faculty and other professionals.
Coaching	The mentor recommends how to successfully navigate departmental politics.
Protection	The mentor shields the protégé's reputation from unproductive criticism.
Challenging assignments	The mentor invites the protégé to participate in challenging projects that increase his or her growing competence and skill level.
Psychosocial functions	
Role modeling	The mentor actively demonstrates how to successfully perform salient professional skills and tasks such as teaching or grant writing.
Acceptance and confirmation	The mentor communicates strong support and confidence in the protégé.
Counseling	The mentor provides advice to the protégé about career goals, balancing academic and personal responsibilities, and developing "dreams" for his or her career.
Friendship/mutuality	The mentor and protégé experience a sense of being appreciated, valued, and trusted by each other.

of experience, advanced rank, and considerable influence among their peers. In other words, the most effective graduate school mentors have the power, resources, and interest to further the protégé's career. When providing career functions, a mentor may help a protégé to gain exposure and recognition from faculty and supervisors, successfully navigate departmental politics, and accept increasingly challenging responsibilities.

Psychosocial functions are the mentoring strategies used by a mentor to enhance a protégé's sense of self-esteem, professional identity, and sense of competence (Kram, 1985). Kram identified psychosocial functions as role modeling, acceptance and confirmation, counseling, and friendship or mutuality. Unlike career benefits, psychosocial functions require a growing sense of trust between the mentor and protégé and are largely based on the mentor's ability to foster a personal relationship with the protégé. Some mentors possess plenty of professional experience and influence, yet are unable to offer their protégés empathy, support, and acceptance during critical transitions. Unlike the career functions that primarily affect graduate students' advancement in the academic, research, or clinical environments, psychosocial functions spill over and affect many different areas of a protégé's life. In fact, it is difficult to receive these benefits without experiencing a change in one's broader sense of self.

The career and psychosocial functions of mentor relationships identified by Kram (1985) have been empirically confirmed and validated in a range of professional fields, including management, psychology, and education. In the following section, we briefly describe each mentor function in more detail. As you read each description, we recommend that you consider how important each career and psychosocial function is likely to be to you. This will be relevant when it comes time for you to identify a suitable faculty mentor (see chapters 4 and 5).

SPONSORSHIP

It is difficult to exaggerate the necessity of sponsorship for success in graduate school. When a mentor sponsors, he or she nominates, endorses, and promotes both within and outside the graduate program. Sponsorship involves sharing one's power, thereby smoothing the way for a student. A recent survey of clinical psychology graduate students demonstrated that sponsorship was among the most significant functions provided by mentors to protégés (Clark et al., 2000). In graduate school, the mentor's sponsorship has two primary components. First, the successful graduate school mentor sponsors the protégé as he or she advances within the program. A mentor promotes the protégé's advancement (e.g., nominating for awards or special recognition, offering endorsement for research projects, and sponsoring and promoting protégés' work for professional publication or conference presentation) and provides protection should controversy arise. As a sponsor, a mentor might assist the protégé in bypassing bureaucratic obstacles in a graduate program. For example, a skillful mentor may know how to quickly advance a research proposal, thereby saving the protégé significant time and energy. Sponsorship may also be essential for advancement to higher status in the graduate program. Most students applying for predoctoral internships know that promotion to the coveted status of "intern" is extremely difficult without the sponsorship and endorsement of at least one supportive faculty member. Successful advancement and promotion through the ranks of graduate school will be enhanced by the sponsorship of an effective mentor.

Second, sponsorship is vital for the graduate school protégé as he or she seeks postdoctoral training and employment. The significance and necessity of strong endorsements from a graduate school mentor cannot be overstated in today's competitive job market. The mentor's sponsorship at this stage of career development provides what Kanter (1977) called *reflective power*. Reflective power through sponsorship indicates to others that the protégé has the backing of an influential faculty member whose resources are readily available to the protégé to promote his or her ongoing success. This is particularly important for protégés with research-oriented goals. Here, the mentor's research program promotes a sense of continuity and power to outside observers. Sponsorship does come with some risks for the mentor. The protégé and mentor simultaneously risk that the protégé will not be able to fulfill expectations, thereby tarnishing both individuals' reputations. It is important for the graduate student to appreciate the risk assumed by a faculty mentor in this regard. If your mentor sponsors you and promotes you to others for positions, then, by all means, work at proving this risk was well deserved.

EXPOSURE AND VISIBILITY

This function involves the mentor's willingness to provide opportunities for the protégé to demonstrate his or her competence to others (Kram, 1985). In graduate education, such opportunities may come in the form of research opportunities, challenging practica, or teaching and writing opportunities. As in the case of sponsorship, the mentor and protégé both incur a level of risk when the protégé performs novel tasks. However, it is the process of exposing the protégé to new responsibilities and promoting his or her success to others that prepares the protégé for advancement in the program and profession. (See Box 2.1.)

BOX 2.1: HOW IT WORKED FOR US—JENNY'S PERSPECTIVE

I benefited from this mentor function in my relationship with Brad. Over the course of several years, Brad offered me opportunities to participate in research and writing tasks. As my skills and confidence improved, Brad encouraged me to take on increased responsibility. He then intentionally highlighted these accomplishments in conversations with department faculty, to others at professional conferences, and in letters of recommendation. As a protégé initially lacking experience and power, I was unsure how Brad would respond to my inevitable failures in the process of learning new skills. I found that Brad took setbacks in stride, which helped me to do the same. As he continued to create opportunities for me, I began to see myself as a competent junior colleague and someone who could indeed meet these challenges.

COACHING

Although graduate school is much like a complicated athletic event requiring individual and team performance, the scoring of "points" to win the game, penalties and timeouts, and that ever-hoped-for prize (graduate degree) at the final buzzer, many students go through this entire ordeal with no coach. The element of coaching in a mentor relationship is similar to coaching in organized sports. Mentors coach when they provide knowledge, make recommendations, offer consultation, and provide motivation and encouragement. Coaching helps the protégé to avoid a number of hazardous pitfalls in graduate school while navigating toward the goal.

During the initial stages of the relationship, the mentor may provide information about department politics, including who has power and who is trustworthy. The mentor may suggest strategies to deal with interpersonal conflict and recommend short-term goals that promote the protégé's long-term dreams. Good graduate school mentors often coach students in the art of securing a good clinical internship. In this role, they are part teacher—dispensing secret tips for appearing in the most favorable light—and part cheerleader—attempting to convince anxious and overwhelmed students that they can indeed have some control over the outcome in the hunt for an internship.

PROTECTION

Graduate school is occasionally a risky business. At some point in their graduate school careers, most protégés have need of protection or shielding from hostility, nonconstructive criticism, or even threats to their status in the graduate program. During the initial years of training, the mentor's protection may take the form of helping the protégé to avoid tasks that would be beyond his or her abilities. Later on, the mentor may intervene to support the protégé while defending a dissertation or fight to protect the protégé's reputation when conflict arises.

Although most protégés appreciate this critical function, there is always a risk that the mentor will overprotect the protégé and promote a sense that he or she is unable to function independently from the mentor. This may be particularly problematic for female protégés in cross-gender mentor relationships. The same gender stereotypes that create a need for protection and coaching within a graduate school organization may also surface in cross-gender mentor relationships. In this case, the female protégé must determine the level of protection she deems appropriate for the situation while taking responsibility for confronting conflict and addressing the issue of overprotectiveness directly with her mentor.

CHALLENGING ASSIGNMENTS

Kevin's example clearly demonstrates the liability associated with not having a mentor who provides challenging assignments that develop the protégé's skills. Although many employment environments tolerate minimal competence, in the competitive world of graduate education, students must demonstrate incrementally increasing competence in order to survive. Except in rare situations, only those students who steadily improve their skills ultimately advance. Graduate students who understand this expectation work to find faculty willing to provide challenging opportunities that promote their development. In Kevin's experience, continuing to engage in menial laboratory tasks resulted in a sense that he was not adequately prepared for postdoctoral training. We strongly believe, given the structured and time-limited nature of graduate school, that the protégé's long-term career success depends on this critical function.

ROLE MODELING

Research in business and education leaves no doubt that role modeling is an extremely important function provided by mentors (Blackwell, 1989; Bolton, 1980; Burke, 1984; Kram, 1985; Torrance, 1984). The entire graduate school education experience is often predicated on availability of excellent faculty role models. For example, medical students watch accomplished physicians perform difficult procedures, law students observe practicing attorneys in action, and psychology students absorb the techniques of skilled therapists. It is significant that role modeling includes the routine demonstration of professional tasks as well as a sense of strong identification with the mentor, and perhaps the mentor's own style and approach to the task. Through role modeling, graduate school mentors become objects of admiration, idealization, emulation, and respect (Kram, 1985). Mentors personally demonstrate the skills that protégés seek to master. As the relationship progresses and the protégé becomes more accomplished, role modeling may slowly decline in importance to the protégé. In graduate school, faculty mentors often model critical professional skills such as teaching, supervising, writing, grant-getting, maintaining professional boundaries, and managing conflict.

ACCEPTANCE AND CONFIRMATION

Acceptance and confirmation is the most frequently reported psychosocial function provided to graduate students in psychology (Clark et al., 2000). Protégés who receive acceptance from their mentors are more willing to trust their mentors and engage in new and challenging tasks. These students have confidence that they will be supported if they fail. As a result, protégés are able to risk stretching their skills further than they previously believed possible (Kram, 1985). Reflecting on the encouragement experienced by many protégés, Phillips-Jones (1982, p. 35) stated, "Their best mentors encouraged them to be all they could be, with prejudiced, unfailing confidence in them. This unflagging faith boosted their self-esteem in a way that mere advice or a pat on the head never could." (See Box 2.2.)

BOX 2.2: HOW IT WORKED FOR US—JENNY'S PERSPECTIVE

I benefited significantly from this function around the time of my dissertation defense. Just prior to my final oral, I felt very anxious (to say the least) and was only moderately successful in lowering my anxiety about the defense outcome. Although Brad lived on the other side of the country at the time, he phoned me several days before flying back to chair the exam, normalized my feelings of anxiety, and offered me assurance about my level of preparedness. This act of acceptance and confirmation made a tremendous difference in my ability to refocus and successfully complete the task (I passed!).

COUNSELING

Counseling is a function that allows the protégé to explore personal and professional issues within the context of the relationship. Kram (1985) identified three primary areas for counseling in mentor–protégé relationships: (a) developing competence and a sense of satisfaction with regard to the protégé's career activities, (b) incorporating personal values and a sense of individuality into his or her professional relationships, and (c) integrating career responsibilities with other areas of his or her life. Graduate education is a developmental process that promotes both pragmatic and existential questions. Good mentors assist in this process by actively listening and reflecting feelings, clarifying protégés' decision-making strategies, assisting in goal setting, helping to fight and conquer inner doubts and obstacles, and working with protégés to articulate their personal and professional dreams (O'Neil & Wrightsman, 2001).

FRIENDSHIP/MUTUALITY

Mutuality is the sense of respect, trust, and affection reciprocally shared by a mentor and a protégé (O'Neil & Wrightsman, 2001). One survey revealed that graduate students in education believe mutual support is a critical component of successful mentor relationships (Wilde & Schau, 1991). Mutuality implies that both mentor and protégé intentionally offer each other positive regard and trust while remaining sensitive to the other's personal and professional needs. The mentor and protégé value each other as individuals and professionals in much the same way that faculty colleagues value one another. Although mutuality requires a certain level of authenticity in the relationship, it does not assume that the mentor and the protégé share a more common or familiar sort of friendship. Instead, mutuality allows for a well-boundaried and professional collegiality to develop between the mentor and protégé. Ideally, the pair is able to protect and manage personal and professional boundaries while also demonstrating warmth and congruence. This is particularly crucial in cross-gender relationships or when a portion of the mentor's role is to provide evaluation or feedback to the protégé.

A Word of Caution

Although a list of mentor functions may be very tantalizing to graduate students seeking a mentor relationship, we want to add several words of caution. First, no mentor relationship embodies all of the functions described here. Levinson noted that mentoring "is not defined in terms of formal roles but in terms of the character of the relationship and the functions it serves" (Levinson et al., 1978, p. 98). Because most mentors are not superhuman, most will not be equally skilled with or attentive in providing all of the mentor functions described here. (See Box 2.3.)

Even famous scholars and teachers may be known as particularly skilled at providing certain career or psychosocial functions while being poorly suited to offering others. Consider the case of world-renowned psychologist Albert Ellis, arguably one of the most prolific and influential clinical psychologists of the century. A recent study of postdoctoral fellows of Ellis's own psychotherapy institute revealed that Albert Ellis is a particularly effective mentor when it comes to providing functions such as direct training, role modeling, and acceptance; however, he is not nearly as strong when it comes to functions such as counseling and friendship/mutuality (Johnson, DiGiuseppe, & Ulven, 1999). So what functions are you most likely to receive from a faculty mentor? A recent survey of nearly 800 psychology doctorates indicated that among those mentored, the career function of direct training and sponsorship, and the psychosocial function of acceptance, support, and encouragement, were most consistently present in the mentor relationship (Clark et al., 2000). Table 2.2 summarizes ratings of Kram's (1985) functions in this group of doctorates. The mean number for each function is simply the average rating (from 1 to 5) for the function across all doctorates. It is worth noting that each of the mentor functions received a greater than

---

BOX 2.3: HOW IT WORKED FOR US—BRAD'S PERSPECTIVE

I often become preoccupied with providing my students career functions (e.g., sponsorship, challenge, and visibility) while at times neglecting seemingly simple (yet extremely important) functions such as encouragement and affirmation. For example, when I first encouraged Jenny to consider coauthoring this book with me, I went out of my way to highlight the positive professional exposure she might garner. It wasn't until Jenny confessed some doubts about her ability to make an important contribution that it dawned on me—I had neglected the psychosocial function of acceptance and encouragement. Although I clearly invited Jenny to be my coauthor on the basis of her excellent writing ability, her tenacious work ethic, and her tremendous capacity for organization, I failed to emphasize my confidence in these abilities early on in the project.

TABLE 2.2

Common Mentor Functions Offered to Psychology Graduate Students

Mentoring function	*M*
Direct training or instruction	4.50
Acceptance, support, and encouragement	4.46
Role modeling	4.26
Sponsorship for desirable positions	3.86
Provision of opportunities for research	3.76
Career exposure and visibility	3.61
Protection	3.46
Personal guidance and counseling	3.46
Friendship	3.36

Note. Ratings based on a 5-point Likert scale. From "Mentor Relationships in Clinical Psychology Doctoral Training: Results of a National Survey," by R. A. Clark, S. L. Harden, and W. B. Johnson, 2000, *Teaching of Psychology, 27,* p. 264. Copyright 2000 by Lawrence Erlbaum Associates. Reprinted with permission.

neutral rating, indicating that all nine mentor functions are likely to be present in mentor relationships at times. Nonetheless, ratings indicate that among these graduates, mentors were least likely to provide protection or to serve as a counselor or friend.

Second, we agree with Kram (1985) that the functions provided in mentor relationships are shaped by factors such as the specific developmental tasks facing the protégé, the mentor's and protégé's level of interpersonal skill, and the manner in which the graduate school environment shapes the range of functions provided. Contemporary graduate students represent a range of age and experience. Whereas one student may enter a program in midlife with years of experience in his or her field, another may enter as a young adult fresh from undergraduate education. Needless to say, the developmental tasks of these two students differ remarkably and will no doubt affect the nature of the student–faculty mentor relationship established. These students will also have unique needs at different stages of the relationship. Unfortunately, not all graduate school environments promote mentoring functions to the same degree. Whereas some departments may actively allocate resources and time for mentor relationships, others may not. In such environments, mentors and protégés are likely to experience more restriction in the range of functions shared in the relationship.

Finally, we encourage graduate students to practice what O'Neil and Wrightsman (2001) referred to as *role flexibility,* or the ability to adapt to different situations. Although the mentor and protégé may anticipate that certain functions will be provided in the relationship, many unexpected factors may influence each individual's needs over time. The protégé, for example, may experience a significant setback from physical illness and benefit from increased acceptance and confirmation as opposed to exposure and visibility. Mentors also experience personal and professional vicissitudes that limit or expand what they have to offer protégés. In sum, the most successful protégés have a clear picture of the functions they hope to receive while simultaneously appreciating the intangible synergy of the relationship, understanding the impact of developmental and environmental factors, and demonstrating that ever-valued quality of flexibility.

On the Benefits of Being Mentored: What the Right Mentor Can Do For You

When Levinson and his colleagues first studied the nature of mentoring in a sample of early to mid-career men, they made this striking claim:

> The mentor relationship is one of the most complex, and developmentally important, a [person] can have in early adulthood. . . . No word currently in use is adequate to convey the nature of the relationship we have in mind here. . . . Mentoring is defined not in terms of formal roles, but in terms of the character of the relationship and functions it serves.
> (Levinson et al., 1978, pp. 97–98)

Most scholars in the area conclude unequivocally that strong mentor relationships are essential for maximal career success and satisfaction. Torrance (1984) noted, "numerous researchers have observed that generally, whenever independence and creativity flourished, there has been some kind of 'sponsor' or 'patron'" (p. 2). On reviewing mentoring research in the field of management, Russell and Adams (1997) concluded: "the benefits to the protégé can be so valuable that identification with a mentor should be considered a major developmental task of the early career" (p. 3). The first empirical data regarding the benefits of mentoring was a large-scale survey of successful executives whose names appeared in the *Wall Street Journal* (Roche, 1979). Among 1,250 executives, two thirds had been mentored. Strikingly, those who reported a mentor earned more money at a younger age, were more likely to adhere to a clear career plan, and were significantly more satisfied with both their careers and their lives in general.

Our own review of the literature generally supports these bold claims. A variety of research designs used with professionals from a diverse range of disciplines consistently yield evidence supporting the claim that mentoring produces both career and personal benefits for protégés. In this section, we summarize the main research findings regarding the effects of being mentored. We have divided our summary into *predoctoral benefits* (those accruing prior to graduation) and *postdoctoral benefits* (those emerging following graduation). It is also important to recognize that some of the outcomes we discuss are clearly *extrinsic* and easy to document (e.g., salary, promotions, publications), whereas others are more *intrinsic* (e.g., satisfaction, professional identity). We believe intrinsic and extrinsic benefits are equally important outcomes of good mentoring relationships.

Finally, it is important to note that the benefits we discuss below apply to *informal* mentor relationships. Informal mentorships develop without external (graduate department) intervention, whereas formal mentorships develop as a result of assignment or some other intervention by the organization. Research among social workers, engineers, and journalists indicates that informal mentors provide protégés with more career and psychosocial functions than protégés in formal relationships (Ragins & Cotton, 1999). Also, protégés of informal mentors experience their mentors as more helpful, are more satisfied with the relationship, and subsequently earn higher salaries than professionals in formal or assigned mentorships (Chao, Gardner, & Walz, 1992; Ragins & Cotton, 1999). We believe that when graduate departments assign students to faculty mentors, these relationships are likely to be shorter in duration and ultimately less beneficial to the student protégé. This is simply because the mentor and protégé have less opportunity for developing comfort and identification with one another prior to entering into a mentorship. It is not surprising then that formally assigned mentors are less motivated to offer mentor functions than informal mentors (Ragins & Cotton, 1999).

Predoctoral Benefits

PROFESSIONAL SKILL DEVELOPMENT

As a graduate student, it is essential that you "learn the ropes" of your particular discipline. A good mentor will go out of his or her way to provide opportunities for you to observe and participate in his or her work. At times, these opportunities will take the form of intentional teaching and training, such as when a clinical psychologist asks a student to observe a therapy session or when a political science professor coaches his or her protégé on the art of presenting data to a community political group. At other times, opportunities for professional skill development are less intentional and more vicarious. This is the case whenever a graduate student observes the mentor "in action" around the department, in the classroom, at professional meetings, or in individual advising sessions.

The faculty mentor uses functions such as teaching, coaching, and the provision of support, guidance, and counsel to help the protégé accomplish initial mastery of the professional requirements of the profession (Kram, 1985; Newby & Heide, 1992; Phillips-Jones, 1982; Wright & Wright, 1987). As one example, some graduate departments have instituted teaching mentorships in which students are paired with excellent teaching mentors for the explicit purpose of preparing them for careers in academia (Murray, 1997). In such programs, mentors serve as role models, provide explicit instruction in the art of teaching, and later, help connect them with job contacts, often working to familiarize them with the university faculty culture. Mentors also embody the professional standards of the profession and (intentionally or not) serve as powerful models of how to be a colleague, how to interact with other professionals, and how to develop and apply strategies for ethical decision making (Johnson & Nelson, 1999).

PROFESSIONAL CONFIDENCE AND IDENTITY DEVELOPMENT

In addition to training and role modeling of specific professional skills, mentors assist protégés in the development of professional confidence and identity. So important is a mentor to this process of identity formation in graduate school that a leading educator argued that good mentoring represents one of the most important factors in graduate training and is essential for fostering long-term career competence and confidence for both scientists and professionals (Ellis, 1992). Graduate school mentors who support, encourage, and express confidence in a protégé are communicating a vision of the protégé as junior professional. As the protégé begins to understand and adopt this vision, professional identity and personal confidence emerge. Functions such as acceptance and confirmation enhance the self-image of the graduate student. When the student fails or errs (as is always the case), tolerance and affirmation are particularly important (Wright & Wright, 1997) and allow the student to consolidate a sense of identity independent from the ups and downs of specific performances.

It is often the case that even the most talented graduate students feel as though they are not nearly talented enough to be in graduate school and that they must surely have gained admission by mistake. This *imposter syndrome* is a common phenomenon among protégés, and good mentors patiently address this experience through consistent application of acceptance, affirmation, and the strong expression of confidence. In most cases, the imposter syndrome dissipates and the well-mentored protégé begins to view himself or herself through the lens of the mentor, eventually adopting a reasonably confident sense of professional self.

NETWORKING

Although many junior graduate students are happy simply to succeed academically in the first years of a graduate program, they will come to appreciate the remarkable significance of making connections, both with their own faculty and with those in the field more broadly. This will be especially salient as students approach graduation and the search for the initial job or postdoctoral fellowship. An effective graduate school mentor will be "on the lookout" for opportunities and introductions that might serve a protégé well. For instance, a social psychology professor may invite a protégé to be a copresenter of a conference paper. At the conference, the mentor may introduce his or her protégé to several important scholars who share the student's area of specialization. The mentor might also alert his or her protégé to job possibilities, which are informal or word-of-mouth. The net effect of this mentor behavior will be that the protégé is likely to have opportunities for employment and advancement that will not be shared by nonmentored students. Research with a range of professionals confirms the notion that professional networking (and the benefits that follow) is significantly enhanced by a mentor, particularly a mentor who is well respected and who holds position and power in the field (Chao, 1997; Orpen, 1995; Wright & Wright, 1987).

PREDOCTORAL PRODUCTIVITY

It is no secret that productive mentors beget productive protégés. One of the by-products of being mentored in graduate school is scholarly productivity as measured by conference presentations and journal publications. In samples of engineering (Reskin, 1979) and psychology (Cronan-Hillix et al., 1986) doctoral students, those mentored were significantly more likely to have published and presented. Of course, scholarly productivity is often an important component of becoming a competitive fellowship and job applicant. It appears that one salient component of mentoring in graduate school is the intentional collaboration between mentor and protégé around research and writing projects. An effective mentor works to involve protégés in ongoing research projects. In this way, a student learns the research enterprise and develops confidence as a researcher, writer, and presenter. In plain terms, you are likely to have more to show from your graduate school experience if you are mentored by a productive faculty member.

DISSERTATION SUCCESS

Excellent graduate school mentors have a track record of getting their students graduated in a timely manner. Of course, the most important ingredient in expeditious program completion is successful navigation of the dissertation project. A good mentor will carefully assess your dissertation-relevant traits and abilities early in the program (e.g., integrative writing skills, organization, tenacity). If you appear lacking in these areas, the mentor may work hard at helping you to organize and develop a project, perhaps setting clear deadlines for subtasks. If, on the other hand, you are highly skilled and possess diligent work habits, the mentor may simply offer encouragement and affirmation as you charge ahead. In most cases, you will depend on your mentor to assist you in developing an interesting idea, formulating a well-defined hypothesis, making contacts for data gathering, and managing any conflict with dissertation committee members.

SECURING INTERNSHIPS AND OTHER TRAINING OPPORTUNITIES

Graduate school mentors open doors for their protégés. A recent article for clinical psychology graduate students offered several important tips for preparing for the all-important and extremely competitive internship application process (Mellott, Arden, & Cho, 1997). Not surprisingly, the number one recommendation for students was to establish mentor relationships. These authors understood that mentors provide graduate students with several essential functions when applying for internships, fellowships, and other training opportunities. These include assistance in selecting sites that "match" the student and the student's career goals, writing very strong letters of recommendation that honestly but clearly promote the protégé, and making introductions for the protégé when the mentor has colleagues or other connections in the field. In our experience, a mentor who unabashedly endorses and promotes a student through letters and phone calls significantly increases the probability that the student will be successful in securing desirable training and early-career positions.

AFFIRMED TALENTS AND FOSTERED DREAMS

Perhaps one of the most important, yet difficult to assess, benefits of being mentored is the experience of having your talents affirmed and your dreams or visions regarding the future fostered and encouraged. Ask enough successful professionals what made the difference for them in graduate school, and most will describe the influence of a mentor who took time to both discern their unique mix of talents and then named and affirmed these. Until your gifts are recognized and praised by a respected mentor, you may have difficulty owning and trusting in them yourself.

Levinson and his colleagues described the *dream* as "a vague sense of self-in-adult-world. It has the quality of a vision, and imagined possibility that generates excitement and vitality" (Levinson et al., 1978, p. 91). You also have a dream, a sense of what you might accomplish and where you might be headed as a professional. You need a mentor who is interested in your dream and who takes time to understand it, examine it in light of your talents, and assist you with refining it. Ultimately, a good mentor will share your dream and will help you discover avenues for getting there. Because good mentors affirm talents and foster dreams, it is not surprising that later in life, protégés often reflect that their mentors were extraordinarily helpful personally as well as professionally (Burke, 1984).

SATISFACTION WITH DOCTORAL PROGRAM

All of the research bearing on graduate school mentoring indicates that mentored students are significantly more satisfied with their graduate programs than nonmentored students. Three large-scale surveys from the field of psychology show unequivocally that graduate students who are mentored by a faculty member report significantly higher levels of satisfaction with their program than those who are not mentored (Clark et al., 2000; Cronan-Hillix et al., 1986; Johnson, Koch, Fallow, & Huwe, 2000). Considering what mentors do for graduate students and the benefits mentored students tend to reap, this probably comes as no surprise to you. Although there are many factors that may contribute to your satisfaction with graduate training, we recommend that you take control of the mentorship factor and increase the probability that you will have a positive graduate school experience.

Postdoctoral Benefits

INCOME AND EARLY EMPLOYMENT

Mentored professionals tend to make more money. As a graduate student, you are probably interested in more than just your eventual in-

come. However, it is worth noting that research with a range of professionals in different settings confirms a robust relationship between
mentoring and eventual financial reward (Chao, 1997; Dreher & Ash,
1990; Roche, 1979; Russell & Adams, 1997; Scandura, 1992). In one
study of over 700 newly minted PhDs from a range of fields, studying
with a well-cited mentor was the single strongest predictor of postdoctoral employment (Sanders & Wong, 1985). Because a mentor will typically sponsor protégés for the best early-career jobs (Ellis, 1992), it is
not surprising that protégés of graduate school mentors enjoy a wider
range of postgraduate job options. Mentors open doors, promote protégés to colleagues, and notify protégés of informal openings and opportunities. Of course, it is also probably the case that well-mentored
graduate students are more confident and competent entering the job
market and that these traits serve them well in the competitive job-
hunting landscape.

PROMOTION AND CAREER MOBILITY

In addition to making more money, you are likely to enjoy more rapid
career promotion and receive more career opportunities than graduate
students who go without a mentor. Across a range of professional fields
from management to engineering to law, mentored professionals report
more rapid promotion and more frequent job offers than those without
mentors (Chao, 1997; Dreher & Ash, 1990; Fagenson, 1989; Mobley,
Jaret, Marsh, & Lim, 1994; Orpen, 1995; Roche, 1979; Russell & Adams,
1997; Scandura, 1992; Whitely & Coetsier, 1993; Wright & Wright,
1987). Of particular interest is the finding that junior lawyers who are
mentored in law school and shortly after are significantly more likely to
achieve partner status than those without mentors (Laband & Lentz,
1999). In the same way that mentored students are likely to experience
more success securing an initial job, they are also likely to rise more
rapidly through the ranks and to be viewed as more desirable job candidates, particularly if the mentor is eminent in the field. By the way,
career mobility is a good thing. Mobility does not imply that you are
obligated to move frequently because you were mentored, rather only
that you will have more opportunities and the luxury of choosing. We
think choices are good.

CAREER "EMINENCE"

If you want to be famous in your field, secure a solid mentoring relationship during graduate school. Cameron and Blackburn (1981) found
that sponsorship by a mentor during graduate school is an important
predictor of career success and notoriety or "eminence." Of course, men-

toring alone is not enough to ensure your success. Nonetheless, other things being equal, mentoring will likely better your odds of not only surviving but also thriving in your discipline. Having the support, confidence, modeling, and formal endorsement of a well-cited and successful graduate school faculty member will enhance your chances of getting opportunities and "breaks" early in your career, which often lead to greater success and perhaps even "fame" later on.

CAREER SATISFACTION

A more intrinsic or personally defined outcome of mentoring is satisfaction with one's work and career. In light of the functions provided by mentors, and the foregoing tangible career benefits, it may not be especially surprising to learn that mentored individuals are also more satisfied with their chosen careers in general and their day-to-day work more specifically (Chao, 1997; P. M. Collins, 1994; Fagenson, 1989; Roche, 1979; Russell & Adams, 1997; Whitely & Coetsier, 1993). This outcome holds true in a range of fields from business to social work. In one study, practicing attorneys reported that having been mentored early in the profession was a stronger predictor of career satisfaction than actual salary (Mobley et al., 1994). If you find a graduate school mentor who takes your dream seriously, communicates confidence and affirmation, helps instill within you a strong sense of professional confidence and identity, and works hard at connecting you with the right opportunities and jobs, you can reasonably expect to experience greater happiness and satisfaction with your chosen work than colleagues who are not mentored. We note with interest that in the original mentoring outcome study by Roche (1979), mentored executives reported not only higher career satisfaction but also greater satisfaction with their personal lives than nonmentored executives.

CREATIVE ACHIEVEMENT

Although there is very little research literature in this area, preliminary evidence suggests that good mentors foster and promote creativity and innovation on the part of protégés (Haensley & Parsons, 1993; Torrance, 1984). A graduate school mentor is likely to select you as a protégé because you are intelligent, are motivated, and show strong promise as a junior colleague and collaborator. Although the mentor clearly possesses superior knowledge and profession-specific skill, he or she is likely to be attracted to a protégé who brings fresh and innovative thinking to the research or scholarly enterprise. Rather than squelch your creativity, an excellent (and personally secure) mentor will nurture it, even while helping you to shape and direct this creative spirit. Mentors often describe working with capable and creative protégés as one of the single most rewarding components of graduate school teaching. Good mentors enjoy the synergy and intellectual stimulation that arises from working with talented students. In sum, a good mentor will honor and facilitate your good ideas, help you to get credit for innovative work, and encourage you to pursue creative projects that may ultimately lead to tremendous success professionally.

LEARNING TO MENTOR OTHERS

Mentored professionals tend to mentor others themselves. For instance, surveys of psychologists (Clark et al., 2000; Johnson, Koch, Fallow, & Huwe, 2000) and managers (Roche, 1979; Russell & Adams, 1997) show clearly that those who were mentored during graduate school, or early in their careers, are significantly more likely to go on to offer mentor relationships to others. This may at first seem like an odd thing to list as an important outcome or benefit of mentoring; however, there are two important reasons why learning to be an effective mentor yourself is important. First, those who mentor derive many benefits from the process. In chapter 3, we highlight several of the top reasons why faculty choose to mentor. One of these is a sense of generativity or pleasure connected with the experience of guiding and developing the next generation of professionals. In one innovative and revealing study, obituaries from eminent psychologists published in the profession's flagship journal—the *American Psychologist*—were content analyzed for common themes (Kinnier, Metha, Buki, & Rawa, 1994). Interestingly, one of the most common reflections regarding these famous psychologists was that they were good mentors. Being mentored may be the most effective way to really learn how to become a mentor yourself, and being a mentor is likely to be rich and rewarding for you. Finally, mentoring is good for your profession. When a profession places substantial emphasis on mentoring junior professionals, then professionals in the field enjoy strong identities, professional confidence, and greater career success and enjoyment.

Mentoring Benefits for Nontraditional (Second-Career) Students

In many scholarly fields, graduate students are increasingly likely to be nontraditional or older men and women who are changing career tracks, often after a successful career in another field. These students may be experiencing what psychologist Daniel Levinson described as the midlife phase of development (Levinson, 1996; Levinson et al., 1978). Graduate students returning to school in midlife or beyond may be pursuing a life-long dream, may have become disillusioned with another career, and may or may not be struggling with a number of common stressors at midlife, including the obvious career transition, biological or health changes, and relationship transitions (e.g., divorce, children leaving home).

Personally seasoned and professionally experienced, the nontraditional graduate student may believe that he or she does not require mentorship. In most cases, we disagree. Although older graduate students may feel awkward seeking mentoring from a same-age or younger faculty member, and although their identity may be quite secure and well developed, nontraditional students may face a number of obstacles that make good mentoring essential. For instance, age bias in academia may cause some faculty and prospective employers to regard the older student with disdain or suspicion—believing that because this student may have a shorter career span, they will be less productive, less likely to make a contribution, and therefore less attractive as a protégé (Dreher & Ash, 1990). Occasionally, younger faculty members may feel threatened by and uncomfortable mentoring more seasoned and accomplished second-career students. Also, some second-career graduate students may have difficulty shifting from a position of power and career mastery to one of subordinate neophyte. They require conscientious support and encouragement in adopting and mastering a new professional identity and (sometimes) entirely new skill sets. Returning women graduate students, in particular, may feel a loss of power and status at midlife (McQuaide, 1998).

For all of these reasons, we encourage nontraditional graduate students to actively seek a well-matched mentor, preferably one who is not threatened by the student's expertise and experience and one who demonstrates sensitivity to the trials of midlife and the stressors inherent in career transitions. We recommend discussing age difference concerns directly with a prospective mentor, as well as any concerns on the part of the mentor about committing to mentor a second-career student.

Who Gets Mentored and Why

3

Case 3.1

From the day he received his acceptance letter to a clinical psychology PhD program, Tom knew it would be important to seek out and develop a mentor relationship with a faculty member. On starting his first semester, he wasted no time asking advanced students for their recommendations about faculty who could offer him coaching and strong support during his academic career. Tom had a clear idea of his long-term professional goals and believed it was his responsibility to find a faculty mentor to help him achieve these goals. Because he was confident that he could offer some form of assistance to a mentor as well, he assertively arranged appointments with faculty to discuss their professional interests. He was disappointed but not distressed when several faculty communicated that they were not able to provide mentoring because of busy schedules. However, he persisted and was gratified when Dr. Able expressed a willingness to begin advising him and an interest in ultimately serving as his mentor. Dr. Able was impressed with Tom's good interpersonal skills, his clear interest in Dr. Able's research area, and his obvious forethought regarding how their research and clinical interests matched. Tom's positive demeanor, strong work habits, and initiative in pursuing a mentorship were key to launching a productive and fulfilling mentor relationship.

Case 3.2

Pam was in the 4th year of doctoral study in music theory when she began to pursue a mentor relationship. At this advanced stage in her graduate school career, she hoped a mentor could provide her with a dissertation topic. Pam was concerned about prospects for developing a mentor relationship in her department. She knew that several faculty were irritated with her long-standing habit of handing in major assignments late—a habit that resulted in frequent "incomplete" grades. Although Pam always completed the paper (often earning As), and although she attempted to cast

her habit in a humorous light ("I'm just deadline challenged!"),
she knew that many of her professors were not amused. As a
result of her chronic lateness, Pam was rarely sought out or
invited to participate in projects with faculty. She began to feel
anxious when each faculty member she approached politely
declined to serve as her dissertation chair. Some were honest and
admitted they could not count on her to get the work done,
whereas others offered less clear rationale.

Why is it that some graduate students seem to attract good mentors?
Graduate students often complain: "All of the good faculty already have
protégés" or "Finding a mentor is too hard!" Finding a good mentor does
not need to be a frustrating process that raises a sense of helplessness.
In fact, most graduate students do not fully appreciate the amount of
influence they have in the process of developing graduate mentorships.
You can get the type of mentor you want by understanding the type of
protégés that most good mentors seek and by strengthening and highlighting these characteristics in yourself. In this chapter, we examine the
personality traits and behaviors of graduate students who get mentored.
We then summarize the literature bearing on what most mentors want
in their relationships with graduate protégés. Finally, we offer suggestions for becoming a more "attractive" candidate when seeking out a
graduate school mentor.

Characteristics of Mentored Graduate Students

Research ranging from higher education to business clearly demonstrates a fundamental core of *personality characteristics* (e.g., emotional
stability, emotional intelligence, and commitment) and *behavior patterns*
(e.g., taking initiative, demonstrating high standards of performance,
and engagement in career planning) exhibited by students who tend to
get mentored (see Table 3.1). We summarize these important qualities
in this section. As you read, we suggest that you consider which characteristics you naturally demonstrate and those that you may need to
strengthen.

PERSONALITY CHARACTERISTICS

Emotional Stability

Emotionally stable graduate students are more likely to get mentored
(Turban & Dougherty, 1994). Emotional stability includes self-awareness, self-esteem, and a tendency to express few negative emotions. As

TABLE 3.1

Personality and Behavioral Characteristics of Mentored Graduate Students

Characteristic	Description
Personality characteristics	
Emotional stability	The student has a good sense of self-awareness, self-esteem, and positive emotional affect.
Internal locus of control	The student believes that he or she can positively influence events.
Coachable	The student shows that he or she is willing to learn and develop new skills and use constructive feedback.
Emotional intelligence	The student is able to successfully develop relationships with others.
Commitment (achievement focus)	The student demonstrates dedication, commitment to the profession, and tenacious work habits.
Similarity to the mentor	The student and mentor share similar traits, goals, and interests.
Behavior patterns	
Initiating the relationship	The student identifies potential mentors, initiates interaction, and works to develop a mentorship with a well-matched faculty member.
Articulating the match	The student is able to convincingly demonstrate how both parties will benefit from the mentor relationship.
Demonstrating ability and achievement	The student demonstrates high potential and works tenaciously to meet or exceed the mentor's expectations.
Career planning	The student establishes short-term and long-term career goals and works methodically toward those objectives.
Communication	The student communicates directly and clearly with the mentor, and others, without becoming either passive or aggressive.

a graduate student, it is important that you have a good sense of your personal strengths and abilities. Self-awareness and personal insight suggest to faculty that you may be open to feedback, flexible, and stable in the face of stressful circumstances. Ideal protégés are tolerant of their needs and vulnerabilities. They skillfully walk a delicate middle ground between arrogant denial of need and dependent expression of neediness. Similarly, faculty are attracted to graduate students who evidence a reasonably healthy level of self-esteem and personal confidence. Confident graduate students recognize that becoming a part of a particular profession involves risks to their self-esteem because learning to master new tasks naturally results in failure at times. For example, grant proposals and articles are frequently rejected at first. Students with a healthy self-esteem choose to learn from failure rather than accept failure as evidence of their incompetence or worthlessness.

Although mentors understand that graduate education is full of new experiences that challenge students' self-confidence, they are most attracted to students who present a sturdy sense of self-esteem and self-confidence (Allen, Poteet, & Burroughs, 1997; Kalbfleisch & Davies, 1993; Noe, 1988a, 1988b). There is also evidence that expressing a great deal of negative emotion will significantly decrease your chances of getting mentored. People high in negative affectivity tend to focus on the negative aspects of other people, themselves, and situations. They may express hostility, and in relationships, they are often demanding or distant (Turban & Dougherty, 1994). Graduate students low in negative affect are most likely to receive mentoring.

Internal Locus of Control

It will come as no surprise that mentors are attracted to students who believe that graduate school performance and events that occur during training are contingent on their own behavior and under their personal control. Students with an internal locus of control have learned that through their own efforts and initiative, they can achieve a good deal of academic and relational success. Locus of control is a stable personality trait that predicts greater motivation to improve oneself and greater probability that one will initiate a mentor relationship in graduate school (Aryee, Lo, & Kang, 1999; Noe, 1988b; Turban & Dougherty, 1994). In Case 3.1, Tom's belief that he could exert initiative and find a good graduate mentor resulted in just that. Not surprisingly, mentors appreciate the initiative and achievement motivation that often accompany an internal locus of control (Allen et al., 1997). Faculty predict that internally motivated graduate students will be more initiative taking, achieving, and likely to contribute importantly to the faculty mentor's own scholarly work.

Coachable

In addition to demonstrating emotional stability and internal control, mentored graduate students also demonstrate that they are coachable and willing to learn from their mentors. In her research with managers, Kram (1985) found this key characteristic extremely important to mentors as they selected protégés. Coachable graduate students pay attention to and express appreciation for both positive feedback and constructive criticism. They subsequently modify their behavior accordingly and avoid responding to mentor coaching with either defensive anger or fragile depression. There are several reasons why mentors prefer coachable protégés. First, mentors know that unless protégés want to learn, their efforts to provide career and psychosocial functions will likely be wasted (Allen et al., 1997). Second, mentors understand that protégés make mistakes as they learn new skills; however, they also want protégés to learn from their mistakes, accept correction, and modify their behavior. A protégé who consistently makes the same error can become a burden or embarrassment to the mentor. Third, excellent mentors possess a natural sense of generativity and experience great satisfaction from successfully developing graduate students into professionals (Burke, 1984; Busch, 1985). In sum, openness to advice and willingness to learn from constructive feedback are key characteristics of students who attract mentors.

Emotional Intelligence

You should also be aware that mentors prefer protégés who demonstrate high levels of interpersonal competence or what has more recently been termed *emotional intelligence* (Goleman, 1997). We use this term to describe the student's ability to understand and successfully manage interpersonal relationships. Students high in emotional intelligence (EQ) are particularly skilled at self-monitoring (Aryee et al., 1999). They are quite sensitive to interpersonal cues and are able to adapt their behavior to the requirements of a situation. Students with high EQ are able to quickly assess unspoken boundaries that exist as a result of the structure of an academic department or the relationships between individuals in this setting. Although structural boundaries may be more overt and easier to define (e.g., a student learns that a dissertation proposal must first be approved by the dissertation chair and then the department chairperson), interpersonal boundaries are frequently changeable and difficult to discern (e.g., a student determines that faculty does not want to be disturbed because he or she is working to meet an important deadline). As a result, the student with high EQ uses a variety of cues, such as nonverbal behavior, direct communication, and emotional tone of the conversation, to determine what the other individual needs or wants.

Potential mentors are likely to be attracted to graduate students with high levels of EQ. EQ is correlated with other desirable interpersonal skills such as empathy, flexibility, and a good sense of humor. These students tend to intuit their mentor's interpersonal preferences (e.g., for more formal or more collegial interactions), and when mentors are overwhelmed or particularly harried, high EQ students can demonstrate flexibility, appropriately adjust their expectations, and offer appropriate empathy.

Commitment (Achievement Focus)

Want to draw the attention of a good mentor? Research suggests that junior professionals who are committed to the profession and dependable in performance are noticed by mentors (Allen et al., 1997; Green & Bauer, 1995). Research with both graduate students (Hirschberg & Itkin, 1978) and managers (Fagenson, 1992) suggests that successful protégés demonstrate a high need for achievement, conscientiousness, and commitment to their profession. Students who are ambitious and possess a strong desire to excel are most likely to seek and receive mentoring. A tendency toward hard work and rapid task completion are also important characteristics. These traits signify to a professor that the student is capable of delaying gratification and tolerating frustration—both of which are essential ingredients to successfully completing graduate school and making a contribution to the field. (See Box 3.1.)

As a student in a graduate program, there are several tried-and-true ways to demonstrate that you are committed. First, complete assignments on time or ahead of time. Second, mentors anticipate that they will come to rely on protégés' productivity to enhance their own performance and work output (Phillips-Jones, 1982). As a result, they have their eyes open for students who produce top-notch work. You can increase your attractiveness in the eyes of potential mentors by doing superior work that clearly shows the mentor what you are capable of achieving. In other words, some degree of compulsiveness and Type A personality functioning is desired when it comes to finding a mentor.

BOX 3.1: HOW IT WORKED FOR US — BRAD'S PERSPECTIVE

During my career, I have been most willing to serve as mentor to students who are highly organized, articulate a clear commitment to the profession of psychology, and are willing to work exceptionally hard to meet deadlines and accomplish difficult tasks. Jenny came to my attention during her first year of graduate training by achieving the top grade in each of two courses she took from me. As a professor, I noticed that Jenny turned in assignments ahead of deadlines, gave extra attention to the quality of her work, and demonstrated her preparedness by making excellent contributions to class discussions. She demonstrated commitment and reliability. I therefore had no reservations about inviting her to join my research team and committing to serve as her graduate school mentor.

Similarity to the Mentor

As a graduate student seeking a mentor, you should be aware that a significant driving force affecting the initiation of the relationship is similarity between the mentor and protégé. Research in the field of graduate psychology suggests that protégés seek mentors who have similar career interests (Cronan-Hillix et al., 1986). Similarity between the mentor and protégé is also a characteristic of mentorships in business (Burke, McKenna, & McKeen, 1991). In fact, research suggests that when the mentor and protégé share similar career interests, the protégé experiences more career functions in the relationship (Burke, McKeen, & McKenna, 1993). This *similarity attraction* is not surprising given the inherent dynamics of the relationship. Specifically, the protégé seeks a reliable guide, and the mentor hopes for a protégé to carry on his or her legacy (Kram, 1985). In a fascinating study, Blackburn, Chapman, and Cameron (1981) asked highly productive graduate school mentors to nominate their most "successful" protégé. These mentors overwhelmingly nominated those students whose careers were essentially identical to their own. This tendency to "clone" one's graduate students is a common, if seldom acknowledged, process among mentors. Although some mentors intentionally seek out protégés who possess different interests or personality characteristics as a way to enhance the creative synergy in the relationship (Phillips-Jones, 1982), most will be attracted to students who remind them of themselves. Like other astute protégés, you will be best served by seeking a mentor who shares reasonably similar career interests, research interests, and interpersonal style.

BEHAVIOR PATTERNS

Initiating the Relationship

If you want to get mentored in graduate school, you had better take initiative for finding a mentor. Research clearly demonstrates that graduate students who target and initiate mentor relationships are more likely to get mentored (Clark et al., 2000; Cronan-Hillix et al., 1986) and to receive more of the important mentor functions during the course of the relationship (Green & Bauer, 1995). This strongly suggests that graduate faculty respond positively to students who take the lead in forming a relationship. As a graduate student, you may feel intimidated by the thought of approaching an esteemed faculty member to discuss the possibility of mentoring. You should know that you are not alone. Most graduate students have many questions and self-doubts when seeking a mentor: "Will I be perceived as annoying or arrogant if I initiate the discussion about a mentorship?" or "How can I simultaneously communicate self-confidence and my sincere need for guidance?" Successful protégés overcome these normal insecurities, move forward, and actively approach faculty they believe may make a good match. This is not especially surprising. Social psychological research shows that frequency of contact and proximity build mutual familiarity and liking. Thus, protégés who actively seek opportunities for interaction with faculty early in graduate school are most likely to get mentored (Aryee et al., 1999). In fact, we believe that this first step is so important that we have dedicated an entire chapter (chapter 5) to equip you with basic strategies for intentionally initiating your own graduate school mentorship.

Articulating the Match

Successful protégés can clearly articulate how the mentorship will likely prove beneficial to both themselves and their faculty mentors. Although faculty are often inherently interested in helping graduate students succeed, they must also frankly consider how mentoring a particular student will help them meet their own needs (Allen et al., 1997; Allen, Poteet, & Russell, 2000). Emotionally "needy" students are especially unattractive to faculty members. In contrast, faculty will be drawn to students with strong potential and clear interest in the faculty member's area of scholarship. Before embarking on a mentor relationship, the faculty member must ask himself or herself, "How is mentoring this student at this point in my career going to help me get where I am going?" Graduate students are wise to consider both their own needs and those of the faculty mentor.

Demonstrating Ability and Achievement

In addition to initiating behaviors, graduate students who get mentored demonstrate high levels of ability to potential mentors. In a longitudinal study of graduate students in the physical sciences, Green and Bauer (1995) found that students who entered their programs with positive attitudes and high levels of ability (e.g., superior GRE scores, high GPA, and prior research experience) received more mentoring during their graduate careers. Similarly, mentors in business organizations indicated that they are most likely to select protégés who they believe are high in potential and ability (Allen et al., 2000). Potential protégés who demonstrate high capacity and ability are simply more likely to come to the attention of potential mentors and ultimately land mentor relationships (Allen et al., 1997; Olian, Carroll, & Giannantonio, 1993). Given the potential costs of mentoring graduate students (e.g., time expenditure, risk of failure), it goes without saying that mentors prefer protégés who are talented and most likely to excel in graduate school and the profession beyond.

Career Planning Activities

Successful graduate school protégés are often those who show a clear identification with the profession, including a habit of developing both short-term and long-term career goals. Graduate faculty are often more attracted to students who demonstrate a clear psychological identification with the profession as opposed to students whose identity and commitment are more nebulous. Research suggests that protégés who show high levels of involvement in planning their professional careers receive more mentoring (Noe, 1988a). It is common for mentors to become vicariously excited by and invested in a promising protégé's career plans (Allen et al., 1997), particularly when the anticipated career trajectory is similar to the mentor's. Committed and invested protégés are most likely to succeed in their careers, thereby creating more visibility and satisfaction on the part of their mentor. If you want to impress a potential faculty mentor, you should actively seek career planning advice early in the relationship and then clearly pursue the short-term steps necessary to achieve ultimate career interests.

Good Communication

It is difficult to overstate the importance of good communication skills in attracting a graduate school mentor. Students from a range of disciplines from education and business to psychology and law know that effective communication can be among the most important predictors of career success. Research indicates that "communication competence" is a reliable predictor of whether or not a student will be mentored in academic settings (Kalbfleisch & Davies, 1993, p. 399). Protégés with strong communication skills maintain their composure even in tough social situations. They articulate their thoughts and feelings clearly and directly without becoming either aggressive or passive in the process. When discussing personal matters, they use discretion and consider how the disclosure will be received. They have also mastered the art of appropriately using wit and humor to set others at ease.

If you are skilled at interpersonal communication, you are the type of protégé that most mentors seek. As a skilled communicator, you signal to potential mentors that you will be able to address potential conflict with the mentor, faculty, and peers; that you will represent your mentor well in classes and professional meetings; that you can provide honest feedback in the relationship in a balanced, straightforward man-

---

BOX 3.2: HOW IT WORKED FOR US — BRAD'S
PERSPECTIVE

Early in her graduate school career, I found Jenny to be a poised
and mature communicator. It was clear that Jenny had natural
gifts in the area of communication, but it was also clear that she
prepared her presentations so that they appeared very polished.
When colleagues approached me at national conventions just to
comment on Jenny's excellent presentations, I knew that my se-
lectivity and judgment in choosing Jenny and protégés with similar characteristics were affirmed.

---

ner; and that you have the ability to clearly articulate career goals and
dreams. (See Box 3.2.)

DEGREE STATUS

Although unrelated to personality characteristics or behavior traits, it is
important to understand that graduate faculty are often most prone to
invest in relationships with doctoral- (versus) master's-degree students.
In graduate departments offering both master's- and doctoral-degree
programs, master's students are often disadvantaged with regard to getting mentored. There are several reasons for this. First, doctoral students
are fewer in number and are often admitted to doctoral study by a
faculty member who has tentatively committed to sponsor and mentor
them. Second, doctoral students work closely with faculty around research—culminating in the dissertation project—and this interaction is
longer in duration (4 to 6 years) than is typical in master's-degree programs. Third, doctoral students are typically preparing for a career similar to that of the mentor. This perceived similarity is attractive to mentors who see much of themselves in doctoral protégés.

If you are a master's-degree student, you have less time and fewer
opportunities than your doctoral-degree counterparts to secure a useful
mentorship. Therefore, you will need to be more intentional in searching for, and more assertive in initiating, a mentor relationship. You will
need to expedite many of the initiation strategies recommended in chapter 5. Nonetheless, master's students can bring themselves to the attention of prospective mentors early on by initiating conversations, taking
elective courses from desired mentors, volunteering for research tasks,
and discussing future career or doctoral program plans—eliciting faculty
interest in their desired career trajectory.

Characteristics of Unmentored Graduate Students

Many graduate students are never mentored. A very small proportion of these students actually prefer to do without a mentor (Clark et al., 2000). However, most unmentored graduate students have personality traits or behavior patterns that prevent them from being noticed or, worse, cause them to be actively rejected by faculty. As you refer to some of these characteristics (highlighted in Table 3.2), we encourage you to give attention to traits and patterns that you may need to address to become a more "mentorable" protégé.

Before considering the characteristics and behaviors of unmentored

TABLE 3.2

Personality and Behavioral Charcteristics of Unmentored Graduate Students

Characteristic	Description
Personality characteristics	
Dependent/needy	The student feels helpless, requires excessive assurance and support from the mentor, and has difficulty expressing his or her own opinions.
Narcissistic/arrogant	The student has an exaggerated sense of self-importance, requires excessive admiration, and is preoccupied with his or her own talents and abilities.
Detached/avoidant	The student is aloof, avoids contact, and appears disinterested in or excessively anxious about contact with faculty.
Emotionally unstable	The student has difficulty tolerating the mentor's honest feedback, demonstrates mood swings, and inappropriately expresses intense emotions (i.e., anger, fear).
Behavior patterns	
Procrastination	The student fails to take initiative in the relationship or to meet deadlines.
Underachievement	The student consistently performs below his or her ability level, resulting in mediocre grades and little respect from faculty and peers.
Disorganization	The student has difficulty organizing time and resources to effectively complete projects.
Inappropriate boundaries	The student fails to recognize and respect the mentor's personal space by asking inappropriate personal questions, disclosing too much, sexualizing the relationship, or disregarding boundaries established by the mentor.

graduate students, please recognize that these are not black-and-white (all-or-none) factors. Instead, each of us exists somewhere along the continuum of each positive and negative characteristic, and our place on the continuum often changes with circumstances. For example, an excellent graduate student may be quite introverted—strongly preferring solitary activities—without coming across as problematically detached or emotionally aloof. Similarly, a typically well-adjusted student may suffer bouts of anxiety or depression without allowing these episodes to become all encompassing or hamper his or her relationships or performance.

PERSONALITY CHARACTERISTICS

Dependent/Needy

Graduate students who are excessively dependent and needy are not likely to attract a mentor. A survey of over 1,000 college professors demonstrated that these mentors most frequently identified excessive dependency in students as the most negative aspect of mentoring (Busch, 1985). Mentors know that needy protégés require more time and effort when compared with self-reliant protégés. Needy and overtly insecure protégés are fearful of criticism, and therefore unlikely to assert new perspectives or offer opinions that diverge from those of the mentor. The mentor and protégé become primarily focused on the protégé's emotional needs at the expense of other important relationship tasks.

Narcissistic/Arrogant

Graduate students who demonstrate high levels of arrogance (or what clinicians refer to as *narcissism*) are likely to alienate potential mentors. Students with an exaggerated sense of self-esteem and high needs for admiration frequently exploit important mentor relationship dynamics such as power, control, and competition (O'Neil & Wrightsman, 2001). Narcissistic students, for example, are more likely to threaten their mentors to achieve a desired outcome (i.e., gain inappropriate authorship credit). They may be unwilling to compromise, devalue other students or faculty, or view their needs as paramount in the relationship. Given their interpersonal style, it is easy to see why such students are perceived as difficult to work with. Mentors will actively avoid narcissistic students.

Detached/Avoidant

You may be the most talented graduate student ever admitted to your doctoral program. However, if you are either so disinterested in relationships (detached) or anxious about relationships (avoidant) that you seldom initiate interaction with program faculty, you are unlikely to be mentored. Professors have seldom mentored a student who did not actively bring themselves to the professor's attention either through collaborative research projects or through clinical supervision. Mentored students display consistent efforts to seek advice, contribute importantly to faculty scholarly projects, and drop by for more informal conversations now and then—often over a cup of coffee. Graduate faculty are remarkably busy. Highly introverted or anxiety-ridden students will be at a tremendous disadvantage when it comes to mentoring unless they work at actively overcoming these traits.

Emotionally Unstable

In addition to dependency, narcissism, and avoidance, we believe the student who is emotionally unstable tarnishes his or her attractiveness to potential mentors. Features such as emotional reactivity in response to constructive feedback may communicate to faculty that you lack the internal "ballast" to weather the demands of graduate education. Graduate mentors understand that students face myriad trials and stressors. Although they anticipate that students will experience the normal ebb and flow of emotions, they are not attracted to students who demonstrate extreme mood swings or poorly modulated reactions to adversity. Faculty understand that poor emotional stability interferes with meeting deadlines, responding positively to feedback, and tolerating anxiety related to new tasks.

BEHAVIOR PATTERNS

Procrastination

Most graduate students learned during their undergraduate careers that procrastination could be deadly for academic success. In the search for a graduate school mentor, procrastination is simply fatal. The primary reason for this is that graduate students who procrastinate in completing academic assignments or other tasks send a clear message to faculty that they are unreliable. These students generally do not compete for higher rank or status in their programs and are likely to require a significant amount of additional work on the part of faculty. Students who procrastinate or expect to be pursued by potential mentors will be severely disappointed.

Underachievement

Although underachievement may be correlated with procrastination, we believe other bad habits may also come into play, such as inattention to details and sloppy work habits. Whatever the case, students who underachieve rarely receive respect from faculty or their peers. These students may have innovative ideas and untapped potential; however, unless this potential is highlighted in consistently excellent performance—academically and otherwise—potential mentors often avoid the risks associated with mediocre or poorly performing students.

Disorganization

Not surprisingly, poor organizational skills may also detract from a student's ability to get mentored in graduate school. Good mentors understand that organizational skills are essential for productivity. Students who lack these skills are at a deficit when compared with peers who are organized and proficient. Fortunately, organization is a skill that can be improved. Keep in mind that faculty are attracted to students who remind them of themselves. Most graduate school faculty are remarkably well organized.

Inappropriate Boundaries

One reliable method for scaring off potential mentors is to demonstrate poor interpersonal boundaries. By this we mean behaviors such as disregarding others' personal (physical) space, disregarding schedule boundaries (i.e., knocking on doors that say "do not disturb"), asking inappropriately personal questions, and disclosing personal information about which the faculty member may feel uncomfortable. In the worst cases, students may make overt romantic overtures or attempt to sexualize the relationship with faculty. In sum, these behaviors communicate to potential mentors that the student does not bring to the relationship the maturity and sense of appropriate interpersonal boundaries that most good mentors seek in a protégé.

If you find that you have identified any areas of deficiency while reading this section on characteristics of unmentored students, we refer you to the last portion of this chapter, which highlights several recommendations for improving your presentation and becoming a more competitive graduate student.

Understanding What Mentors Want

You might be wondering why we would include a section focused on how mentors hope to benefit from mentorships with graduate students.

We believe that you will stand a better chance of attracting a good mentor if you understand how mentor relationships are beneficial to faculty. When Levinson and his colleagues (Levinson et al., 1978) began to observe the benefits that male mentors in their study experienced, they illuminated the similarity between mentoring and the process that Erikson (1963) called *generativity*.

> There is a measure of altruism in mentoring—a sense of meeting an obligation, of doing something for another being. But much more than altruism is involved: the mentor is doing something for himself. He is making productive use of his own knowledge and skill. . . . He is maintaining a connection with the forces of youthful energy in the world and in himself. He needs the recipient as much as the recipient needs him. (p. 253)

Although you may find it difficult to imagine that a graduate school professor could actually experience tremendous reward from mentoring you, a solid mentorship could be very meaningful to both you and your mentor.

In addition to the experience of generativity, Kram (1985) suggested that mentors receive tangible benefits from the relationship, including technical and psychological support and a loyal base of followers who assist the mentor in improving his or her own work performance. Following a large-scale survey of business executives, Ragins and Cotton (1999) proposed five primary benefits that mentors experience: (a) rewarding experiences, including a sense of fulfillment, satisfaction, and creativity; (b) improved job performance as a result of rejuvenation and increased innovation; (c) a loyal base of support; (d) recognition by others when protégés demonstrate talent; and (e) generativity through transmission of skills and identity to protégés.

Graduate faculty are more likely to enter mentorships when they anticipate some benefit for doing so. As a prospective protégé, you should understand which benefits graduate school mentors find most attractive. In this section, we briefly summarize the major research findings regarding the benefits anticipated most by mentors. Consistent with our review of the benefits available to protégés, we divide these benefits into *extrinsic* or more easily observed benefits (e.g., salary, promotions, publications) and *intrinsic* and less tangible benefits (e.g., satisfaction, generativity).

EXTRINSIC BENEFITS

Career Productivity

Believe it or not, you can anticipate that as a graduate protégé you will assist your mentor with his or her own career development (Allen et al., 2000; Busch, 1985; Newby & Heide, 1992; Phillips-Jones, 1982;

Ragins & Scandura, 1999). Graduate protégés join their mentors in a variety of tasks, including writing research grants, collecting and analyzing research data, lecturing and grading undergraduate courses, and writing articles for professional publication. As protégés become increasingly competent and confident with these tasks, mentors feel more comfortable allowing them greater autonomy, thus creating more time and energy to devote to other career tasks. Protégés' creative and fresh input may generate new and innovative ideas (Newby & Heide, 1992). The joint effort of a well-matched mentor–protégé dyad can also significantly increase the graduate mentor's productivity and work quality, thereby leading to special awards, increased recognition, or tenure status. (See Box 3.3.)

Valued Information

In addition to career development, graduate protégés provide valuable information to their mentors about specific programs or grants, the graduate school as a whole, or particular individuals in the program (Newby & Heide, 1992). For example, a protégé may express loyalty by passing on important information to the mentor that promotes a different perspective on departmental politics, or a protégé may offer constructive criticism of the mentor's teaching or writing. As a graduate protégé, your mentor will likely value and benefit from the confidential information exchange that often characterizes strong mentorships.

Increased Power Base and Visibility

As a graduate protégé, you are a trusted ally for your mentor (Newby & Heide, 1992; Ragins & Scandura, 1999). This means that your mentor can count on you to be a loyal supporter. Loyalty may be particularly

---

BOX 3.3: HOW IT WORKED FOR US — BRAD'S PERSPECTIVE

I have benefited tremendously from mentoring Jenny and a few other students who happen to be very proficient writers. Although I enjoy many facets of mentoring, I find that I work most closely with those students who become actively engaged in my current scholarly projects. For example, Jenny has often taken the lead in developing an outline for an article, conducting the literature review, or writing large segments on her own, thus helping me to generate considerably more work than I could alone.

important when the mentor faces critical review during important career milestones such as tenure. In addition to loyalty, your mentor may benefit when you perform well (Phillips-Jones, 1982). When you succeed, your excellent performance increases your mentor's visibility and reflects well on him or her. Successful protégés form their own power base and network that can also benefit the mentor. Even the most experienced protégés may feel pressured knowing how much their performance reflects on the mentor; however, good mentors are aware of this pressure and work to alleviate unnecessary anxiety or unreasonable expectations.

Creative Synergy

Although inexperience can frequently feel like a deficit for protégés, good mentors understand that inexperience is often accompanied by energetic drive and fresh perspectives (Burke, 1984). Trends in the high-tech and scientific fields show a growing tendency for senior staff to be linked with the company's newest PhDs (Zey, 1988). These companies seem to appreciate that mentors and protégés often experience a creative synergy that acts as a catalyst for innovation. We believe that this synergy is more likely to occur when the relationship promotes free exchange of ideas and opinions. As with any profession, graduate professors experience times of fatigue when new ideas for research and writing seem few and far between. At these times, the protégé's fresh ideas are particularly important and beneficial for the mentor.

INTRINSIC BENEFITS

Satisfaction

In addition to extrinsic rewards, mentors experience an intrinsic sense of satisfaction when they invest in their protégés (Allen et al., 1997; Kram, 1983, 1985; Phillips-Jones, 1982). There are limitless reasons why you may offer your mentor a sense of satisfaction. For example, your graduate mentor may enjoy seeing you benefit from his or her advice and counsel and knowing that your growth and advancement will be a positive reflection of the relationship. From an altruistic perspective, your mentor may experience satisfaction from simply knowing that you benefited from the relationship. When you accomplish milestones in your academic career, your mentor will feel a sense of nostalgia, vicariously recalling his or her own accomplishments (Phillips-Jones, 1982). Finally, serving as a mentor can help graduate faculty to resolve what Erik Erikson (1963) argued was an important adult developmental stage of generativity versus stagnation. In the process of helping you with your development, your mentor is able to see himself or herself in a positive light. In her book *Mentors and Protégés* (1982), Phillips-Jones noted:

> [Mentors] take on protégés as an indirect way of paying their debts to society as a whole, or to the specific people who once helped them. They feel that they were given a break at just the right time and now are morally obligated to provide the same helping hand for others. (p. 59)

Although mentors experience a host of extrinsic and intrinsic benefits, the sense of generativity or building one's legacy is among the most profound and long-lasting rewards.

Friendship/Mutuality

Graduate mentors typically enjoy some degree of friendship or mutuality with their protégés (Allen et al., 1997; Kram, 1985). The sense of camaraderie and closeness may require time to develop; however, the ideal outcome for the mentor and protégé is a relationship between colleagues (Kram, 1985). Although excessive familiarity between mentor and protégé may lead to ethical concerns (Johnson & Nelson, 1999), most mentors enjoy close working relationships with protégés. Good relationships with faculty colleagues and excellent graduate students help ease the burden and isolation common of the "publish or perish" world of university-based graduate departments.

Becoming the Protégé Mentors Are Looking For

PROTÉGÉ SELF-ASSESSMENT INVENTORY

Now that you understand the type of protégé most graduate mentors actively seek, it is time to evaluate yourself as a prospective protégé. To help you with this process, we have included a Protégé Self-Assessment Inventory (see Table 3.3) for your use. Although this is not a standardized or normed test, the items reflect the main points from this chapter, and your score should be instructive as you prepare for a mentor relationship.

Read each statement and circle whether you *strongly disagree* (0), *disagree* (1), *agree* (2), or *strongly agree* (3) with the item. You will find this inventory to be the most useful if you honestly reflect on your current characteristics rather than respond as an ideal protégé. Tally the total score after responding to each item. A self-rated score in the range

TABLE 3.3

Protégé Self-Assessment Inventory

Item	Strongly disagree	Disagree	Agree	Strongly agree
1. I have a good sense of my personal abilities and strengths.	0	1	2	3
2. I believe that I can positively influence events in my life.	0	1	2	3
3. I am open to constructive feedback and learning new skills.	0	1	2	3
4. I actively seek and maintain collegial relationships with peers and faculty.	0	1	2	3
5. I establish high standards for my academic performance.	0	1	2	3
6. I am willing to seek out and initiate a mentor relationship.	0	1	2	3
7. I demonstrate a high degree of academic achievement.	0	1	2	3
8. I have a clear plan for my professional development.	0	1	2	3
9. My style of communication is honest and direct.	0	1	2	3
10. I am capable of telling a prospective mentor how the relationship will likely benefit me.	0	1	2	3
11. I am not overly dependent or in need of excessive amounts of assurance from a mentor.	0	1	2	3
12. I have a good understanding of my professional strengths and weaknesses.	0	1	2	3
13. I am unlikely to become extremely emotional or reactive under stress.	0	1	2	3
14. I have clear boundaries and respect others' boundaries.	0	1	2	3
15. I generally meet professional deadlines.	0	1	2	3
16. I am generally well organized in the use of time and resources.	0	1	2	3

of 37 to 48 indicates that you are an excellent prospective protégé. It is likely that you have many of the skills to develop a mutually rewarding and productive graduate school mentorship.

A score in the range of 25 to 36 suggests that you are a good prospective protégé; however, it is likely that there are several skill areas that could benefit from further development. For example, you may need to give attention to developing a clear sense of your personal abilities and strengths, refining your communication skills, or improving your use of time and resources. It is important to target particular deficits (any item to which you circled a 0 or 1 should be cause for concern). Once identified, these relative deficits can be intentionally developed. We talk more about this in the next section.

If you scored in the 13 to 24 range, it is likely that there are multiple skill areas, either personally or professionally, that you find to be particularly challenging. Given the magnitude of these deficits, we recommend that you seek assistance either from experienced students in your program or from faculty who are willing to provide you with coaching. If the pattern of low marks on this inventory suggests long-term personal or emotional difficulty, it may also be useful to consult a mental health professional. This may be done through your university counseling center or through another source. Mental health practitioners can be useful to you as consultants in several ways. For instance, if you have difficulty with initiating relationships, some coaching in assertiveness techniques may be helpful. Alternatively, if you have a history of procrastinating and missing important deadlines, you may benefit from some cognitive and behavioral interventions designed to attack the beliefs and behaviors that keep you locked in this self-defeating cycle. Finally, a score of 12 or lower suggests that you are not likely to be ready for a graduate-level mentor relationship at this time.

Extremely low scores may indicate that you cannot visualize yourself in a mentor relationship as a result of poor self-esteem, chronic relationship problems, or irrational beliefs about yourself or potential mentors. These irrational beliefs are very important to understand and dispute (see chapter 8). Again, we recommend consultation with a professional. Although not every graduate student is mentored, it is our position that graduate students can actively enhance their chances of being mentored, even when they have certain personal or professional weaknesses.

ACTION STRATEGIES

If the Protégé Self-Assessment Inventory (Table 3.3) reveals areas that you wish to polish, we have several suggestions for you. Although peers and professional consultation may still be most helpful, these action strategies should get you started.

Carefully Observe Mentored Peers

The first strategy is to keep your eyes open for well-mentored graduate students who you believe demonstrate the positive characteristics we have discussed in this chapter. Many complex tasks are much easier to learn when another person models them. Successful students who are more advanced in their academic or dissertation work may serve as excellent models. Be bold in asking them for tips and advice. Ask them to share several of the most important things they learned when finding their own mentor. Chances are they will enjoy the opportunity to pass on some knowledge to you.

Target and Develop Areas of Weakness

Make a list of the areas that you want to improve. For example, you may want to develop a more direct style of communication or procrastinate less. Write these goals in a clear and objective manner so that you can measure your progress and will know when you have accomplished them. In Case 2.3, Pam could set the following goals to improve her attractiveness to potential mentors: (a) "Turn in all assignments by the due date for a full term" and (b) "Participate in at least one formal faculty–student meeting in which I brainstorm methods for improving my standing in the program." We believe that you will be more likely to follow through with these goals if they are reasonable and if you plan to reward yourself for accomplishing them. Simple strategies to improve your own performance and smooth rough edges can do wonders when it comes to attracting a good mentor.

Ask for Honest Feedback From Faculty

If the Protégé Self-Assessment Inventory was not helpful in identifying areas for improvement, yet you have received several rejections from potential faculty mentors, we suggest asking for honest feedback from one or two well-respected faculty members. Requesting honest feedback about how you are perceived, both in terms of personality and performance, can be extremely intimidating to say the least. One way to structure this discussion is to ask faculty for feedback about both your strengths and areas that need further development. Tell faculty that you are interested in being mentored and want to know what improvements you can make to increase the chances that this will happen in the department. Many faculty would rather stay focused on your strengths so you may need to communicate clearly that you want suggestions for improvement as well. We believe that if you choose faculty who are insightful as well as patient, this exercise can be extremely useful in revealing your own strengths and limitations more clearly. For many, this may be the first step in becoming a graduate student who develops a solid mentorship.

Be Tolerant of Yourself

We have made many assertions in this chapter about the graduate student who gets mentored. Our final suggestion is to be willing to accept yourself despite your imperfections. Although it is certainly wise to target deficits and improve yourself where possible, efforts at improvement must be balanced by self-acceptance. Although ideal protégés possess several important characteristics, no graduate student can meet all of these standards at all times. Incidentally, it is also unlikely that a graduate mentor will be ideal at all times. These realizations may come as a shock or disappointment to some; nevertheless, we believe it is best to be realistic about personal limitations. Most importantly, this means that you should not allow an awareness of your personal limits to prevent you from initiating a relationship with a potential mentor.

II

How to Find a Mentor

What to Look For in a Mentor

4

Case 4.1

Prior to applying to doctoral programs in industrial psychology, Greg had researched the characteristics of good mentors. He knew that he wanted to work with a mentor with a well-established research program—one that closely matched his own research interests. Because he was interested in publishing during graduate school, Greg was determined to seek a mentor who had published extensively and had experience presenting research at professional conferences. Greg was also aware that a close working relationship with a mentor would be more effective if his mentor had a good sense of humor and excellent communication skills. Finally, Greg knew that he wanted an opportunity to work with a mentor who would be sensitive to his orthodox Jewish beliefs and practices.

Armed with a list of desired personal and professional characteristics, Greg identified several potential mentors by asking relevant questions in timely and sensitive ways during his interviews. After identifying key faculty from each program, Greg did not hesitate to ask current students in these programs if the faculty were well respected and had good track records as mentors. He also spoke directly to potential mentors about their experience with mentoring and willingness to develop a mentorship with him, if he was accepted into the program. His hard work paid off when he identified several faculty from two different programs who were an excellent match with the characteristics he prioritized. When offered a position in one of these programs, Greg felt confident about accepting the position, knowing that he had already established the groundwork for a successful and fulfilling mentor relationship at that university.

Case 4.2

During her first weeks of graduate training, Nancy never seriously considered working with any faculty member in the department other than Dr. Grant. Dr. Grant had just what Nancy was looking for: a well-established research program, plenty of funding, and a long list of publications. Nancy was ecstatic to receive an invitation from Dr. Grant to join his research team and she immediately accepted. She did not consider asking more experienced students about Dr. Grant's track record on such matters as his reputation for helping students to complete dissertation work in a timely manner, his interpersonal style, or his level of influence with other faculty in the department. Nancy also failed to obtain any information about Dr. Grant's personality, communication style, or personal health.

Although the relationship began on a positive note, Nancy soon became concerned to learn that Dr. Grant worked nearly 70 hours a week and expected students to do the same. She also learned through more advanced students that Dr. Grant had a string of failed marriages, in part, because of his compulsive work ethic. When discussing differences in their work habits, Dr. Grant dismissed Nancy's concerns and angrily informed her that she needed to "pay her dues" if she expected to have her dissertation proposal supported. Nancy also learned that many students who began dissertation work with Dr. Grant worked an average of 8 years before defending because of pressure to remain singularly focused on Dr. Grant's projects.

Finding a good mentor in graduate school can be difficult. Students such as Nancy find themselves initially thrilled to work with a specific faculty member, only to discover later that incompatibilities between the two make the match unproductive or dysfunctional. Poor matches may result from personality differences, dissimilarity in work styles, disparate research interests, unethical or unprofessional conduct by the mentor, or in the worst case, the mentor's exploitative behavior (see chapter 8). It can be difficult to discern indicators of incompatibility prior to establishing a mentor relationship. Inattention to important mentor matching variables may stem from stressors inherent in the graduate school experience. These include getting accepted, producing excellent work, performing well in practica, and carving out a dissertation. In addition, students may initially be in awe of faculty members, seeing only their strengths and accomplishments. Because initial impressions may lack accuracy, graduate students must intentionally work at discerning key faculty traits and carefully determining what implications these may have for mentoring.

The Ideal Mentor: Fact or Fantasy?

Before discussing the characteristics of good mentors, let us acknowledge a critical fact: The ideal mentor does not exist. No matter how sophisticated your approach to finding the right mentor, it is highly unlikely that any one mentor can meet all your needs and expectations.

Students who demand an ideal mentor generally experience two unsatisfying outcomes. First, they never settle for a well-matched (though imperfect) mentor, hence missing out on mentoring altogether. Second, their tendency to initially idealize faculty may cause them to disregard important red flags—signals of a potentially bad match between the mentor and protégé. Our message: After you accept the disappointing truth that no ideal mentor exists, you can begin the process of searching for a good mentor who suits you well.

It is also worth mentioning that although most successful alumni of graduate programs can identify one particularly important (primary) mentor, it is likely that you will have several influential advisors and career helpers during graduate school. Some of these will be secondary faculty mentors, some peer mentors, and some external professionals in your field of study (see chapter 11). Rather than expect your primary mentor to meet each of your mentoring needs, recognize that you will be guided, coached, counseled, protected, and supported by a range of helpers in graduate school.

Although mentor perfection is a myth, research does point to several highly desirable mentor characteristics. Allen et al. (2000) asked mentors working in business settings to describe the traits or behaviors of ideal mentors. These individuals, most of whom were also protégés at one time, ranked the following five characteristics as most important: (a) listening and communication skills, (b) patience, (c) knowledge of the organization and industry, (d) ability to read and understand others, and (e) honesty/trustworthiness. In a recent large-scale survey, more than 600 psychology doctoral students were asked to describe their ideal mentor (Rose, 1999). Results of the survey (see Table 4.1) suggest that doctoral students see an ideal mentor as one who is experienced and reliable, demonstrates intellectual curiosity and professional ethics, and possesses good communication skills. This mentor is also available to the student, offers honest and constructive feedback, and conveys a sense of confidence in the student's abilities.

In this chapter, we describe the personality characteristics and behaviors of good mentors. To heighten the reader's sensitivity to certain "red flags," we also describe some characteristics of bad mentors. Finding a good mentor may be serendipitous for a few lucky students. However, you are more likely to get the mentor you want by intentionally considering who you envision a good mentor to be.

Characteristics of Good Graduate School Mentors

What makes a good graduate school mentor? It may come as no surprise that research from a range of disciplines is consistent in describing a core

TABLE 4.1

Mean Importance Ratings of Ideal Mentor Characteristics

Characteristic	M
Provide honest feedback (both good and bad) about the quality of my work	4.75
Communicate openly, clearly, and effectively	4.75
Be experienced in his or her field	4.55
Treat me like an adult who has the right to be involved in decisions affecting me	4.55
Show me how to use relevant research techniques	4.45
Be available to me to discuss academic problems	4.45
Respect intellectual property of others	4.44
See my potential	4.40
Treat research data in an ethical fashion	4.38
Always be counted on to follow through when he/she makes a commitment	4.36

Note. From *What Do Doctoral Students Want in a Mentor? Development of the Ideal Mentor Scale*, by G. L. Rose (1999), unpublished doctoral dissertation, University of Iowa. Adapted with permission.

set of personality and behavioral characteristics of good mentors (see Table 4.2). In this section, we summarize these important characteristics. We hope that the following descriptions will serve as a benchmark, a starting place in searching for a good mentor. As you read this section, keep a list of those characteristics that are most important to you.

PERSONALITY CHARACTERISTICS

Personality Traits

There is strong support for the notion that personality and interpersonal competence are among the most important factors influencing initial attraction between mentor and protégé (Olian et al., 1993). When choosing a graduate school mentor, it is important to remember that your mentor's personality style will probably have a significant impact on your satisfaction with the relationship. Thoughtful consideration of the personality traits you are most drawn to can help you to get the most out of this relationship. Most of us do not intentionally nurture close relationships with people that we find noxious or irritating. Unfortunately, many anecdotal reports suggest that annoying and even pathological mentors do exist. Unlike Greg, who had a strong sense about the type of personality that he was attracted to, Nancy failed to appreciate Dr. Grant's "quirky" personality. We address personality red flags later in the chapter.

TABLE 4.2

Personality and Behavioral Characteristics of Good Graduate School Mentors

Characteristic	Description
Personality characteristics	
Personality traits	The mentor possesses a likable personality characterized by warmth, humor, support, encouragement, flexibility, dedication, patience, and empathy.
Healthy work habits	The mentor possesses a high level of self-awareness and strives to maintain balance between his or her work and personal needs and responsibilities.
Attitude and values	The mentor is aware of potential exploitation in the relationship and models values such as integrity and honesty.
Behavioral characteristics	
Productivity	The mentor is actively engaged in research, professional writing, and publishing and invites the protégé to join him or her in this process.
Professional influence and power	The mentor is well respected by students and colleagues as a result of his or her professional accomplishments.
Effective communication	The mentor is a skilled communicator and endeavors to model communication skills for the protégé.
Availability	The mentor is deliberate about scheduling and maintaining time for supervision, feedback, or other important mentoring functions.
Mentoring track record	The mentor has mentored several successful and satisfied protégés, and previous protégés offer favorable mentor performance evaluations.

Two surveys have focused on the personality traits of good graduate school mentors. Cronan-Hillix and her colleagues (Cronan-Hillix et al., 1986) asked graduate psychology students to describe the five most important characteristics of good mentors. Interestingly, of all the different characteristics listed by these students, personality was rated second only to the mentor's support and interest in the protégé. Students participating in this study identified a good sense of humor, honesty, dedication, empathy, compassion, genuineness, patience, nonsexism, flexibility, and loyalty as the most important characteristics to seek in a mentor. A second survey of psychology graduate students yielded remarkably similar results. Clark et al. (2000) found that good mentors were described as supportive, intelligent, knowledgeable, humorous, encouraging, honest, warm, available, caring, and accepting. In sum, good mentors are kind, competent, and enjoyable to be with.

These findings show that good mentors consistently demonstrate certain personality features. Still, there is some variability regarding those personality features most attractive and important in a prospective mentor. The key is to have a good sense of your own personality style and how this may blend (or not) with the various personalities among the faculty in your graduate school. Most of all, we suggest that you not settle for a mentor who lacks most of the characteristics that are important to you.

Healthy Work Habits

You will learn many different skills from your mentor. Among the most important skills is learning to develop a lifestyle that promotes a long and satisfying career. In the "publish or perish" climate of academia, it is easy to wonder how you could reasonably expect characteristics of personal health and life balance in a mentor.

A recent study of master therapists by Jennings and Skovholt (1999) suggests some clues to solving this mystery. These researchers interviewed psychologists and social workers nominated by their peers as being experts in their respective fields. When asked to describe the essential characteristics of these accomplished professionals, their responses fell into three broad domains described as cognitive, emotional, and relational. In the cognitive domain, master therapists were described as voracious learners who value the cognitive complexity and ambiguity of the work they perform. In the emotional domain, they are self-aware, nondefensive, and open to feedback. They attend to their own emotional well-being and are aware of how their emotional health affects the quality of their work. In the relational domain, master therapists possess strong relationship skills, and they regularly use these to promote positive change in others. In summary, these highly skilled professionals are well-rounded, self-aware, emotionally integrated individuals who enjoy being in relationship with others.

Although most mentors are not master therapists, good mentoring can be therapeutic, or growth-producing, for the protégé. We believe that healthy mentors help their protégés to grow in several ways. First, they model self-awareness and good boundaries between personal and professional roles. Second, they talk explicitly with their protégés about how they define and maintain these boundaries. Finally, good mentors help their protégés recognize and effectively address unhealthy professional work habits (e.g., compulsive overworking, social isolation) that are likely to interfere with long-term personal health.

Attitudes and Values

It is quite helpful to find a mentor who shares your fundamental attitudes and values. Cronan-Hillix et al. (1986) found that values of sharing, giving, and being nonexploitive were among the most important characteristics of good mentors. Good mentors hold clearly positive attitudes about students and their roles as mentors. They are fair, egalitarian, and professional.

It is particularly important to find a mentor who values and behaviorally supports professional ethics and codes of conduct. Recent research suggests that more than 1 in 10 graduate students have ethical concerns about their mentor relationships (Clark et al., 2000). Frequently cited ethical concerns in this study included the mentor sexualizing relationships with other students or the protégé, research-related concerns including publishing questionable findings, or the mentor becoming too emotionally involved with the protégé. Surveys consistently show that graduate students desire faculty mentors who demonstrate honesty, fairness, and integrity in their work with students. These should be key criteria in your own mentor search.

BEHAVIORAL CHARACTERISTICS

Productivity

Evaluating the professional and research performance of potential mentors is remarkably similar to car shopping after winning the lottery. Imagine that you are shopping for a car—a fantasy for many graduate students. As you walk up and down the rows of excellent, high-performance cars, the salesperson says "let me show you the used cars, some of them even start with luck!" Do you imagine yourself choosing something dependable and fun to drive, or a high-maintenance model —something temperamental, unreliable, and slow to respond? When shopping for a mentor, we hope that you will be as discriminating about the professional performance of potential mentors.

If you are seeking a graduate school mentor who is actively involved in research, consistently publishes professional work, and values continued sharpening of professional skills, you are not alone. Most graduate students believe that ongoing involvement in research and professional interests is a key characteristic of a good mentor (Cronan-Hillix et al., 1986). There are several reasons why most graduate students should carefully consider a potential mentor's level of involvement in professional research and publication. First, mentors involved in research usually have ongoing projects that can stimulate new research and dissertation hypotheses. Frequently, this can shave years off the laborious process of defining a dissertation topic and research method. Second, research skills, which are necessary for the professional careers of many academicians and clinicians, are best learned through direct observation. Watching your mentor design and perform innovative research is likely to be better than any coursework on the topic. Finally, a potential mentor's lack of involvement in research and writing may be a "red flag" indicating undesirable personality traits such as professional disengagement, lack of motivation, or poor self-esteem. Whatever the case, we hope you will carefully consider a potential mentor's research and professional engagement.

Professional Influence and Power

Do you want a mentor who will be invested in developing your skills and potential? Research suggests that high-ranking and influential individuals are more likely to mentor than their lower ranking counterparts (Ragins & Cotton, 1993). Furthermore, prominent mentors will likely have more positive effects on your career. Wise protégés appear to understand the importance of considering a potential mentor's influence and power within his or her department and profession. Olian and her colleagues (Olian et al., 1988) asked protégés in the field of business what characteristics they prized in mentors. They were significantly more attracted to mentors who were influential and involved in the organization's decision-making structure.

Why choose a mentor with professional power? Kanter (1977) proposed that protégés with influential mentors benefit from *reflective power*. That is, when a mentor sponsors you and your work, this indicates to others that you have the support of an influential person who is ready to back you up. Support and sponsorship from a resourceful mentor is important in several ways during graduate school. Mentors with departmental influence can expedite the dissertation process for their protégés by skillfully smoothing out conflict that inevitably arises among dissertation committee members. Influential mentors protect their protégés from unfair treatment that could damage the protégé's reputation or standing in the program. They are also highly networked with professionals from other departments and disciplines and are able to facilitate their protégés' applications for research, postdoctoral, and employment positions.

Although power and influence are important characteristics to prioritize when seeking a mentor, we want to add an important caveat. The best mentors temper professional success and prominence with a dose of humility and empathy for protégés. This means that no matter how well known and famous your mentor is, he or she should not forget that you are engaged in a learning process during graduate school. Narcissistic or self-absorbed mentors who fail to balance power with empathy for their protégé are generally best avoided, despite their highly influential status.

Effective Communication

A recent survey of managers revealed that listening and communication skills are some of the most important characteristics mentors can possess (Allen et al., 2000). Unfortunately, many graduate students understand the frustration that results from interacting with a professor who has poor communication skills. Professors who are vague about expectations, unclear about due dates, and unable to articulate exam topics are frequently avoided by experienced students. After all, graduate school is difficult enough as it is. Just as good communication is important in the classroom, it is essential in a relationship.

Several indicators suggest that a mentor possesses strong communication skills. First, good mentors communicate directly with their students and protégés rather than becoming passive and unclear or aggressive and demeaning. Subsequently, their protégés rarely leave important conversations with questions such as "What does my mentor expect of me in this situation?" or "What did I do to deserve that tirade?" Second, because of their direct communication skills, good mentors handle conflict in a constructive manner. Finally, good mentors offer positive and constructive feedback, feedback that is simultaneously encouraging and challenging.

Availability

In addition to being effective communicators, good graduate school mentors make themselves available to their protégés. It may come as no surprise that mentors who are inattentive, fail to schedule time for protégés, or disregard commitments are rarely seen as successful. Research consistently shows that mentor availability is very important to protégés. Cronan-Hillix et al. (1986) found that graduate psychology students were quite critical of mentor unavailability or inaccessibility. A study by Ensher and Murphy (1997) revealed that protégés who spent more time with their mentors were more satisfied with the relationship. We believe that you are wise to carefully consider availability and accountability when choosing a mentor. (See Box 4.1.)

Mentoring Track Record

Good graduate school mentors have consistently mentored students, and their protégés are consistently satisfied with the mentorship. Most graduate school mentors do not publish a list of their most famous or satisfied protégés; however, they can easily identify their protégés and they frequently maintain less formal peer relationships long after the formal relationships have ended. Because they inherently enjoy the pro-

BOX 4.1: HOW IT WORKED FOR US—JENNY'S PERSPECTIVE

As a graduate student, I valued having regular meetings with Brad, especially when working intensely on my dissertation. These meetings provided accountability, support, encouragement, and, most importantly, helped me to complete the task on time. Although I know Brad prizes time for writing (solitude), he worked at being particularly available to students he had committed to mentor.

cess of mentoring and are serious about the commitments they make to protégés, they are unlikely to mentor more than a few graduate students at any one time. Good mentors see each protégé as unique and important. They commit to knowing each protégé and discerning the unique mix of talents and dreams each of their students brings to graduate school. They value the opportunity to intentionally teach, coach, and model for their protégés, and they enjoy both their protégés and the mentoring process. For these reasons, excellent mentors are selective and avoid accepting too many protégés.

A Warning About Bad Mentors

Now that you have a strong sense of the characteristics that make a mentor truly excellent, we draw your attention to warning signs that a mentor may be less than desirable. It is difficult to estimate how many bad mentors are lurking in the world of graduate education. Clark et al. (2000) surveyed graduate psychology students about their negative experiences with mentors and found that up to 25% of students had some form of negative experience with their mentor. Primary problems included mentor unavailability, difficulty with termination, being unable to meet the mentor's expectations, and the mentor's unethical behavior (i.e., taking credit for the student's work, sexualizing the relationship). Although we believe that most faculty are not malignant—seeking to exploit vulnerable and naive graduate students—we highlight several negative personality and behavioral characteristics (see Table 4.3) so that you can carefully "weed out" and avoid problem faculty.

TABLE 4.3

Personality and Behavioral Characteristics of Bad Graduate School Mentors

Characteristic	Description
Personality characteristics	
Personality traits	The mentor possesses noxious personality traits such as narcissism, emotional detachment, avoidance, and immaturity.
Unhealthy work habits	The mentor possesses a low level of self-awareness about his or her personal needs or has compulsive work habits that interfere with personal health.
Attitude and values	The mentor is unaware or unconcerned about exploitation of the protégé, demonstrates sexist or racist attitudes, or does not adhere to professional and ethical values.
Behavioral characteristics	
Lack of productivity	The mentor is not actively engaged in research and other professional activities and therefore is unable to invite the protégé's participation in this process.
Unethical behavior	The mentor engages in unethical professional behaviors such as claiming credit for the protégé's work, sexualizing the relationship, or being racially insensitive.
Ineffective communication	The mentor is a poor communicator who fails to listen, is unable to articulate clear expectations, or cannot appropriately self-disclose or affirm the protégé.
Unavailable/unsupportive	The mentor fails to schedule or maintain time for supervision, feedback, or other important mentoring activities.
Poor mentoring track record	The mentor has several current or previous protégés who are unsatisfied or displeased with the outcome of the mentorship.

PERSONALITY CHARACTERISTICS

Personality Traits

Bad mentors may have noxious or unlikable personality traits. There are a range of personality styles that would likely make working with a mentor difficult. For example, extremely avoidant or detached mentors struggle to provide important psychosocial functions in the relationship. Narcissistic or excessively arrogant mentors have difficulty supporting their protégés because they are engaged in dominating or competing with their protégés. Mentors who are personally immature often struggle to establish appropriate boundaries and challenge protégés. You can probably add other annoying personality traits to this list based on your own experience and preferences. We caution you to carefully exclude faculty with these traits when selecting a mentor.

Unhealthy Work Habits

In addition to noxious personality traits, mentors with poor work habits are worth avoiding. These mentors frequently lack an essential awareness of their personal needs, including needs for intimacy and balance between personal and professional roles. As a result, these mentors may demonstrate destructively compulsive work habits and expect their protégés to adopt them as well. They may also seek to fulfill personal needs for intimacy through their relationships with protégés. Although it is natural for some personal needs to be met through the relationship, an unbalanced approach may lead to uncomfortable boundary violations (e.g., excessive self-disclosure) or even attempts to sexualize the mentor relationship.

Attitudes and Values

Bad mentors are either unconcerned about how their attitudes and values affect protégés or actively adhere to negative and harmful attitudes and values that undermine a good mentorship. These mentors may be dishonest and deceptive toward their protégés, exploitative of their protégés, and purely utilitarian in attempts to maximize their own benefit from the relationship. Faculty with disparaging attitudes about women, racist views, or clear hostility toward other program faculty are best avoided. Finally, you should be cautious about faculty who hold largely pessimistic or antagonistic views about their own profession or discipline.

BEHAVIORAL CHARACTERISTICS

Lack of Productivity

Unproductive faculty are not actively engaged in research or salient professional activities. Although they may profess expertise, they have few publications, have few cutting-edge professional contributions, and may not be highly respected by their peers. They are what many refer to as "dead weight" in the department, using up valuable resources without offering any substantial returns to the institution or the students who pay tuition. Although they may be well intended and even interpersonally gifted, research suggests that graduate students—particularly those interested in careers in academia—will be best served by a mentor who is productive as a scholar. We suggest that you find a mentor who is whole-heartedly pursuing the types of professional activities that are consistent with your professional aspirations.

Unethical Behavior

Mentors who engage in unprofessional conduct should be avoided at all costs. Unfortunately, we have heard too many stories about students who found their mentors taking credit for their work, providing minimal supervision, or sexualizing their relationship. Many students complain that their mentors' unprofessional behavior was not apparent early in the relationship. We recommend that you carefully observe your prospective mentor's professional behavior and that you engage in good reconnaissance—asking other students, program graduates, and professionals, about your potential mentor (see chapter 5). It goes without saying that evidence of unprofessional or unethical conduct should serve as a clear red flag. In this case, you should pursue other options.

Ineffective Communication

We have already discussed the importance of good communication to promote a successful mentorship. We won't belabor the point here, except to restate that if you have concerns about a potential mentor's communication style, you should address them before committing to the relationship. If a faculty member is a poor listener, fails to articulate expectations, appears unable to communicate praise and satisfaction with your performance, or has great trouble understanding or expressing his or her own emotional state, you should be cautious. Although communication generally improves as a mentor and protégé get to know one another, do not expect to retrain or "fix" a mentor's passive or aggressive style of communication. If the potential mentor responds defensively to your questions about his or her style of communication, this is further evidence that you are better off investing in another mentor.

Unavailable/Unsupportive

Unavailable or inattentive mentors fail to provide support for their protégés and should be avoided. These faculty are chronically late or fail entirely at establishing and maintaining regular meetings with their protégés. When confronted about their failure to maintain these commitments, they are quick to suggest that demands on their own time and resources are simply too great to make time for protégés' needs. As a result, protégés often feel that they are completely on their own. Fortunately, tendencies toward inattentiveness and lack of support are relatively easy to determine by checking the mentor's track record with other protégés.

Poor Mentoring Track Record

Lousy mentors have poor track records; they leave a trail of angry or dissatisfied graduate students. Although their previous protégés may be unwilling to discuss the details of their relationship, most will be willing to pass on a cautionary note or point out the mentor's weaknesses— particularly those that were most problematic for them. It is important to note that poor track records are not established by one dissatisfied protégé. In fact, most mentors with more than a few years of experience have one or two disenchanted protégés for one reason or another. Nevertheless, if in the process of gathering feedback from past protégés you discover a string of unhappy consumers, we suggest that you consider this a red flag and move on to better options.

The Intentional Protégé: Initiating a Mentor Relationship

5

Case 5.1

Once she decided to pursue a PhD in education, Maria began aggressively researching the many PhD programs around the country. In addition to information about program prestige and quality, she researched faculty interests and carefully noted which programs had faculty with interests in multicultural educational models—her own primary interest. She contacted several of these programs and requested additional information about program emphasis. She even asked to speak to a current graduate student at each program. On the basis of the data gathered from this research, she applied to 12 programs and was accepted to 4. Maria then went to work gathering more in-depth information about the 4 programs, including specific faculty interests. Three of the programs had at least one Hispanic faculty member. Because finding a Hispanic mentor was important to her, she narrowed her search to the 2 programs with Hispanic faculty who also had interests in multicultural education models. She then contacted each of these faculty members and explored their availability and willingness to take on new graduate students. She further asked for the names of a current student of each faculty member and contacted these students, asking questions about their experience working with the faculty mentor. On the basis of this information, she selected one of the programs. During her first semester, Maria assertively gathered additional information about the two faculty she viewed as strong potential mentors. She attended research team meetings run by these faculty, signed up for classes taught by each, and arranged a formal meeting with both to discuss their research program and approach to working with graduate student advisees. Convinced she wished to work with Dr. Chavez, Maria scheduled a formal meeting with him to request that he become her advisor and, ultimately, her graduate school mentor. She clearly described her interests in working with him and explained how she thought both might benefit from their collaboration. Dr. Chavez was delighted with her thoughtful consideration of this match and they quickly formed a productive and rewarding mentorship.

Case 5.2

When Stewart began thinking about a graduate program in economics, his primary concern was getting into one of the top programs listed in a recent magazine ranking. His undergraduate peers confirmed the notion that just "getting in" to one of these programs was all that mattered. He used several helpful guides to gaining admission to graduate school and was successful in getting an offer from one of the top 10 schools in the national ranking. He quickly confirmed his acceptance of this offer. During his first 2 years in the graduate program, Stewart was overwhelmed with the many demands on his time. Occasionally, he felt he was barely keeping up and he remained focused on just getting through each semester. Toward the end of his 3rd year in the program, Stewart began to worry about his dissertation. He began talking to peers and was alarmed to hear that many faculty were already "full" when it came to taking on new students in his year group. Not especially committed to any specific scholarly interest, Stewart (now frantically) began asking several faculty if they would consider chairing his dissertation project. Most confirmed that they were committed but kindly offered to serve as a committee member (though not his chair). After a great deal of frustration, Stewart found that only Dr. Arctic was willing to chair his dissertation—as long as it was in Dr. Arctic's area of interest, a very obscure theoretical area of economic theory in which Stewart had almost no interest. Furthermore, Dr. Arctic was known for being cold, aloof, arrogant, and difficult to communicate with. He had only one other graduate advisee. Stewart's dissertation experience was very unpleasant and it took him a year longer than he had planned. He and Dr. Arctic had very few interactions beyond those required for completion of his project, and Dr. Arctic was slow to return drafts of his work. When Stewart graduated and required letters of recommendation for job applications, he was so ambivalent about his relationship with Dr. Arctic that he had to approach other program faculty for letters—none of which knew Stewart particularly well. Stewart had trouble landing his first job and remained bitter about his graduate school experience for many years.

Mentorships don't just "happen." Rather, one or both members of the pair actively create them. Although some graduate school mentorships may appear to form magically and effortlessly—as though fate or chemistry exerted a magnetic pull between student and professor—research suggests this is rarely the case. In fact, most graduate school mentorships are actively initiated by the graduate student (Atkinson et al., 1994; Clark et al., 2000; Cronan-Hillix et al., 1986). This is true even in large research-oriented PhD programs (Blackburn et al., 1981). Approximately half of all mentorships in the field of psychology are formed almost exclusively through the active initiative of the student, whereas another 30% to 40% are formed mutually, with both student and professor taking some initiative. Thus, in the vast majority of cases, mentorships would be unlikely to develop without the intentional investment and activity of the prospective protégé. Even when programs attempt to match incoming students with specific faculty advisors, students can take an assertive role in ensuring the best match.

Hirshberg and Itkin (1978) found that the success of PhD students in several graduate programs at the University of Illinois was best predicted by factors such as achievement orientation, persistence, commitment to the discipline, and competence with research. They concluded: "The constellation of such Protestant ethic traits as industriousness, commitment, and conscientiousness characterized the student who obtained the degree and went on to publish" (Hirshberg & Itkin, 1978, p. 1091). We believe it is no coincidence that high-achieving and tenacious students are most successful in their graduate programs and in their careers. Students with these traits will also be most successful in arranging to be mentored by the right faculty member.

In this chapter, we hope you pick up a singular and salient message: If you want to be mentored, you had better be intentional about finding the right mentor and tenacious in initiating the mentor relationship. Not only should you be intentional and assertive in finding a mentor, but you should also do this as early as possible in your graduate student career. The greater the duration of your mentorship, the greater the probability that your mentor will truly *know* you. The mentor will be in a better position to provide essential training experiences and, ultimately, address your unique qualities in strong letters of recommendation for internships and jobs (Mellott et al., 1997).

We consider this one of the most important chapters in the book, and we hope you use it as a manual for developing a personal strategy for getting mentored. In addition to our mantra that getting mentored will require intentional planning and tenacious commitment, we offer another indispensable theme: *Reconnaissance pays*. Not all graduate programs take mentoring seriously, and not all faculty are well suited to the mentor role. For these reasons, it is essential that you gather good "intelligence" about graduate programs and individual faculty members as you prepare to initiate a mentorship. We have organized this chapter into four sections using the consistent theme of *reconnaissance* or intelligence gathering (see Exhibit 5.1). The sections include Preapplication reconnaissance, Postadmission reconnaissance, First-Semester reconnaissance, and Initiating the mentorship ("Operation Initiation").

Initiating a Mentor Relationship

Phase 1: Preapplication reconnaissance
  Determine the current interests of faculty in your field.
  Determine if the doctoral programs of interest demonstrate adequate
    attention to mentoring.
  Make inquiries about the program to faculty and current students.
Phase 2: Postadmission reconnaissance
  Carefully assess each program's specific mentoring structure.
  Gather in-depth information about faculty interests and productivity.
  Gather information about the program's mentoring structure from
    current students.
Phase 3: First-semester reconnaissance
  Watch, listen, and learn about the personal and professional
    characteristics of faculty who could potentially fill the role of a
    mentor.
  Talk with current and former students about the faculty member's track
    record as a mentor.
  Arrange introductory meetings with top faculty prospects to discuss the
    possibility of developing a mentorship.
Phase 4: Initiating the mentorship ("Operation Initiation")
  Create opportunities for informal interaction (e.g., assisting with
    teaching or research projects, attending the faculty member's research
    seminars, or enrolling for courses offered by the faculty member) with
    your "top choice" faculty mentor.
  Formalize the mentorship by scheduling a meeting, identifying mutual
    goals, and obtaining an affirmative commitment from the mentor.

Phase 1: Preapplication Reconnaissance

The decision to apply to graduate school is a weighty one. In deciding
to embark on this arduous journey, you have undoubtedly chosen a
career, considered the financial and personal costs of graduate education, and examined specific graduate program characteristics such as
reputation and admission criteria, geographic location, and time required to achieve the graduate degree. We hope that you have also
considered more specific variables, such as program specialty, the productivity and reputation of individual faculty, and the extent to which
your research and career interests appear to match those of faculty in
each program you consider.

There are a number of excellent guides to gaining admission to graduate school in a range of fields. In Exhibit 5.2, we list several of the best of these guides. These books will show you how to select the best schools, how to make yourself a desirable candidate, how to prepare for entrance examinations and interviews, and how to increase your acceptance rate when applying for admission.

These guides to gaining admission to graduate school are essential in our opinion. If you are still preparing for the application process, we recommend that you purchase and carefully use the guide most relevant to your field of interest. You will certainly be more informed, and probably more competitive. Keep in mind, however, that these guides say very little about the importance of selecting graduate programs with mentoring in mind. Therefore, you will need to use the strategies recommended in this chapter in concert with the good advice provided in these admission guides.

We understand that as one facing the trial of application to graduate school, you may be focused more on just "getting in." Many doctoral programs and law schools are extremely competitive, and only a small proportion of applicants will gain admission. However, in many disciplines, there are literally hundreds of graduate programs to choose from, and there are probably several well suited to your skills, interests, and career goals. We encourage you to become an assertive consumer—even at the application stage. By this we mean that you should not select programs based merely on prestige, rankings in popular magazines, or percentage of applicants admitted. Although you should consider these factors, why not also investigate variables related to the probability of finding a good mentor once admitted? We recommend seeking information in the following areas before applying to a program.

EXHIBIT 5.2

Guides to Getting Into Graduate School

American Psychological Association. (1994). *Getting-in: A step-by-step plan for gaining admission to graduate school in psychology.* Washington, DC: Author.

Castellucci, M. (2000). *Peterson's game plan for getting into graduate school.* Lawrenceville, NJ: Peterson's Guides.

Falcon, A. (1998). *Planet law school: What you need to know (before you go) . . . but didn't know to ask.* Honolulu, HI: Fine Print Press.

Martinson, T. H., Waldherr, D. P., & Martinson, T. E. (1998). *Getting into graduate business school today.* New York: Arco Publishing.

Plantz, S. H., Lorenzo, N. Y., & Cole, J. A. (1998). *Getting into medical school (4th ed.).* New York: Arco Publishing.

WHAT ARE THE CURRENT INTERESTS OF FACULTY?

If you are pursuing a doctoral degree in any field, you will be required to engage in at least one major scholarly research endeavor (typically the doctoral dissertation). In addition, you may be required to engage in research in some form throughout your graduate school career (e.g., you may be funded as a research assistant to a particular faculty member). If you are interested in a career in academia or research, this early career research experience will significantly affect your subsequent career success. Working with a faculty mentor who shares your interests and brings seasoned scholarly wisdom and topical expertise to bear on your projects will prove invaluable. If you are intensely interested in the sociology of adolescent gangs, the neurobiology of gender differences, or the novels of Walker Percy, then does it not stand to reason that your graduate school experience, as well as your ability to develop true expertise in your area of interest, will be facilitated by finding a mentor who is a clear expert in it as well? Not only will you benefit immediately from your mentor's expertise, but you will also receive the benefits of what social psychologists call the *halo effect*—meaning that the expertise attributed to your mentor may also be attributed to you when your mentor recommends you for research funding or academic positions.

Finding a graduate school mentor begins when you intentionally apply to a program because at least some of the faculty share your research and scholarly interests. This is true even if you plan a professional career as opposed to a career in academia. For example, applicants to clinical psychology programs who are specifically interested in learning psychodynamic approaches to treatment should avoid applying to programs that clearly describe themselves as behavioral or cognitive in theoretical orientation. Information about individual program faculty will be available in promotional materials, and usually, on the university's Web page. Various guides may also summarize salient theoretical or research orientations in doctoral programs. For example, the annual guide *Graduate Study in Psychology* (Braswell, 2000) summarizes such information for over 500 graduate programs in the field of psychology.

DOES THE PROGRAM DEMONSTRATE ATTENTION TO MENTORING?

In its promotional brochures and curriculum summary, does the program articulate a coherent approach to mentoring? Excellent graduate programs may use one of two approaches to ensure that incoming students find faculty mentors early in their education. First, more traditional doctoral programs often admit students whom they believe are specifically matched to the research interests of a particular faculty member (Ellis, 1992). This professor is assigned as the student's faculty advisor, and ideally, develops a mentorship with the student. When applying to such programs, wise applicants are careful to specify the faculty member or members with whom they are most interested in working. A second approach to mentoring sometimes articulated by graduate programs is a group or team approach. In such programs—often programs with larger student-to-faculty ratios—students are encouraged to "sample" various faculty-led research teams before choosing one to join permanently. Faculty-led advising teams can sometimes offset the effects of large student-to-faculty ratios. Although they do not guarantee that faculty will develop mentorships with students, the regular contact and collaboration around research or professional tasks helps foster mentoring.

Graduate programs that articulate some structure for facilitating mentorships should receive particular attention as you narrow your list of desirable programs. Unfortunately, many programs will not address this issue either in their materials or in their contact with applicants. You should be somewhat concerned about a graduate program that either ignores mentoring altogether or, worse, openly disparages mentoring or insists that finding a faculty advisor is the sole responsibility of the student.

IS THE PROGRAM RESPONSIVE TO DIRECT INQUIRIES?

Once you have researched prospective graduate programs and determined that at least one of the program faculty members has professional or research interests similar to your own, why not call or write individual faculty or program chairs to gather further information? If your calls or letters are answered in a timely fashion and in a respectful tone, this is a good sign. Even information gleaned from a department secretary or program administrator may be immensely helpful in your decision to ultimately apply to the program. Besides, direct contact with a graduate program helps to establish your role as an assertive consumer.

In your inquiry, it may be useful to ask more about how admitted students are assigned to advisors; that is, what is the structure for facilitating mentoring? It is entirely reasonable to ask for the address or phone number of a current student and a recent graduate of the program. What was their experience? Were they mentored? If not, why? Finally, if you are specifically interested in working with a single faculty member, we recommend contacting this person directly and asking if he or she is accepting new students. Not only will this serve to inform you about the reality of actually working with the professor if admitted, but it will also allow you to briefly introduce yourself and inform the prospective mentor of your interest and intention to apply to the program and your specific interests in his or her work. Keep in mind that graduate school faculty and administrators are notoriously busy; the more successful they are, the busier they will be. Still, making contact with the program may give you a clearer sense of whether it is wise to spend your time and money on an application.

Phase 2: Postadmission Reconnaissance

Congratulations. We will now assume that you have received several offers for admission to graduate schools in your discipline. However, even if you have been admitted to only one program (and plan to attend), much of the advice we offer in this section will still apply. Following an offer of admission, and prior to making a commitment to a graduate program, you have more intelligence gathering work to do. Whether you have one offer or are deciding between several, we recommend that you engage in the following reconnaissance activities before finalizing your decision.

CAREFULLY ASSESS EACH PROGRAM'S SPECIFIC MENTORING STRUCTURE

As noted earlier in this chapter, graduate programs may address faculty–student mentoring through one of two broad program structures. Programs that rely on *formal structures* are intentional about pairing each incoming student with a faculty advisor/mentor (Cunic, McLaughlin, Phipps, & Evans, 2000). This structure is most common in traditional PhD programs, and the assigned relationships are clearly based on shared interest and are intended to last the duration of the graduate student's tenure in the program. Not only will the faculty mentor help the first-year student through the trials of adjusting to graduate school, but he or she will ultimately serve as the thesis and dissertation chair. It is rare for students in these programs to switch advisors once assigned.

Positive elements of formal structures include the quality and quantity of research supervision, the ability to focus one's research on a single coherent area as long as it is within the mentor's area of interest and expertise, and an increased probability of getting published, funded for research, and access to academic positions at graduation (Cunic et al., 2000). On the down side, there may be limited opportunity to focus on

---

BOX 5.1: HOW IT WORKED FOR US — JENNY'S PERSPECTIVE

When I joined Brad's research team during my 2nd year in graduate school, I committed to attend biweekly research meetings. As a new team member, I initially collaborated on group research projects and offered feedback to other team members about their dissertation work. Later, as I began focused work on my own dissertation, I received important advice and encouragement from Brad and other team members. Frequent team meetings allowed Brad and I the opportunity for interacting and deepening our mentoring connection. Simultaneously, I enjoyed the collegial friendship and support of my peers in the group.

---

research and professional interests outside the mentor's interests and little exposure to the supervision styles and interests of other program faculty.

Another programmatic approach to mentoring graduate students is the *informal structure* (Cunic et al., 2000). In such programs, new graduate students may be encouraged to visit faculty-led supervision or research "teams" during the initial semester or entire first year. Once a student determines which faculty member he or she would most like to work with, the student is responsible for discussing this with the faculty member and—if the match is desirable to both parties and a team opening exists—the student is assigned to the faculty member for the duration of the graduate program. Often, teams meet weekly or biweekly, and the team leader ultimately oversees the student's dissertation. Informal team models offer the advantage of strong peer support and greater freedom to pursue various projects and interests. On the down side, informal structures may offer less depth in research training, and there may be less opportunity for development of individual mentorships (particularly as teams grow in size). (See Box 5.1.)

Again, if a program cannot articulate any approach to mentoring, we recommend considerable caution. When a graduate program explicitly values mentoring, there will be some intentional design for facilitating mentorships.

GATHER IN-DEPTH INFORMATION ABOUT FACULTY INTERESTS AND PRODUCTIVITY

It is now time to get all published program material, get on the program's Web page, and carefully assess each faculty member's primary interests and qualifications. If the graduate school is research oriented —particularly if you are interested in a career in academia—then by all means, look up each faculty member in a literature database and review each of his or her publications. How often do they coauthor articles? We find that the best mentors are often the most prolific coauthors, frequently inviting their students to gain valuable writing experience during graduate school. Is there one or more faculty in a program with whom you would be interested in collaborating? Do their interests match your own? Are their credentials impressive?

It is now time to make personal (preferably phone) contact with the one or two faculty in each program with whom you are most interested in working. Although this interest in no way commits you to working with them, a direct conversation will allow you an initial opportunity to gauge factors such as responsiveness, interpersonal skill, excitement about your interest, and attitudes toward working with graduate students more broadly. Now that you have gained the status of admission, good mentors will respond cordially to your call, and ideally, will encourage continued dialog about collaborating once you arrive. If a prospective mentor fails to return your calls, is brusque interpersonally, or worse, insulting or demeaning, we recommend extreme caution in considering the graduate program's offer of admission.

GATHER INFORMATION FROM CURRENT GRADUATE STUDENTS

Now that you have assessed each program's mentoring structure and evaluated each faculty member's unique interests and expertise, it is essential that you gather some first-hand information from the "inside." Dr. X may be remarkably productive in an area of great interest to you, but does she take time to get to know her advisees? Dr. Y is a high-profile leader in the field, but is he supportive and encouraging of graduate students? Is he emotionally abusive and without a sense of humor? After all of the glossy brochures and impressive promotional packets, it should be refreshing and helpful to hear directly from some current students in each doctoral program.

We recommend that you contact each doctoral program to which you have been admitted, explain your interest in speaking with at least two current students, and contact these students by phone. In addition to inquiring about their experience as graduate students in general, ask about their perceptions of the faculty that most interest you. What are they like as teachers and advisors? How are their interpersonal skills? Are they ethical and professional in their dealings with students? Does the student have any reservations about recommending them as a potential mentor?

Some graduate student unions actually collect data on faculty performance as mentors. For example, graduate students at the University of Southern California (Cesa & Fraser, 1989) collected annual student ratings of faculty mentors and published the ratings for all students and faculty. Students rated their faculty mentors on dimensions such as accessibility, friendliness, and skill as a research supervisor. Not surprisingly, this annual assessment caused ratings to soar as faculty began to take mentoring seriously! Although most graduate students will be less formal about assessing faculty in their program, they should still be able to provide you with crucial information about the graduate program and individual faculty members.

Finally, we recommend that you carefully consider the importance of mentor gender and race or ethnicity at this precommitment stage. In most graduate programs, male faculty significantly outnumber women, particularly at the upper ranks (Associate and Full Professor). If finding a female or African American mentor is important to you, for example, then it is important to both apply to programs that employ more women or African American faculty and make your final acceptance decision based to some degree on these important matching variables.

Although each of these strategies will help you to determine which program may offer the best hope for finding a suitable mentor, you will also need to consider those mentor traits and matching variables (see chapter 4) that you consider most important. Once you have officially committed to a graduate program, it will be time to narrow your focus of reconnaissance.

Phase 3: First-Semester Reconnaissance

Now that you have decided on a graduate program, have formally accepted the offer of admission, and have prepared to begin your first semester in an exciting—and sometimes overwhelming—new world, it is time to enter the final phase of intelligence gathering. As an insider, you will have access to first-hand information about each prospective faculty mentor. Your first semester—and certainly your first year—in graduate school should afford you ample time to gain exposure to each of the faculty of interest, time to speak informally with many of their current advisees, and hopefully time to speak formally with each of your top mentor candidates.

As a new graduate student, you may be shocked at the many demands on your time. You will have rigorous courses, and if you have an assistantship, there will be expectations for teaching or research as well. In clinical or applied programs, you will be expected to begin some form of practicum experience. Regardless of your field of study, you will begin to hear startling rumors of stressful hurdles soon to come (e.g., thesis, comprehensive exams, and dissertation). Because you will be stressed, fatigued, and focused (sometimes entirely) on just surviving the first year, you may be tempted to put off thinking about a mentorship. This is a mistake. A solid and maximally useful mentorship will take time to develop—often years. If you join the ranks of graduate students who wait to think about mentoring until they have a dissertation to complete or require a letter of recommendation, you may be disappointed. Instead, be assertive, intentional, and scrutinizing in your approach to gathering information about program faculty—even during your first weeks on campus. As in the previous reconnaissance phases, we recommend several strategies for use in getting the information you need to make an informed decision.

WATCH, LISTEN, AND LEARN

Keeping in mind the desirable mentor traits discussed in chapters 1, 2, and 4, arrange opportunities to watch faculty members in action. What are they like interpersonally? Are they self-aware, socially sophisticated, and interested in graduate students? Are they good communicators? If you have them in class, are they kind, competent, and fun to be around? Are they clear about class expectations and fair when it comes to evaluating students? Are they friendly and warm or distant and aloof? Are they engaging and interesting? Most importantly, are there some you could spend many hours collaborating with around scholarship and your own professional development? It is also important to observe the professional activities of various professors. Those who hold offices in professional organizations, serve as contributing editors for journals in your field, and get grant funding are probably actively engaged professionals who would be excellent models and capable of teaching you what you need to know to successfully enter the profession yourself.

TALK WITH CURRENT AND FORMER STUDENTS

During your first semester in graduate school, you will have opportunity to interact formally and informally with a number of other students across the spectrum of seniority. If your graduate program uses an informal or team structure for mentoring, you should visit as many faculty research teams as possible, always taking time to ask team members about their experiences. What is the faculty member like as an advisor? Does he or she take time to really mentor students? How does the mentor handle expectations, work deadlines, and the various needs of protégés? Do students have any complaints about the mentor, including ethical concerns? Are women and men equally satisfied with the faculty member as a mentor? Even if your graduate program is more formal and you have been assigned to a faculty advisor at admission, you should still gather this sort of student reconnaissance from the current and former advisees of the two or three faculty you view as potential mentors. In essence, you want to learn as much as you can about how current "consumers" evaluate their mentor.

If you are particularly drawn to a faculty member because he or she represents your own group (based on gender, race, religion, sexual orientation, etc.), you should carefully consider how this person's minority status affects his or her ability to function as a mentor. For example, in many doctoral programs around the country, women and racial minority faculty may be difficult both to attract and retain. One of the reasons for this is simple burnout. For example, if your doctoral program has only one or two women faculty, they will probably be assigned to more than their share of committees and will be overburdened as mentors by a large cadre of women students who prefer a same-gender mentor. You should realistically evaluate each faculty member's current student advising load and frankly consider the resources (e.g., time and energy) this person has to offer.

ARRANGE INTRODUCTORY MEETINGS

After observing faculty firsthand and interviewing current advisees of various faculty members, you will begin to formulate clear impressions regarding each faculty member's mentor-related assets and liabilities. These experiences should help narrow your search to a few strong mentor candidates. On the basis of your own impressions, the confirmatory opinions of other students, and the compatibility of your research and career interests, it is time to select two or more faculty as top prospects. Having done so, we recommend that you take initiative for scheduling a formal meeting with each prospective mentor. Because we value honesty and deliberate clarity in communication, we recommend a straightforward discussion of your interest in exploring the prospective mentor's research and professional interests, willingness to take on new graduate students, and any criteria he or she may use in deciding to accept new advisees. This meeting can be valuable as a mechanism for further assessing the faculty member's apparent interest, interpersonal savvy, and clarity with respect to expectations.

Having completed these first-semester reconnaissance tasks, you are now ready to make the all-important decision about who you want to become your graduate school mentor. At this point, you will probably feel fairly certain about which faculty member is the best fit. However, rather than move ahead instantly to initiate a mentorship, we recommend taking time to rank-order your top faculty selections. This way, you will be prepared to quickly proceed to your next choice if your highest-rated faculty member is unable or unwilling to take you on as a new advisee and protégé. If you have difficulty deciding between two excellent professors, we encourage you to revisit chapter 4 and use these matching variable categories to create a list of pros and cons for each person on your list. When you have successfully rank-ordered prospective mentors, it is time for you to proceed to one of the most important steps in the entire mentoring process: initiating the relationship. It is with a sense of vicarious excitement that we urge you to read on!

Phase 4: Initiating the Mentorship ("Operation Initiation")

Now that you have done the hard work of finding a well-suited faculty mentor, it is time to take the lead in getting this mentorship off the ground. Continuing with our military reconnaissance theme, we dub this phase "Operation Initiation." It has two important components. The first is the *intentional interaction* stage, which will emphasize creation of opportunities for interaction and relationship development. The second component of initiation is the *formal contracting* stage. This involves explicit formalization of the mentor–protégé relationship. As you read this section, let us remind you once again that mentoring will not just "happen." It is one thing to find an ideal faculty mentor. It is quite another to actually develop a strong and collaborative mentorship with this person. Research on mentor relationship formation in graduate school clearly confirms that unless you are assertive and intentional at this phase, it is unlikely you will reap the benefits of mentoring.

INTENTIONAL INTERACTION

Now that you are certain whom you would like for a mentor, it is essential that you are deliberate in creating opportunities for interaction with this person. Kram (1985) referred to this as the initiation phase of mentorship. Although other authors use different terms such as the interaction (N. W. Collins, 1983) or entry (O'Neil & Wrightsman, 2001) phase, the meaning is the same. Like all interpersonal relationships, mentorships depend on a period of introduction and positive social exchange in order for both parties to develop interest in the other.

O'Neil and Wrightsman (2001) noted that the potential mentor relationship will be viewed more positively if both parties find the other to fulfill some of his or her own needs. Although you have clearly considered your own needs as a graduate student (guidance, direct coaching, support, encouragement, etc.), it is essential to now consider what needs your faculty mentor may have. Of course, these may vary widely depending on your mentor. Some of the most common include (a) assistance with teaching or administrative tasks, (b) assistance with research or writing projects, (c) creative synergy—the joy of collaborating with a sharp graduate student who shares his or her interests, (d) generativity—the satisfaction that accompanies contributing to the next generation, and (e) development of a new collegial relationship as the protégé matures and develops professionally. You should attempt to discern which of these needs might be most prominent for your prospective mentor.

Mentorships, like nearly every other interpersonal relationship type, will hinge to some extent on simple principles of attraction. That is, like all human beings, mentors and protégés are more likely to form a relationship when both members are attracted to the other in some way. Of course, it is important to distinguish general interpersonal attraction from romantic or erotic attraction. Later in this book (see chapter 8), we address various problems associated with mentoring, one of which is the potential development of a romantic component and how this should be addressed. Social psychologists have been researching the fundamental elements of interpersonal attraction for decades (Dion, Berscheid, & Walster, 1972; Zajonc, 1968). As a prospective protégé, you should be aware of these key contributors to mentor relationship formation.

1. *Proximity*. One of the most reliable findings in the psychology of attraction is that we are generally friendliest with those with whom we live and work closely. That is, simple proximity clearly leads to liking (Festinger, Schacter, & Back, 1950). What does this mean to you? It means you will be well served to find ways to work with your desired faculty mentor. Sign up for seminars and classes taught by this person, get permission to attend his or her research meetings, and volunteer to work in his or her lab. Above all, PERFORM WELL in these endeavors! Research suggests that working closely with this person will enhance his or her liking of you.

2. *Mere exposure*. Another reliable strand of research from social psychology shows that repeated exposure to another person is itself

enough to significantly increase liking (Zajonc, 1968). That is, familiarity with another person evokes positive feelings. There is one exception to this rule: When initial interactions are strongly negative, repeated exposure is unlikely to enhance attraction. As in the case of proximity, this principle suggests that maximizing positive interaction with a prospective mentor will enhance the probability of mentorship formation.

3. *Similarity.* Each of us tends to like those whom we perceive as similar to us. Discovering similarities in attitudes, values, or traits promotes liking. The more similar, the more the liking (Byrne, 1969). This does not mean that you should feign similar traits and interests to attract a mentor. However, it does indicate that you should intentionally pursue prospective mentors with whom you believe you hold some things in common (e.g., research and professional interests, personal values).

4. *Liking those who like us.* Researchers in the area of attraction note another consistent interpersonal attraction effect. We tend to like those people who express liking of us. That is, knowing that someone evaluates us positively will promote attraction to that person. The fact that you have selected a prospective mentor from among all faculty members in your program indicates that you like a good number of things about him or her. Without evidencing fawning attention or excessive praise, why not take opportunities to note the things you like about this person? If you find them to be a good teacher or a helpful research supervisor, why not say so?

5. *Physical attractiveness.* The final component of interpersonal attraction is simple physical beauty. Although we define mentorship as a clearly professional relationship, we must also acknowledge that in our culture, we live by the rule "what is beautiful is good" (Dion et al., 1972). Research on attraction consistently shows that physically attractive people are assumed to possess more socially desirable personality traits and are expected to lead better lives (e.g., be more competent in relationships and more successful occupationally; Dion et al., 1972). Physical attractiveness tends to be most important early in a relationship, and its significance lessens as the relationship develops (Hatfield & Sprecher, 1986). We include this final component of attraction merely to bring it to your attention. By doing so, we do not mean to imply that you should work hard at becoming more physically appealing to attract a mentor. Rather, you should simply be aware of this principle and perhaps pay close attention to obvious details such as maintaining a professional and well-groomed appearance when interacting with your prospective mentor.

FORMALIZING THE MENTORSHIP

You have carefully searched for a prospective faculty mentor, and you have sought out opportunities to interact with him or her in courses, research endeavors, and perhaps even committees or noontime student–faculty brown bag lunches. Certain this is the right mentor for you, you are ready to formally initiate the mentorship. After all of your efforts at reconnaissance and selection, this single (perhaps brief) meeting may feel anticlimactic. Although it is quite important, it is certainly only the start.

We recommend that you schedule a formal meeting time with the prospective mentor and that you boldly and assertively state your interest in having him or her become your faculty advisor and ultimately your graduate school mentor. This is a good time for you to disclose some of your efforts at intelligence gathering, the reasons why you are most interested in having him or her serve as your mentor, and the interests and commonalities that you think make you well matched for a mentorship. We encourage you to speak openly and boldly about the things you most hope to get from a mentorship (see chapter 2), as well as those things you believe you have to offer the mentor (e.g., eagerness to learn, shared scholarly interests, a commitment to assist with research projects).

In our experience, most graduate school faculty members will be both impressed and flattered by such a direct and articulate presentation on the part of a junior graduate student. The fact that you have taken the time to research his or her scholarship and interests and carefully consider the potential for a solid and productive relationship will signal several positive things about you, including industriousness, initiative, assertiveness, good communication skills, and forethought regarding your graduate school and professional career.

Your goal, of course, is to get an affirmative response from this person—a commitment to serve as your advisor, with an understanding that you hope the relationship will evolve into a mentorship. Assuming this occurs, and we hope it does, you are ready to proceed to chapter 6 and begin consideration of how to intentionally design this new relationship such that it is healthy, productive, and rewarding for both you and your mentor. If your top pick says no, it is usually valuable to ask why. We recommend some nondefensive exploration of the faculty member's rationale. Are there misguided concerns or erroneous beliefs about you or mentoring in general that you can help clear up? If so, we recommend continuing the dialogue as long as the person is willing. He or she may request additional time to consider the request or may ask to delay taking you on as an advisee until a current student graduates. Ultimately, you will have to decide whether these requests sound reasonable and whether you are still interested in pursuing the relationship.

If it is clear that a mentorship will not be feasible with your top-rated faculty member, or if in the process of engaging him or her in a meeting it becomes clear that this person is not the best fit for you, then we recommend wasting little time in moving to the next faculty member on your list and repeating the process outlined in this section. It is essential that you refrain from becoming hopeless or self-critical during this phase and that you maintain your assertive consumer stance. Successful protégés will persist until they are mentored.

III

How to Manage the
Mentor Relationship

Designing the Mentor Relationship 6

Case 6.1

Early in his 2nd year of doctoral studies in economics, Todd knew it was time to establish a mentor relationship. There was little question in Todd's mind that he wanted to work with Dr. Capital, the department's sharpest faculty member. Todd had done his research on making a good match with a mentor. He knew that Dr. Capital had a good track record as a mentor. Nearly all of her protégés completed their dissertations on time and spoke highly of her ability to "coach" students through this difficult process. Dr. Capital's area of expertise was quite interesting to Todd, and numerous interactions in the classroom suggested to Todd that the two had similar personality traits and senses of humor.

Confident that initial indicators suggested the two could enjoy a productive mentorship, Todd set up a meeting with Dr. Capital to discuss the possibility. Aware that the best mentorships involve shared expectations and goals, Todd brought a list of his short- and long-term goals to the meeting with Dr. Capital (e.g., publishing several scholarly articles, completing his dissertation, obtaining an academic appointment following graduation). He specifically described how a mentorship with Dr. Capital could help him achieve these goals, as well as how he might contribute to Dr. Capital's professional projects along the way. Todd was thrilled with Dr. Capital's overwhelmingly positive response, and the two decided to arrange a second meeting to specifically discuss the "nuts and bolts" of the mentorship.

Todd approached the second meeting with the same amount of preparedness and articulated the specific short- and long-term goals he hoped to achieve during the next 3 years of graduate school. To reach these goals, both believed it was important to meet twice a month to monitor progress. A recent public dispute in the department between another faculty member and student also prompted Todd and Dr. Capital to identify how they planned to handle conflict and safeguard confidential information in the relationship to prevent either party from feeling compromised.

The pair also openly discussed the inherent challenges of developing a close working relationship with someone of the opposite gender. Both wanted to avoid the appearance of any impropriety and agreed to hold meetings in Dr. Capital's office during the day rather than working or socializing in the evenings. Finally, they agreed to evaluate progress toward Todd's goals as well as the state of the mentorship after 6 months to determine if changes in course were necessary. Although they decided it was not necessary to draft a formal "contract" of their agreements, both kept notes regarding the details of their arrangement and believed it would be helpful to refer to these specifically during the first formal evaluation of their new mentorship.

Case 6.2

Lucy was surprised and thrilled when Dr. Spontaneity, a young, energetic, and sometimes unpredictable faculty member asked her to become his advisee during her 2nd year of graduate studies in biology. Dr. Spontaneity was, at times, a controversial professor in the department who was known for having many research projects running simultaneously. Lucy wasn't quite sure that Dr. Spontaneity's research interests matched her own. However, she had not firmed up a plan for dissertation and decided that she would accept his gracious offer. Although Lucy was curious about what to expect from the relationship, the idea of addressing this directly seemed absurd.

From the beginning, Lucy was amazed by Dr. Spontaneity's faith in her abilities. With almost no supervision, she was assigned to direct an ambitious field experiment that would have challenged many postdoctoral colleagues. Lucy did not complain, although she often felt overwhelmed, frequently fell behind in her own studies, and kept late hours in the lab to have time to discuss results with Dr. Spontaneity. Initially, the two met weekly in the evenings to discuss the project. Lucy hoped that Dr. Spontaneity would initiate a conversation about her own needs to establish a dissertation topic or to coauthor a paper prior to graduation. When she meekly raised this issue, hoping that he would take on the role of coach and sponsor, Dr. Spontaneity seemed disinterested and promised her that there would be time for that after the current project was completed. Lucy reluctantly let the issue drop.

At the end of her first year with Dr. Spontaneity, Lucy became increasingly anxious about his lack of involvement in helping her to define a dissertation topic. She was also worried about departmental rumors regarding conflict between Dr. Spontaneity and other faculty members. Unfortunately, there never seemed to be a convenient time to confront him with these concerns. Lucy's anxiety peaked on the day Dr. Spontaneity informed her that he had decided to leave academia in favor of a well-paying industry position. On seeing her shock and dismay, Dr. Spontaneity stated that he was surprised by her response since it was "well-known" that he was only testing the waters of academia. When Lucy asked for his recommendation to work with another faculty member, Dr. Spontaneity laughed and noted that, given recent conflict with other faculty, it was unlikely anyone would offer any special favors to students working in his lab. He apologized for any inconvenience to her but noted, "Life just isn't predictable!"

Good mentorships, like well-built homes, are strong and stable because of careful planning and construction. Although the best contractors may make the construction of a home appear effortless, it would be very unusual to meet a contractor who did not frequently consult blueprints, carefully discuss and plan construction with builders, and evaluate the fortitude of the emerging home. The best mentorships are no different. Good mentors and protégés know that long-term satisfaction is based on more than an initial sense of attraction between two individuals. Successful mentorships emerge from shared expectations and intentional clarification of these expectations. Unfortunately, many graduate students hope that once their ideal mentor is identified, their uncommunicated expectations will magically translate into a common agenda and a solid working relationship. These protégés are likely to be disappointed.

In this chapter, we describe a strategy for intentional mentor relationship formation and development. From the outset, this strategy involves explicit discussions of key issues we refer to as *core expectations*. Core expectations include anticipated duration of the relationship, frequency of contact between mentor and protégé, role expectations, possible cultural and gender concerns, short- and long-term goals, methods for evaluating progress toward goals, and plans for approaching transitions in the relationship, including eventual termination. The critical message for graduate students is this: *It is essential to clarify expectations and process differences in expectations early on in your relationship with a mentor.* Finally, we address the pros and cons of developing formal mentor contracts as one method to solidify expectations for the mentorship. We believe that mentorships formed through careful planning and attention to these issues will be ready for the challenges ahead.

Shared Expectations: The Foundation of Solid Mentorships

THE IMPORTANCE OF SHARED EXPECTATIONS

In the context of human relationships, the term *expectations* often evokes an emotional response—people expect us to meet deadlines, act our age, overcome our weaknesses, look our best, or work to peak capacity. Expectations are often associated with "pressure" of one sort or another. Therefore, it is not surprising that most of us would rather avoid the topic of expectations, particularly when we fear we might not be able to meet expectations or when we are enjoying the idealistic dream that our mentors will magically meet all our expectations. Given the richness and complexity of the hopes and dreams most protégés have for the mentorship, it would be impossible, impractical, and probably unnecessary for the protégé to identify and communicate all of his or her expectations.

Nevertheless, we believe there are several compelling reasons for mentors and protégés to share some core relationship expectations at the outset of the relationship. First, a great deal of literature suggests that similarity in expectations between the mentor and protégés predicts relationship success and satisfaction. Mentors often expect protégés to have preferences, goals, and relationship expectations similar to their own (Burke et al., 1993). Additionally, protégés' satisfaction with their mentorships is related to a sense of similarity and the degree to which they aspire to be like their mentor (Cronan-Hillix et al., 1986). Sharing specific expectations at the onset of the relationship offers both you and your mentor the opportunity to further assess your common goals, interests, and similarities. Just as important, such clarification allows you to evaluate areas of dissimilarity—those places in which relationship expectations diverge.

A second compelling reason for the mutual sharing of expectations early on is to provide either the mentor or protégé a means of an early "no fault" escape if significant incompatibility exists between the two individuals. In her book *Mentors and Protégés*, Phillips-Jones (1982) noted that the early stage of relationship formation is often characterized by strong feelings of mutual admiration:

> Each of you admires and has a highly favorable image of the other. You're both anxious to please, and you both give without being asked and without keeping score. You feel good about yourselves, good about each other and good about your relationship. . . . Both you and your mentor are careful to present only your best sides during this phase. Shortcomings, when you notice them are shrugged off and seem unimportant, particularly when you remember the stakes. (p. 111)

Unfortunately, this strong sense of admiration, coupled with avoidance of areas of dissimilar expectations, may lead to significant problems later in the relationship. Clarifying expectations while isolating discrepancies allows the mentor–protégé pair a variety of options, including negotiating around the differences or "bugging out" of the relationship before too much time and energy have been invested. Although leaving a mentorship early because of differences in expectations may seem harsh, Lucy's example (Case 6.2) clearly demonstrates that early identification of incompatible expectations can result in a better outcome for the protégé.

KNOWING YOURSELF AND DEFINING YOUR EXPECTATIONS

Most graduate students who have followed our advice and carefully researched and initiated a mentor relationship probably have some sense of their expectations for the relationship. However, it is now critical for you to clarify core expectations of the relationship and to clearly communicate these to your mentor. Such clarification will allow negotiation and agreement regarding how the mentorship will "work." In the following section, we discuss several core expectations that need to be explicitly clarified (see Table 6.1). As you consider each of these elements, we suggest that you take your own set of notes, outlining individual needs, wants, hopes, and dreams for your mentorship. At the same time, we encourage you to remember three important truths that we have highlighted numerous times in previous chapters. First, there is no such thing as a perfect mentor. The fact that most students report an average of more than two mentors while in graduate school suggests to us that no mentor can possibly provide for all a protégé's needs (Clark et al., 2000). This does not reflect a mentor's failure per se but rather the normal limits of human beings and human relationships.

Second, it is important for you to remember that expectations are a two-way street. Although it is certainly your responsibility to define and communicate your expectations, you should also be prepared to solicit and consider your mentor's expectations. Good mentors have challenging but reasonable expectations that build protégé confidence and establish a sense of trust in the relationship. For example, mentors will expect hard work, diligence, assistance with research, and increasing willingness to accept responsibility and work independently.

Finally, it is important to approach the topic of expectations in a flexible manner. Although mentors and protégés can do their very best to anticipate core expectations, such as the frequency of contact, duration, goals, and termination, expectations do change over time and changes are unpredictable. Remember that both you and your mentor may need to revisit expectations and modify them as time goes on. We suggest you use the next few pages to deepen your own understanding of what you want, as well as what you are willing to offer your mentor.

TABLE 6.1

Core Relationship Expectations

Core expectation	Descripton
Anticipated duration	The mentor and protégé determine the approximate length of the relationship with the understanding that this may be subject to change.
Frequency of contact	The mentor and protégé determine how frequently they will meet together for scheduled contacts.
Role expectations	The mentor and protégé identify the major roles that the mentor will assume (e.g., coach, sponsor, advisor) and how these roles relate to specific short- and long-term goals.
Short- and long-term goals	The mentor and protégé outline the protégé's short- and long-term goals including time lines for accomplishing goals.
Boundary maintenance and confidentiality	The mentor and protégé decide how they will deal with potential dual roles in the relationship and clarify expectations for confidentiality.
Anticipated separation	The mentor and protégé identify major goals or milestones that will suggest a structural change or redefinition in the relationship and the need for separation.
Cross-gender and cross-race issues	The mentor and protégé openly discuss cross-gender and cross-race concerns and develop a strategy to minimize negative outcomes from these concerns.
Relationship evaluation	The mentor and protégé define how frequently they will evaluate the relationship and what goals or objectives will be evaluated.

Designing the Relationship

ANTICIPATED DURATION

Among the first things to discuss with your mentor is how long the relationship is expected to last. Current research suggests that graduate school mentorships generally last 4 or more years (Clark et al., 2000). This makes sense given that most graduate students require at least that much time to complete coursework and dissertation requirements. The anticipated duration of the relationship is a critical element for discussion for several reasons. First, research projects, including dissertation research, often require years to complete from beginning to final defense. Many graduate students know they will be relocating after completing coursework requirements. Discussing the likely date of reloca-

BOX 6.1: HOW IT WORKED FOR US — BRAD'S
PERSPECTIVE

In our mentorship, my relocation to a new university resulted in a
need to redefine expectations about the duration and nature of
our relationship. It was important for Jenny and I to discuss how
the move was affecting each of us and how the rapid termination
of the active phase of mentoring would affect Jenny and the remainder of her doctoral education. Although this change initially
felt quite stressful, the difficulties of the transition were minimized
by good communication, renegotiation, and flexibility.

tion can help the mentor and protégé determine which projects will
likely be completed or which dissertation components can be finalized
prior to a move. Second, as we discuss in the next chapter, all mentor
relationships pass through relatively predictable stages of development.
Knowing the approximate time frame for termination offers both you
and your mentor a better sense about when you can expect your relationship to pass through each stage. (See Box 6.1.)

FREQUENCY OF CONTACT

Once you and your mentor have established the anticipated duration of
the relationship, you should plan to spend time discussing how frequently you will meet. We believe this is a core expectation that deserves specific attention during this formative stage of the relationship.
When asked about the most negative aspects of their mentorships, 25%
of psychology graduate students reported their mentor was not as available as they would have preferred (Clark et al., 2000). Additionally, Noe
(1988a) reported that among mentor–protégé dyads in his study, time
limitations, incompatible work schedules, and physical distance were the
most frequent reasons for lack of interaction between the two. These
results strongly suggest that intentional discussion and planning for the
frequency of meetings between mentor and protégé is a key element,
particularly with regard to protégés' satisfaction with the relationship.

Rather than recommending a specific number of meetings or precise
amounts of time, we encourage you to consider several important principles regarding the frequency of meetings with your mentor. First,
meetings should be frequent enough (and long enough) to promote
progress toward short- and long-term goals. Because of the tremendous
variation in protégé goals and mentor availability in graduate school,
ideal frequencies will vary considerably. (See Box 6.2.)

BOX 6.2: HOW IT WORKED FOR US — BRAD'S PERSPECTIVE

In our mentorship, Jenny and I established two scheduled meetings a month in addition to a variety of research team meetings and impromptu discussions. During our formally scheduled meetings, we discussed progress on research and writing projects, Jenny's progress on coursework, and dissertation tasks. We also used part of each meeting to chat informally about life, families, and long-term career goals. One of the things I most appreciated about Jenny (and other excellent graduate students) was her good preparation for our scheduled meetings. She was ready to update me on dissertation progress, preparation for internships, and other important graduate school requirements. I was confident that our time together was well utilized.

Second, meetings should create a sense of continuity and stability for the protégé. During times of intensified work on projects or the dissertation, you and your mentor may choose to increase the frequency of your meetings to support you in meeting important goals. Although this intensified contact may be episodically beneficial, your mentor will need to balance mentoring you with a range of other responsibilities. Be realistic in your expectations for time. In sum, specific goals, circumstances, and tasks in the relationship will determine the necessary frequency of contact. It is essential to clarify expectations and remain flexible.

ROLE EXPECTATIONS

There are many different roles that good mentors take on in their relationships with protégés. Consistent with the mentor functions identified by Kram (1985), good mentors serve as sponsors, coaches, teachers, role models, advisors, counselors, and sometimes friends. These roles come naturally to good mentors. Additionally, fine mentors are skilled at moving flexibly between roles, depending on the protégé's needs and goals (O'Neil & Wrightsman, 2001). Although this may come naturally to your mentor, it is still useful to clearly communicate which roles you believe will be most helpful to you. For example, in Case 6.2, Lucy hoped that Dr. Spontaneity would take on the role of coach and sponsor to assist her in defining a dissertation topic. Although Lucy was not successful in articulating this expectation, we recommend that you consider and discuss the specific roles you hope your mentor will adopt in the relationship. Although no mentor can perfectly meet all of your needs, he or she certainly has a better opportunity when aware of the type of support you seek.

SHORT- AND LONG-TERM GOALS

Graduate school is full of challenges and hurdles. At times, it may seem impossible to imagine how you will complete all the requirements to become a full-fledged member of your chosen discipline. Hence, graduate school is a time to become an excellent goal-setter. Ideally, because your mentor has walked this difficult road before, he or she will likely understand the major goals that you need to establish (e.g., completion of coursework, completion of academic work, applications for internships/employment) as well as the tricks of the trade with regard to goal-setting: making goals concrete, breaking larger goals into smaller steps, setting realistic deadlines, and rewarding yourself for accomplishing goals. Although we certainly hope you are fortunate to work with this sort of mentor, we also recommend several proactive steps to establish how your mentor can support your ability to meet goals.

First, it is important for you to set short- and long-term goals that promote successful completion of your graduate work and launch you into your career. Second, we recommend that you clearly communicate these goals to your mentor. You should also let your mentor know how he or she will be called on to help you with the process. For example, you may ask to coauthor a paper with your mentor to meet a short-term goal for obtaining a publication. Third, build accountability for deadlines into your schedule. Accountability is perhaps one of the mentor's most important functions in helping you to successfully accomplish short- and long-term goals in graduate school. Mentors can provide accountability by asking to see progress, helping protégés identify barriers to meeting deadlines, or discouraging protégés from taking on excessive responsibilities. Finally, we suggest that the most important goals in the relationship are your goals. Although your mentor will have goals that the mentorship will facilitate (e.g., getting publications, making tenure, nurturing a future colleague), the relationship should focus primarily on your goals and needs. Faculty who fail to recognize this should be approached with caution.

BOUNDARY MAINTENANCE AND CONFIDENTIALITY

Early identification of the "limits" or terms of confidentiality may seem a bit excessive or unnecessary early on to the mentor–protégé relationship; however, a growing body of literature suggests that this is an important topic for discussion (Clark et al., 2000; Johnson & Nelson, 1999). In addition, it is useful to anticipate the various roles the mentor will likely have in your relationship and whether multiple roles will threaten professional boundaries and the maintenance of confidentiality. Although hypothetical, the following case vignette clearly highlights potential problems that may emerge when mentors and protégés neglect to clearly identify these boundaries.

> A 27-year-old 3rd year counseling psychology graduate student files a complaint against his mentor for "breach of confidentiality" and "destroying my graduate school career." The student charges that his mentor, an unlicensed 2nd year faculty member who has not yet completed his own dissertation, disclosed several confidential and personal pieces of information to the larger faculty resulting in the student's dismissal from the program. The student notes that he and his mentor are the same age, and that over the course of two years, they had socialized together a "great deal." This socialization included meals out, "nights on the town" during which the two would drink together and "pick up women," and several backpacking trips. During the course of the last year, the student disclosed information regarding an extensive history of psychiatric treatment. The student emphasizes that his faculty advisor "was a great mentor. I could tell him anything . . . until he turned on me." Later, the faculty member admits disclosing this information to the faculty and is clear in stating "my primary obligation as a professor is to protect the public and that duty requires me to bring this information to the faculty." (Johnson & Nelson, 1999, pp. 195–196)

As this vignette highlights, dual roles can pose particular problems for mentors and protégés. As a graduate school protégé, it is likely that your mentor may serve several roles in your education process. In addition to being your mentor, it is also quite possible that he or she will at some point be your professor, employer, evaluator, and, potentially, a friend. The fact that many roles can be wrapped up in one relationship means that the relationship can quickly become quite powerful, rewarding, and risky all at the same time.

To minimize the risk of confidentiality breaches or unethical boundary violations (see chapter 8), we recommend that you and your mentor discuss potential role conflict and how much confidentiality is expected in the relationship. In most cases, it is the mentor who holds multiple roles and should take the initiative to define how he or she will resolve conflict between these roles in a manner that protects the mentorship. In other cases, the dual role may belong to the protégé. How would you respond if the department chairperson, in an attempt to fire your mentor, asked you to document examples of poor performance on the mentor's part? To whom do you owe loyalty? Would you feel inclined to protect your mentor? There are no easy answers to such scenarios; however, careful planning for dual roles at the beginning of the relationship will help to minimize the likelihood that role conflicts significantly damage the mentor, protégé, or the mentorship.

PLANNING FOR SEPARATION

Although thoughts of finding a mentor evoke positive feelings in most protégés, thoughts of separating from a mentor seldom induce similar feelings. Generally speaking, separation can be difficult for mentors and protégés alike. Common separation problems noted by Kram (1985) include premature separation resulting in the protégé feeling anxious and unprepared for independence. On the other hand, delayed separation can promote resentment and frustration. Even in the best of circumstances, separation involves some degree of loss. Because the ending phase of your mentorship is likely to require emotional and psychological preparation and adjustment, careful planning is indicated.

You and your mentor first need to plan an approximate, yet flexible, time frame for terminating the most active phase of your relationship. For most graduate students, a natural time for separation and redefinition of the relationship is the completion of graduate education, successful defense of the dissertation, or landing that first job. With your mentor, you should discuss the milestone or time frame that will indicate a need for redefining the relationship. Many protégés feel awkward about predicting when they will no longer require the functions of a mentor. Keep in mind that your need and readiness for increased autonomy is one of the surest signs that your mentor has done a good job. We also believe it is important for mentors and protégés to acknowledge upfront that life is at times unpredictable, despite the best strategizing. Either you or your mentor may need to end the relationship sooner than expected. If this is the case, good communication established at the beginning of the relationship is likely to benefit your adjustment to a new time frame. In other words, plan to be flexible at all costs.

Evaluating the Mentorship

THE IMPORTANCE OF EVALUATION

Periodic evaluation is an important way to ensure growth. Although the concept of "evaluation" typically carries a variety of negative connotations for most graduate students, evaluation of your mentorship is not focused on whether you and your mentor are receiving passing grades.

Rather, it refers to ensuring that the relationship is making steady progress toward defined goals and is meeting the identified needs of both the protégé and mentor. Evaluation also allows the protégé and mentor to air frustrations and to problem solve conflict or areas of disagreement that may have developed in the relationship. Finally, good evaluation is focused on relative strengths and weaknesses and should be motivational—spurring the mentor and protégé to troubleshoot, acknowledge success, and fine-tune.

CHOOSING WHAT TO EVALUATE

Many graduate students are afraid to broach the topic of mentorship evaluation, either because they view this as the mentor's responsibility or because they are timid about the prospect of honestly offering their mentor feedback. By building periodic evaluation into your expectations for the relationship, these fears may be diminished. We recommend that you and your mentor periodically evaluate progress toward both short- and long-term goals. Evaluating this progress may include adjusting time lines, addressing barriers, and identifying new goals. Evaluation of the specific career and psychosocial functions (see chapter 2) that are working well in the mentorship is also helpful. In addition, you should consider identifying specific functions that you could benefit more from (e.g., creation of challenging assignments). Finally, after discussing goals and mentor functions, we highly recommend that you and your mentor openly discuss problematic areas in the relationship. This may include a variety of issues. We have attempted to highlight the most frequent sources of mentorship dysfunction in chapter 8, including strategies for resolving problems with your mentor.

FREQUENCY OF EVALUATION

Although there are no rules regarding how frequently you and your mentor should evaluate the mentorship, two primary recommendations are in order. First, integrate feedback into regular interaction with your mentor. You may do this by noting progress toward goals and identifying ways that your mentor can help you to address obstacles. It is also helpful for mentors to regularly receive positive feedback about what they are doing well (e.g., "I really learned a lot from watching you lead that meeting" or "I appreciated your invitation to work on this project"). Second, we suggest that you and your mentor select specific times when you will more formally discuss how the relationship is progressing. Predictable time frames, such as every 6 months, may be most reasonable and beneficial.

STRATEGIES FOR APPROACHING EVALUATION

When approaching evaluation, sensitive and sophisticated protégés understand the need to balance assertiveness with respect for the mentor's capacities. As we have said before, no mentor is perfect. The purpose of evaluation is not to "ding" the mentor for imperfections or failures. Wise protégés also know that it is much easier to receive corrective feedback when this is balanced, ideally proceeded by praise. Such a balanced perspective may be more elegantly achieved by writing down feedback prior to offering it to the mentor. Additionally, you should consider practicing feedback delivery with an objective third party, particularly if you anticipate that the feedback will be hard to give or difficult for your mentor to receive.

PROBLEMS WITH EVALUATION

We hope that intentional and frequent evaluation will be an affirming and motivating experience for both you and your mentor. However, at times, many protégés find it necessary to deal with more perennial or malignant mentorship problems during times of evaluation. We have proposed a detailed action strategy to help resolve mentorship problems in chapter 8. We also want to remind you of several important guidelines. First, relationship conflict and problems, although difficult and annoying, are a normal part of life and are not necessarily a sign that the mentorship is destined to fail. In fact, many researchers see times of conflict as specific opportunities to reenergize and revitalize the relationship (O'Neil & Wrightsman, 2001; Zey, 1991). In other words, try to visualize this confrontation as an opportunity for growth. Second, while offering feedback to your mentor, stay focused on mentorship agreements and commitments rather than "character flaws." Finally, be prepared to propose solutions to problems in an empathic manner. Don't get stuck in the "blame game," arguing about who is at fault. Rather, focus on positive signs and potential solutions. Although it is unlikely that your mentorship will be continuously free of conflict, following these suggestions should minimize negative consequences or fatal injuries to the mentorship.

On the Pros and Cons of Mentoring Contracts

BENEFITS OF MENTORING CONTRACTS

The notion of a "mentoring contract" may seem unusual to many graduate students. Mentoring contracts formally establish the mentor's and protégé's core expectations in a written format. Although we believe it would be highly atypical (and usually inappropriate) for such a contract to be used for legal purposes, it does offer a clear and public format for articulating the contours of your relationship. We have included a sample mentor contract (see Exhibit 6.1). Keep in mind that this contract template can be customized endlessly to match the personalities and preferences of you and your mentor.

Developing a contract, in either formal (assigned) or informal (less structured) mentorships, may offer several significant benefits. First, committing relationship expectations to paper helps to prevent major misconceptions between the mentor and protégé. When the mentor and protégé work together to negotiate these terms, there is generally a solid understanding of the nature of the commitment both are making. Second, elaborating the terms of the mentorship helps both mentor and protégé to understand his or her own motives, as well as the other individual's motives for entering the relationship. Lucy, in Case 6.2, could potentially have benefited from a clearer understanding of Dr. Spontaneity's motives. Finally, a written contract between a mentor and protégé can assist the two in clearly identifying progress toward established goals. In sum, although a contract cannot possibly capture all of the goals and hopes that each has for the relationship, it can serve as an objective reminder of the core expectations directing the relationship.

LIMITATIONS OF MENTORING CONTRACTS

Despite the benefits that mentoring contracts may offer, graduate protégés should consider several limitations associated with "formalizing" the relationship through the development of such contracts. First, developing a mentoring contract can diminish or dampen the intrinsic motivation associated with the attraction and similarities that initially drew the mentor and protégé together. This dampening of intrinsic motivation is a common problem noted when mentor and protégé are assigned to work together; rather than choosing to form the relationship based on these internal dynamics, the pair may feel "forced" to work together. For example, when comparing formal (assigned) and informal (nonassigned) mentorships, Chao et al. (1992) found that protégés in informal relationships reported more career-related support from their mentors and higher salaries. After reviewing the various ways graduate mentors and protégés formed their relationships, Cronan-Hillix et al. (1986) noted that it is doubtful whether true mentor relationships can ever be assigned.

Second, graduate students who request formal mentoring contracts risk the possibility that their mentors will feel pressured or put off by formalizing the relationship in this manner. Although many graduate

EXHIBIT 6.1

Sample Mentor Contract

Mentor and Protégé Contract

As a mentor and a protégé, we agree that our mentorship can be described as a personal relationship in which a more experienced (usually older) faculty member acts as a guide, role model, teacher, and sponsor of a less experienced (usually younger) graduate student. We agree that our investment in this relationship is voluntary and based on the belief that we will both receive benefits from the relationship. If either of us concludes that the relationship is no longer mutually beneficial, we agree to significantly redefine or terminate the relationship. The following are salient components of the relationship that we agree upon:

- Anticipated duration of the relationship: _____

- Frequency of contact: _____

- Specific roles of the mentor (coach, sponsor, advisor, teacher, etc.): _____
  _____

- Short-term goals: _____
  _____

- Long-term goals: _____
  _____

- Plan to deal with confidential information: _____
  _____

- Frequency of evaluation: _____

❑ We have discussed the terms of this agreement.

❑ We agree to revisit this agreement on the following date: _____

_____   _____
Mentor   Protégé

_____   _____
Date   Date

school faculty enjoy mentoring, they are typically extremely busy with teaching, writing, and research schedules. A mentoring contract may symbolize yet one more mandatory responsibility. This, of course, may cause unwanted resistance (Gibb, 1999). Increased resistance, in turn, can inhibit creativity and flexibility that are essential to an energetic and growth-oriented mentorship.

A BALANCED APPROACH

We began the chapter by emphasizing the importance of shared expectations as the foundation of graduate school mentorships. Throughout this chapter, we have highlighted two salient principles: (a) the necessity of making expectations explicit and concrete and (b) the understanding that expectations may change and evolve over the course of the relationship. Because all graduate mentorships are unique, mentors and protégés may use a variety of creative means to integrate these principles. Although there are inherent limitations associated with formalizing the relationship through mentoring contracts, it is possible that some mentors and protégés will find this tool extremely useful in organizing the formation of the relationship. Other pairs, such as Todd and Dr. Capital (Case 6.1), may prefer to make clear verbal agreements regarding their expectations, which are regularly revisited and modified as the relationship develops. In either case, mentors and protégés should select a strategy that best fits their own personal style, reflects their individual goals for the mentorship, and increases a sense of mutual trust between both individuals.

The Stages of Mentor Relationships (What to Expect)

7

Case 7.1

During his first semester of graduate school, Clark became certain that developing a mentor relationship with Dr. Health would be a great boost to his career. Not only was Dr. Health a noted scholar and fine teacher, his area of expertise fit perfectly with Clark's interests. For the remainder of that first year, Clark worked hard to interact with Dr. Health. He asked to help with Dr. Health's research, took one of his elective seminars, and, whenever possible, informally chatted with him about issues of shared interest. By the end of the year, the two had formed a solid advising relationship and Dr. Health began actively mentoring Clark. During the remainder of Clark's time in graduate school, the two collaborated on several research projects, and Clark eventually served as Dr. Health's primary research and teaching assistant. Dr. Health was extremely supportive and encouraging of Clark, while still pushing him to excel and take an increasingly autonomous role in the department. During his final year in the doctoral program, Clark successfully defended his dissertation and began sending out applications for academic jobs. Although he found himself less dependent on Dr. Health for support, he continued to enjoy their frequent interaction. When Clark landed an academic job in a neighboring state, he was both ecstatic and appreciative of Dr. Health's strong recommendation. Although it was difficult to say goodbye, Clark moved on and the two had little contact during the following year. In subsequent years, they enjoyed seeing one another at conferences, and they continued to collaborate now and then on research projects. On occasion, Clark still solicited advice and career support from his mentor, and both enjoyed the friendship for many years.

Case 7.2

When Tim began working as a graduate assistant to Dr. Narcissus, he was delighted. Dr. Narcissus was a leading English scholar and an accomplished poet. In Tim's view, no professor in the department had more impressive credentials or more fame in the literary community. Although Dr. Narcissus did seem rather vain and self-absorbed, and although students sometimes called him "Dr. Me," Tim decided to overlook these personality concerns. The two quickly developed a strong mentorship, and Dr. Narcissus gave Tim a great deal of personal encouragement as well as careful and constructive criticism of his essays and poems. The mentorship was smooth until a year before Tim was to write his dissertation and graduate. At that time, Tim had several poems and an essay accepted in major literary journals. One was a journal that had never accepted Dr. Narcissus' pieces. Although Dr. Narcissus gave Tim faint praise, the relationship changed at that point to one characterized by distance, and it seemed to Tim, hostility. Dr. Narcissus became quite critical of Tim's work and failed to return drafts of his dissertation proposal. Several student peers commented that Dr. Narcissus seemed jealous of Tim. After several more months of criticism and nonresponsiveness from Dr. Narcissus, Tim requested a new dissertation chair. This enraged Dr. Narcissus, who refused to speak with him any further. Although Tim wrote an excellent dissertation and eventually graduated, he felt abandoned by his mentor and quite angry. The two never interacted again.

Like all relationships, mentorships change. Because graduate school is limited in duration (if it is not, something has gone wrong), so too is the most active phase of most graduate school mentorships. Although many mentor relationships continue in some new form long after graduation, others end when the dissertation is defended or when the student leaves the campus for the final time. In all cases, change in the relationship is inevitable. As a graduate student, it is important for you to appreciate the evolutionary nature of your mentor relationship. Just as circumstances (graduate school) and developmental needs (both yours and your mentor's) fuel the onset of the mentorship, so too will new circumstances (graduation and geographic change) and developmental needs (autonomy and reciprocity) demand an ending or redefinition.

Reflecting on our own lives, most of us can identify the difficult as well as the rewarding experiences that result from changes in important developmental relationships. Teenage children, for example, may be both thrilled and terrified to leave their parents as they head off to college. At times, a graduate student may wish to avoid separation from the mentor, hoping the mentor will continue to respond to all of his or her personal and professional concerns throughout a career. This student will soon become disillusioned. Kram (1985) wisely observed that "mentor relationships are limited in their duration and they can become destructive for one or both individuals if they are maintained beyond the time when individuals' needs are complementary" (pp. 49–50).

In this chapter, we describe the four primary phases of mentor relationships. We believe it is profoundly helpful for graduate student protégés to understand, anticipate, and even welcome these phases. Each phase fits the needs and circumstances of both protégé and mentor, and each shift or phasic change is precipitated by growth and development on the part of the student. Although loss and anxiety may accompany certain of these changes—particularly the separation phase as the protégé prepares to leave graduate school—they are typically reflective of positive growth. Thus, even the end of a close mentorship can be cause for some satisfaction. The well-mentored neophyte has become a confident new professional. In time, gratitude and friendship will replace sadness and anxiety.

Kram (1983) first described mentorship phases in her research with pairs of mentors and protégés from the world of business. Kram found that most mentorships progress through a series of predictable phases. The first phase, *initiation*, is centered on formation of the mentorship. The mentor and protégé have increasingly frequent interaction, get to know one another, and begin a helpful and enjoyable alliance. The second phase, *cultivation*, is the longest phase of a mentorship; during this phase, the majority of the protégé's growth and development occur. Mentors provide the full range of career and psychosocial functions while the protégés' confidence and competence increase. Various developmental and circumstantial changes will eventually trigger *separation*, the third phase of mentorship. Ranging from 6 months to more than a year, separation is characterized by an ending of the relationship in its most active and intense form. Healthy readiness for greater independence, or more tangible markers such as a new job or graduation, requires an ending of sorts. Eventually, the mentor relationship enters a phase described by Kram as *redefinition*. This is an indefinite period after the separation phase when the relationship takes on a new long-term form; the mentorship typically evolves into a more steady, peerlike friendship.

Kram's phasic model of mentorship development is validated by research on mentorships in a range of settings (Chao, 1997; Pollock, 1995). Most mentorships will go through these phases in a predictable sequence. Of course, there will be tremendous variation in how and when each graduate school mentor pair moves through each phase. For some, the pattern may fit perfectly. For others, the mentorship may terminate abruptly, or redefinition may never occur. It is also true that some overlap occurs between phases. For example, the line between initiation and cultivation is not always clear, and in some graduate school mentorships, protégés occasionally work on discrete components of separation (e.g., forming secondary mentorships with other faculty or independently authoring a journal article) while still very much in the cultivation phase of their mentorship. In any case, it is important to flexibly read and understand the phases that follow. In Exhibit 7.1, we highlight the four mentorship phases, emphasizing the time frame, primary characteristics, and essential developmental tasks accompanying each.

Phase 1: Initiation

STRESS AND IDENTITY CRISIS: THE CONTEXT OF GRADUATE SCHOOL MENTORSHIP

Before describing the first phase of mentorship, it is important to paint a picture of the context for mentorship formation. The ideal graduate school mentorship is initiated during the first year of graduate training —a year fraught with stress, anxiety, and marked instability in personal identity. Several authors have summarized the stresses and crises common of the early phase of training (Berger & Buchholz, 1993; Bruss & Kopala, 1993; Kaslow & Rice, 1985; Lamb, Baker, Jennings, & Yarris, 1982). New graduate students are often scrambling for identity. Their hard-won pregraduate identities and friendships are often left behind. They may relocate, terminate romantic relationships, and suffer financial stress. They often experience isolation, role ambiguity, and a sense of personal and professional vulnerability. First-year graduate students frequently score in the "life crisis" category on measures of stress, and, as a result, some will experience serious psychological symptoms such as depression and insomnia (Mallinckrodt, Leong, & Kralj, 1989). Although most early-phase graduate students are stressed, men and women may experience different sources of stress. Mallinckrodt et al. (1989) found that although intense loss was common to most new graduate students, women were often most stressed by outside employment, marriage, and other relationships. In contrast, men were most stressed by economic difficulties and debt.

In addition to these sources of stress, new graduate students are acutely aware of intense scrutiny and evaluation on the part of program faculty. Feeling vulnerable, alone, and overwhelmed, the student now contends with demands to perform academically. Professors may be perceived as critical and unreasonably rigorous in expectations. To make matters worse, the student becomes aware that his or her peers are also quite intelligent and high achieving, thus fueling fear of failure and the sometimes not-so-subtle sense that he or she is an "imposter"—unqualified, inadequate, and perhaps admitted by mistake.

In this context of stress, insecurity, and hypervigilance, the new

EXHIBIT 7.1

Phases of Graduate School Mentorship

Phase 1: Initiation
    Time frame: A period of 6 months to 1 year during which the relationship
        begins and becomes more important to both student and faculty
        member.
    Phase characteristics: In the context of stress and a struggle for identity, the
        graduate student initiates contact and interaction with the mentor. Inter-
        actions are positive, filled with promise, and promote attraction and col-
        laboration. The protégé idealizes the mentor as an exemplar, whereas
        the mentor sees the protégé as a source of creative energy and poten-
        tial. Primary mentor functions include acceptance and confirmation,
        coaching, and role modeling.
    Developmental tasks: Establishing roles, developing competence, construct-
        ing professional boundaries, and identifying a career trajectory.
Phase 2: Cultivation
    Time frame: A period of 2 to 5 years when the mentorship is stable and
        the mentor actively provides a range of career and psychosocial
        functions.
    Phase characteristics: The most stable, productive, and helpful phase of the
        mentorship; cultivation is characterized by rapid personal and profes-
        sional growth on the part of the protégé. The full range of mentor
        functions are used to enhance the protégé' competence and confidence.
        Both mentor and protégé enjoy the relationship as mutuality and trust
        deepen. Increasing protégé autonomy marks the end of this phase.
    Developmental tasks: Solidifying professional identity, taking risks, achiev-
        ing autonomy, developing competence, investing in a career trajectory,
        and establishing professional integrity.
Phase 3: Separation
    Time frame: A period of 6 months to 2 years during which the protégé
        completes graduate school and exits the active phase of the mentorship.
    Phase characteristics: As the protégé completes final graduate school tasks
        (e.g., coursework, dissertation, and internships) and prepares for post-
        graduate employment or training, both mentor and protégé must accept
        and process issues of termination and loss. Strong emotions may range
        from gratitude to sadness or resentment. The active phase of mentorship
        ends, and for a time, interaction may be minimal or nonexistent.
    Developmental tasks: Asserting professional autonomy, accepting loss, say-
        ing goodbye, developing a balanced view of mentor as human, launch-
        ing the early career.
Phase 4: Redefinition
    Time frame: An indefinite period following the separation phase when the
        mentorship ends altogether or is redefined as a collegial friendship.
    Phase characteristics: If the graduate school mentorship continues, and
        many do not, the relationship changes in character to one marked by
        friendship, mutuality, and collegial interaction. Some mentor functions
        (e.g., encouragement, sponsorship) may persist.
    Developmental tasks: Accepting professional identity, including the role of
        colleague to former faculty and supervisors.

graduate student often experiences a heightened sense of dependency, an intense desire for a stable and dependable parent-figure (Bruss & Kopala, 1993; Kaslow & Rice, 1985). Not surprisingly, new graduate students are often quite ready to bond with a faculty mentor, leaning heavily on him or her while the stress and insecurity of the first phase of graduate school lessen. Excellent mentors understand this dependency and the need for what psychologists call a "holding environment," or a relationship characterized by warmth, nurturance, protection, and encouragement.

ATTRACTION, POTENTIAL, AND SYNERGY

In chapter 5, we encouraged you to intentionally interact with the graduate school faculty member you found most promising as a mentor. These interactions may occur in classrooms, research labs, clinics, and, less formally, in the hallway outside the faculty member's office. As a proactive and intentional protégé, you have single-handedly kicked off the first phase of your mentorship.

The first phase of any mentor relationship is marked by elements of attraction, increasing awareness of the potential for an enjoyable and productive relationship, and an accompanying sense of synergy or creative excitement. The first 6 months to 1 year of a mentorship is characterized by excitement and positive interaction (Kram, 1983, 1985; Levinson et al., 1978; O'Neil & Wrightsman, 2001). The graduate student idealizes the mentor as a protector who will guide the protégé into the professional world. Although somewhat clouded by fantasy, the protégé's admiration and sense of awe relative to the mentor help to form the initial relationship bond.

Primary developmental tasks for the protégé during this phase include establishing roles, developing a sense of competence, constructing initial professional boundaries, and identifying a purpose or professional trajectory (Chickering, 1969; Zorich, 1999). Graduate students often struggle to understand and adopt the role of graduate student. They must also balance new academic roles with family or employment roles. During the initiation phase, graduate students work at feeling minimally competent at a range of new activities and creating workable professional boundaries between themselves, peers, and faculty.

A potential obstacle to mentoring in this phase involves unrealistic (often unconscious) expectations and idealized images of the mentor by the protégé (Mehlman & Glickauf-Hughes, 1994). For example, protégés who were disappointed by their own parents may attribute unrealistic attributes and talents to their mentor, ultimately resulting in disappointment and disillusionment. Alternatively, protégés may have strong needs to be exactly like their mentor, resulting in attempts to clone themselves in their mentor's image rather than develop an autonomous professional identity. Finally, some protégés have excessive needs for confirmation and approval from the mentor, resulting in perfectionist expectations of themselves and demands for approval from the mentor. It is easy to see how each of these styles may pose an obstacle to developing a healthy mentorship.

During this phase, the mentor sees the junior as someone with potential, someone coachable, and someone enjoyable to work with. The mentor may be drawn to the student's values, research interests, and potential for offering technical assistance and creative stimulation. He or she is increasingly aware of the potential match between the student's talents and interests and his or her own needs and interests. If the mentor is in the reassessment or reappraisal stage of midlife (Levinson et al., 1978), he or she will be particularly drawn to contribute creatively to the development of a talented graduate student.

Important mentor functions during this phase include acceptance and confirmation, coaching, and role modeling. As the initiation phase of mentorship continues, mentor–protégé interactions will become more reciprocal and mutual. At some point during this first year, the mentorship will enter the second phase, characterized by stability, productivity, and a wide range of protégé-enhancing mentor functions. In the case examples presented at the beginning of this chapter (Cases 7.1 and 7.2), both Clark and Tim experienced a range of positive mentor functions during the initiation phase of the relationship. For many protégés, this is a very exciting time.

Phase 2: Cultivation

Once your mentorship has been initiated and weathered the initial 6 to 12 months, it will enter what Kram (1983) termed the cultivation phase. This phase (typically 2 to 5 years) will usually extend until you exit graduate school. It is the most stable, productive, and enjoyable phase of a mentorship and typically involves the least amount of conflict and turmoil. As a protégé, you will experience a steady increase in security, competence, and accomplishment—feeling confirmed and respected by your mentor. The cultivation phase is marked by several key developmental tasks for the protégé and delivery of most of the essential mentor functions (Kram, 1985). During this productive and meaningful phase in your mentor relationship, your mentor will probably be most active in helping you grow professionally and personally.

KEY DEVELOPMENTAL TASKS

Perhaps the most important developmental task of the cultivation phase is establishment of an early professional identity. Establishing identity involves the assimilation of professional knowledge, skills, and attitudes into a stable sense of self. Identity development also hinges on a sincere appreciation of one's fundamental strengths and weaknesses (Orzek, 1984; Zorich, 1999). Identity formation requires awareness of professional limitations, self-doubt, and self-confrontation, coupled with steadily increasing self-tolerance, self-confidence, and willingness to take risks (Lamb et al., 1982). As you become more confident, first in your role as a graduate student, and later, in your role as junior professional, you might also expect to feel less threatened by corrective feedback and less competitive with peers and faculty. Helping a protégé become confident, competent, and self-aware may be the most salient of all mentor tasks.

Taking risks and achieving autonomy are developmental tasks linked to identity formation. During the years of cultivation, your mentor will often challenge you to try new roles, face daunting tasks, and risk your (sometimes fragile) sense of esteem. As your identity forms and your confidence improves, it is essential that you take on increasing responsibility and function more autonomously. When you present your first professional paper to a conference audience, work at initial drafts of your dissertation, or teach a course section, you will be risking. Keep in mind that your mentor risks here as well. If you refuse to take risks, remain dependent, or fail miserably, your mentor's credibility and reputation may also suffer. It is important that you accept challenges and risk failure on your way to becoming a professional. (See Box 7.1.)

Achieving competence is another critical developmental task during the cultivation phase of mentorship (Chickering, 1969; Orzek, 1984).

BOX 7.1: HOW IT WORKED FOR US — JENNY'S PERSPECTIVE

I can vividly recall my initial sense of anxiety when Brad asked me to present at a large professional conference. Although I thought of many reasons why I was unprepared for this challenge, I knew that accepting the assignment and performing well would likely lead to other opportunities that were important to my training. Although anxious, I prepared and performed well as a presenter (at least I got lots of good feedback). Consequently, my self-confidence and sense of self as a scholar were enhanced.

Competence in any profession will involve both technical and social (interpersonal) dimensions. Not only will an ideal mentorship enhance your knowledge and skill base (e.g., research, teaching, or clinical competence), but it will also prepare you to navigate professional relationships, interpersonal conflict, and organizational requirements. Through interaction with your mentor, and observation of your mentor "in action," you will learn the art of building collegial relationships and how to "be" a good colleague. Competence involves both emotional self-management and expertise with discipline-specific subject matter.

Two final developmental tasks during this phase include investing in a career trajectory and establishing professional integrity (Chickering, 1969; Zorich, 1999). Healthy development in graduate school requires growth of a professional career focus. What do you want to do after you graduate, and how will you do it? Good mentors have walked a similar path and understand the importance of targeting and pursuing desired career goals during this phase. Simultaneously, graduate students in the cultivation phase of mentorship begin to adopt the ethics and values of the profession. Watching the mentor successfully handle ethical dilemmas and hold to the profession's highest standards facilitates professional integrity development.

KEY MENTOR FUNCTIONS

The cultivation phase of your mentorship will be the time when your mentor provides the widest range of important mentor functions. During this time of relative stability in the relationship, your mentor will serve as a strong catalyst in your journey of professional development. Lageman (1986) referred to the mentor as a "midwife" during this phase, helping the protégé to birth a new identity and then helping to crystallize his or her sense of self in the professional landscape.

In most cases, career functions emerge first during the cultivation stage. The most common and important career functions will include challenge, exposure and visibility, sponsorship, and protection. Just as it will be your responsibility to take risks in graduate school, so too will it be your mentor's duty to present you with challenges requiring risk. Asking you to teach a class in his or her absence, coauthor an article, or take on a particularly complicated research task or clinic client are all examples of professional challenge. Although the point is not to overwhelm, a good mentor will work to keep you stretching for the next level of competence. Good mentors provide challenging assignments accompanied by healthy doses of reassurance, support, and confidence.

An excellent mentor will also work to create positive attention for his or her protégé. When your mentor asks you to copresent a paper at a conference, coauthor an article, or attend a professional meeting so that introductions to other professionals can be made, your visibility within the discipline is enhanced. "Insiders" in any discipline will tell you that hiring for most jobs and access to other career opportunities are strongly influenced by informal networking. When a mentor introduces you to colleagues at other universities or mentions your achievements and abilities to other faculty within the graduate department, your professional exposure is vitally enhanced. In other words, your professional stock goes up each time you are given visibility (and you perform well in response). A related and equally important mentor function during this phase is sponsorship. Mentors sponsor protégés for society memberships, assistantships (teaching or research), grant funding, and internship and postdoctoral fellowship positions. The more well known or respected your mentor, the more potent his or her sponsorship will be.

During the cultivation phase, it is also true that the majority of psychosocial functions (Kram, 1985) emerge. One of the primary tasks of the early cultivation phase is establishment of mutual trust between mentor and protégé. Once the initial commitment is made, trust will emerge as mentor and protégé gradually and reciprocally self-disclose and come to confidently rely on each other. Several mentor functions will facilitate trust in the mentorship and both the personal and professional growth of the protégé during the cultivation phase. First, the mentor must continue to provide acceptance and confirmation of the protégé. Regardless of how confident you become, and how many challenges you successfully meet, it is likely that you will continue to benefit from your mentor's affirmation and encouragement—particularly on those occasions when all is not going well. Second, in some mentorships, the mentor may offer counseling when this is appropriate. This may take the form of advice, disputation of seemingly crazy or catastrophic thinking, or reflection and observation. Although the mentor should avoid entering into a clinical role with any protégé, there may be times during graduate school (e.g., personal crises, critical decision points) when your mentor can serve as a helpful informal counselor. Finally, mentors may increasingly come to be seen as friends or colleagues to protégés. Although during the cultivation phase, you are most likely to see your mentor as quite separate from you in terms of expertise, competence, and power, it is both natural and healthy for this perceived "gulf" to gradually narrow as you approach the separation phase. Part of maturing as a professional in any field is accepting one's increasing competence and entering into colleague status with faculty. Eventually, this will include your mentor.

AS THE END DRAWS NEAR

At some point during this productive and enjoyable phase of mentorship, you will become aware that ending is in sight. That is, an end to the cultivation work of mentoring is near. This phase may end gradually, seamlessly merging into separation. More often, however, the end is more severe; the protégé graduates and contact between mentor and protégé sharply declines.

In the ideal case, your mentorship will have shifted from one-way helping (on the part of your mentor) to a mutual exchange. As you develop competence, self-worth, and technical mastery, your mentor trusts you with increasing autonomy, and the relationship becomes more reciprocal and collegial (Kram, 1985). As an emerging professional (Lamb et al., 1982), you may be aware of "needing" your mentor less intensely. You may pursue jobs, fellowships, and research or professional endeavors without seeking consultation from your mentor. This increasing autonomy is not only healthy; it is essential as you prepare for the separation phase of mentorship. Also, toward the end of the cultivation phase, you should be forming a more critical and realistic view of your mentor. More mature and independent in your own professional perspective, it is now safe to see your mentor as human and imperfect. Each of these important maturational changes will serve to disrupt the equilibrium in the mentorship, a disruption that will come to fruition when you exit graduate school.

Phase 3: Separation

In her study, Kram (1983) found that most mentorships move from cultivation to a phase marked by leave-taking and distancing in the relationship. This separation phase typically lasts between 6 months and 2 years and often begins for graduate school mentorships during the protégé's final year in the program. Several milestones or rites of passage herald the onset of the separation phase. First, you will finish work on the dissertation, and (we hope) weather your final defense. You will wrap up coursework and other program requirements and may spend less time on campus. Second, you will become engaged in the hunt for postdegree employment or advanced training. Applications for internships, fellowships, and initial jobs will force you to look beyond graduate school to life in the profession. Third, as you discuss postdegree plans with your mentor, your pending exit from the program should become a growing reality for both of you.

Navigating the separation phase will be crucial to your professional development. It is imperative that you focus ahead and anticipate new responsibilities and challenges. Time that you had previously devoted to coursework, dissertation research, and perhaps time with your mentor should now be directed at the tasks associated with exiting graduate school. Simultaneously, you must acknowledge and accept the pending loss of the mentorship, as you have known it.

The exit phase of graduate education is often quite stressful for a variety of reasons. As you prepare to leave the familiar terrain of graduate school, you must reorient to reality in some ways. Student loans, the job hunt, and geographic relocation constitute common stressors. In addition, many students question their preparedness for functioning as a professional, and some question the value of their education and the sacrifices required to achieve it.

ACCEPTING LOSS AND SAYING GOODBYE

If your mentorship has been helpful, productive, enjoyable, and personally meaningful, it is hard to imagine that you will not experience a sense of real loss when you take leave to begin your career. In fact, if there are no pangs of sadness, or no sense that the mentor will be missed, we wonder about the depth and quality of the mentor bond. During the separation phase, both mentor and protégé become aware of the protégé's pending exit from the program, and both need to find ways to acknowledge this. More importantly, both must find ways to accept this loss and arrange to say goodbye to the most active phase of the relationship.

As you prepare to leave graduate school and your mentor, do not be surprised by feelings ranging from sadness to anger and resentment. Protégés sometimes feel abandoned by mentors who quickly turn their attention to new students or who minimize the significance of leave-taking. They sometimes experience a strange sense of "stuckness" or ambivalence—on the one hand wanting to move on, and on the other hand afraid to do so (Kram, 1985; Lamb et al., 1982). Most commonly, however, they are temporarily melancholy with loss and the real sense of ending. Among graduate students in psychology programs, 17% found termination of the relationship to be quite difficult (Clark et al., 2000). If you have mixed feelings about saying goodbye, you are very normal.

We highly recommend that you find a way to say thank you and goodbye to your mentor before formally exiting your program. Just as you were intentional in initiating the mentorship, you should now be intentional in accepting its end. You must arrange a format by which you and your mentor can process how your relationship has evolved, what it has achieved, its meaning for you, and how it might change in the months and years ahead. Of course, some mentors will be more self-aware, relationally savvy, and capable of processing strong emotions than others. Even if your mentor has trouble with saying goodbye, it is important for you to go through this process in some way. Ideally, you will be able to discuss your separation several times before it occurs. A final lunch, dinner, or meeting for the explicit purpose of saying good-bye to this phase of the mentorship is a nice way to end.

During the separation phase, good mentors work at facilitating a protégé's growing sense of individuality and independence (Kaslow & Rice, 1985). They allow the relationship to become more collegial, in a sense welcoming the protégé into the profession and endorsing his or her status as more than a student—a colleague. Rather than stifle the protégé's growing autonomy, the mentor encourages and reinforces it. Friendship may be more characteristic of the separation phase of mentorship as self-disclosure and support become more mutual. Excellent mentors also aggressively promote their protégés in strong letters of recommendation, and perhaps in phone calls to colleagues and prospective employers. The mentor will continue to coach—now for job interviews, dissertation hurdles, and other end-of-program obstacles. He or she will continue to affirm and endorse the protégé when self-doubts and disappointments occur. Above all, the excellent mentor will attend to the significance of separation, will accept feelings of loss, and will openly discuss these with protégés.

SEPARATION PROBLEMS

The separation phase is sometimes problematic. In fact, this is typically the phase of mentorship most likely to result in conflict and relational turmoil (Bruss & Kopala, 1993; Kram, 1985). When there is a problem, it is most likely to stem from insecurity, dependence, or anger on the part of a mentor who has difficulty accepting loss or who feels competitive with protégés who become increasingly successful and self-sufficient. Such a mentor may resent the student's separation and cease offering encouragement and support. In the worst case, a mentor might actively block student advancement by prolonging dissertation work, discouraging moves out of state, or delaying postgraduation planning in general. In response to feeling threatened with loss, the pathologic mentor may become rejecting, critical, or (perhaps worst of all) indifferent. As a protégé, it is important that you recognize each of these as a sign of relationship pathology. In the next chapter, we offer a range of strategies for addressing problems in mentorships. If your mentor shows signs of difficulty with separation, it will be important for you to address this directly.

Another potential separation problem involves sudden or premature separation. Like other professionals, graduate school professors often move on to new positions as they advance in their careers. In other cases, a mentor may be fired, retire, become seriously ill, or even die. A sudden separation or termination of the mentorship may pose several

BOX 7.2: HOW IT WORKED FOR US—JENNY'S PERSPECTIVE

When Brad departed George Fox University for a new position, our mentorship was squarely within the cultivation phase. As a result of his decision to leave, our relationship was forced into a premature separation status. Although Brad continued as my dissertation chair, and although we continued to collaborate and interact by phone and e-mail, his physical exit from the program posed a number of unexpected challenges for me. Like many students faced with similar circumstances, I initially found this transition to be frustrating and anxiety provoking. Only continued long-distance collaboration resulted in a more natural and rewarding close of the cultivation phase.

problems for you as protégé. First, there may be significant disruption in crucial mentor functions (e.g., support, protection, challenge). Second, loss of a mentor may involve loss of your dissertation chair and subsequent difficulty completing graduate school on time. Finally, sudden mentor loss may pose emotional problems—experience akin to loss of any other important relationship. (See Box 7.2.)

Finally, protégés themselves can block healthy mentorship separation. Most often, this occurs through a range of self-defeating and self-sabotaging behaviors designed to prolong graduate school and avoid separation. Whether conscious or unconscious, behaviors such as turning in job or internship applications late, failing to get the dissertation written, or putting off remaining coursework may all be indicative of difficulty with separation. Protégés who have difficulty with separation may also attempt to avoid it altogether by refusing to discuss the changing mentorship with their mentor or exiting graduate school without ever saying goodbye.

Phase 4: Redefinition

Some mentor relationships end altogether when the protégé leaves graduate school, with the mentor and protégé having no further contact. In other cases, the mentor and protégé correspond or meet from time to time at conferences to get caught up and renew their friendship. In still other cases, a mentorship may transform into a new collegial connection characterized by frequent interaction, often in the context of

> ### BOX 7.3: HOW IT WORKED FOR US—BRAD'S PERSPECTIVE
>
> Although Jenny has now become a postdoctoral fellow and I have moved 3,000 miles away, we continue to collaborate on scholarly projects, including this book. Increasingly, I see Jenny as a valued and trusted colleague. I also enjoy our friendship and appreciate Jenny's excellent creative contributions to our joint research and writing projects.

shared scholarly projects. Kram (1983) referred to this final phase of mentorship as the period of redefinition. During this indefinite phase, the relationship ends altogether or takes on a substantially different character as the two become more peerlike and the relationship settles into a long-term friendship. Here the stresses and turmoil common of the separation phase diminish while gratitude and appreciation replace any lingering loss or resentment.

In all probability, you are unlikely to interact frequently with your mentor once you leave graduate school. Although you may remain grateful to your mentor, and your mentor proud of your accomplishments, time, geography, and the demands of new protégés (for your mentor) and new professional responsibilities (for you) make regular contact difficult. This is most often a healthy sign that you and your mentor have done good work together, despite the fact that it can also be disappointing or sad. To acclimate to autonomous functioning and to close the previous chapter of the mentorship, you will find that a period of separation and infrequent contact is likely useful.

It is also true that many solid mentorships result in an ongoing though redefined connection. Although the mentor may continue to provide specific mentor functions (e.g., encouragement, support, and promotion in the form of recommendations), these redefined relationships are typically more mutual and centered around ongoing friendship and professional collaboration. Ideally, such redefined mentorships can be enjoyable, rewarding, and mutually beneficial for years. Some excellent predictors of whether your mentorship will result in this kind of ongoing relationship include (a) the quality and depth of the relational bond, (b) the maturity of both parties, (c) clarity of communication, (d) relationship reciprocity, and (e) the extent to which you continue to share interests and enjoy interaction. (See Box 7.3.)

Potential Problems (and How to Handle Them)

8

Case 8.1

Marsha was in her 3rd year of doctoral studies in political science when her relationship with Dr. Angst began to make her uncomfortable. Dr. Angst was a senior faculty member in the department and was an excellent scholar and teacher. He and Marsha had worked well together for 2 years in what Marsha viewed as a tremendously helpful mentor relationship. Dr. Angst was supportive and encouraging, and he frequently presented Marsha with new professional opportunities and challenges. During her 3rd year in the program, however, Marsha began to notice subtle changes in Dr. Angst's behavior and appearance. He was distracted, emotionally fragile, and sometimes disheveled. He began to miss meetings, writing deadlines, and even some class sessions. Worse, Dr. Angst began to confide in Marsha that his marriage was failing. He requested that Marsha hold this information in confidence and stated that he "just needed some support" from her. Marsha became increasingly uncomfortable with Dr. Angst's disclosures and his growing emotional dependency. On two or three occasions, he even called her at home to seek reassurance. During the final phone call, Dr. Angst said, "I just wish I had found someone like you when I was younger." Although Marsha had been sharing her concerns about Dr. Angst with a trusted friend outside the department, she now sought consultation from a faculty member at her undergraduate university. The faculty member assured Marsha that her concerns were legitimate and helped Marsha outline a plan for kindly but clearly confronting Dr. Angst. Marsha then scheduled a formal meeting with her mentor and clearly described how his blurring of personal and professional boundaries in the mentorship had made her feel uncomfortable. Although she was empathic with Dr. Angst, she was also clear and concrete in describing what she required from him to remain in the mentorship. For example, she requested that the two only have contact in the department and that Dr. Angst refrain from disclosing further information about

29

his marriage. Although initially startled by Marsha's confrontation, Dr. Angst responded appropriately and later complimented Marsha for her kindness and thanked her for her loyalty. Dr. Angst sought emotional support elsewhere, and the two enjoyed a productive mentorship for the remainder of Marsha's program.

Case 8.2

When Paula began doctoral studies in engineering at a major research university, she was simultaneously thrilled and terrified. Although Paula had excellent grades and recommendations as an undergraduate, she lacked confidence and harbored a nagging belief that she had "slipped through" the admissions grid by mistake. She was particularly anxious about pleasing her faculty advisor Dr. Frosty, a renowned engineer. Throughout her first year in the program, Paula worked extremely long hours and performed exceptionally well academically and as a contributor to Dr. Frosty's research lab projects. Nonetheless, Dr. Frosty's demeanor remained stiff, cold, and brusque. He displayed annoyance whenever Paula broached personal concerns, and he never complimented her good work. It became clear to Paula that Dr. Frosty lacked the interpersonal skills and the familiarity with the concept of mentoring to offer her any psychosocial mentor functions (e.g., the encouragement, support, and affirmation she desperately wanted from a mentor). Angered and disheartened, Paula began complaining to other students and faculty within the department about Dr. Frosty, calling him "Dr. Cold Blood" behind his back. Rather than take initiative for discussing the bad match with Dr. Frosty and pursuing a different mentor, Paula began avoiding him and intentionally neglecting research lab tasks, even though her behavior caused havoc for Dr. Frosty. When Dr. Frosty angrily confronted her negligence, she impulsively filed a formal complaint with the academic dean, accusing Dr. Frosty of "emotional abuse."

Alas, all human relationships, like all human beings, suffer from imperfection. Every significant and worthwhile relationship involves some mixture of joy, pleasure, error, success, anger, regret, and forgiveness. An important component of building and sustaining relationships is the recognition—and often acceptance—of our partner's faults and imperfections (Duck, 1994). In spite of the normalcy and pervasiveness of relationship imperfection, most scholarly research and writing on the topic of interpersonal relationships focus nearly exclusively on the pleasant, healthy, and ideal side of relationship functioning (Duck, 1994; Feldman, 1999; Merriam, 1983; Scandura, 1998). Of this trend, Duck (1994) wrote, "the focus on the favorable, positive, close, and nice side of relating misses entirely the point that, at the very least, such behavior and the processes of cognition that go with it are always implicitly contrasted with something else in human life" (p. 14), and "relational life can be nasty, brutish, and short, certainly insofar as it is practiced" (p. 4).

The Dark Side of Mentorship

Avoidance of what we call the "dark side" of relationship functioning is also prevalent in literature bearing on mentoring (Johnson & Huwe, 2002). Most mentorship research uses small samples of long-term relationships characterized by both strong emotional ties and close working partnerships (Feldman, 1999). Even the term *mentoring* itself implies a positive relational activity; to be mentored is to be cared for, nurtured, and protected. Although some mentor relationships are clearly unhealthy (Levinson et al., 1978) and destructive (Kram, 1985), research remains largely focused on the bright, productive, and functional side of mentorships.

In spite of this avoidance of the dark side of mentoring, preliminary data indicate that, like other relationships, mentorships are prone to imperfection and, at times, negative outcomes. Studies of manager protégés (Eby, McManus, Simon, & Russell, 2000) and both graduate and undergraduate protégés (Kalbfleisch, 1997) suggest that at least half of protégés have experienced at least one problematic mentor relationship. A significant percentage of recent doctorates in clinical psychology also noted clearly negative aspects of their primary graduate school mentorship (Clark et al., 2000). The most common problems included (a) mentor unavailability, (b) difficult termination, (c) feeling unable to meet the mentor's expectations, (d) maintaining a relationship that required unpleasant activities, and (e) exploitation by the mentor (e.g., mentor took credit for protégé work). Together, these findings confirm that negative experiences in mentorships are neither aberrant nor necessarily pathologic but rather indicative of the same human foibles and shortcomings that plague all relationship forms.

In this chapter, we explore common forms of dysfunction in graduate school mentorships. We begin with a definition of relationship dysfunction and consider the various contributing factors to relationships gone awry. We consider 11 distinct mentorship problems and how each may be manifest in a graduate school mentorship. We then highlight what *not* to do when problems develop and conclude by outlining strategies for handling mentorship dysfunction once it is detected.

Before you read further, it is important to acknowledge two truths about problematic graduate school mentorships. First, the "dark side" of mentoring is not always dark in its effects (Duck, 1994). In fact, handling conflict effectively may produce surprisingly positive outcomes, both for your own development and for the life of your mentorship. As in other chapters of this book (see chapter 5), we encourage you to be assertive and intentional in your response to dysfunction once you determine it exists. Effectively handling mentorship problems will be an indicator of growth, maturity, and relational resilience. It will additionally bode well for your ultimate success in life and career.

The second truth about any dysfunctional graduate school mentor-ship is that it is seldom the exclusive result of pathology or incompe-tence on the part of the mentor. Mentoring involves a process of mutual influence, and protégés are often co-contributors to both positive and negative mentorship outcomes. Although some problems will be clearly linked to your mentor's poor planning, inexperience, or bad behavior, your response to these mentor failings will influence the ultimate health and value of the relationship.

Defining Mentorship Dysfunction

When is a mentor relationship dysfunctional? In the first study of men-tor relationships, Levinson et al. (1978) connected dysfunction primarily with the mentor's behavior. For example, these authors described men-tors with corrosively critical, demanding, or authoritarian personal traits, as well as mentors who became jealous of protégé success, ultimately sabotaging careers. However, not all problems in mentor relationship emanate from the mentor. Some stem from protégé traits or behavior, whereas others are rooted in circumstances, poor matching, or even the effects of normal development and healthy growth.

Several authors have attempted to clarify and define the character-istics of relationships that are no longer rewarding, productive, or healthy (Eby et al., 2000; Feldman, 1999; Ragins & Scandura, 1997, 1998). We borrowed from each of these authors in creating our own definition of dysfunctional mentorship. Although the term *dysfunctional* has become somewhat faddish, we simply use it to refer to a mentorship that has become unproductive or characterized by conflict. In short, the relationship is no longer working. Specifically, the following are the cri-teria for dysfunctional mentorships:

1. The primary needs of one or both partners are not being met.
2. The long-term costs for one or both partners outweigh the long-term benefits.
3. One or both partners are suffering distress as a result of being in the mentorship.

The first indicator of mentorship dysfunction is evidence that the primary developmental or professional needs of either the protégé or the mentor are not being addressed by the relationship. For example, your mentor may be exceptional at providing career coaching and op-portunities for research but may fail entirely at offering support and emo-tional encouragement. If you have significant needs for psychosocial mentor functions, you may feel dissatisfied with this mentor relationship. Similarly, a faculty mentor may become frustrated if the protégé resists his or her attempts to offer career guidance or job recommendations, thereby thwarting the mentor's need to feel generative and helpful.

Second, mentorship in which either the protégé or the mentor senses that the long-term costs of the relationship outweigh the long-term benefits is likely to become dysfunctional. For example, if it becomes clear that your mentor expects long-term commitment to his or her research program—including numerous hours working on his or her projects each week and a commitment to work on a dissertation topic of his or her choosing—you may sense that the costs to you in terms of time, flexibility, and independence outweigh the potential benefits of being mentored by this professor. When faculty sense a dysfunctional cost–benefit ratio with protégés, it is usually because they see a protégé as demanding excessive time or emotional resources. Graduate students who are extremely emotionally needy, are slow to grasp research procedures, procrastinate, and require frequent intervention are likely to contribute to mentorship dysfunction.

Finally, dysfunction may occur when either the protégé or the mentor is distressed or feels harmed as a result of the relationship. Protégés are likely to feel distressed when they are sharply criticized, publicly humiliated, entirely neglected, sabotaged (e.g., with negative letters of recommendation), or approached sexually by their mentor. Mentors may feel dysfunctional distress when a protégé is continually critical, demanding, or disloyal (e.g., complaining about the mentor to other students or faculty).

In the balance of this chapter, we describe the primary sources of conflict and dissatisfaction in graduate school mentor relationships. Some of the problems described can be subtle and hard to discern (e.g., matching, boundary maintenance), whereas others are more egregious and obviously prone to producing dysfunction (e.g., exploitation, conflict). We strongly encourage you to become familiar with each problem category (summarized in Table 8.1), recognizing how each could present a serious obstacle to the life of your mentorship.

Sources of Mentorship Dysfunction

PROBLEM 1: A BAD MATCH

Poorly matched partners often experience relationship problems. Distinct differences in personality, communication style, work patterns, ca-

TABLE 8.1

Sources of Mentorship Dysfunction

Problem	Description
Bad matching	Mentor and protégé are poorly matched along key dimensions such as personality, communication style, work style, career stage, and career interest.
Mentor technical incompetence	The mentor lacks necessary competence in his or her field or lacks competence with respect to understanding and managing mentorships.
Mentor relational incompetence	The mentor lacks relational skills and emotional intelligence. In addition, dysfunctional personality characteristics and emotional problems may interfere with mentorships.
Mentor neglect	The mentor offers the protégé inadequate time and attention. Important protégé needs are not addressed, and few mentor functions are evident.
Conflict	Arguments, binds, distancing, or venting of negative affect (e.g., anger) characterize the mentorship. Rather than problem-solve, the parties accuse and sabotage.
Boundary violations	The boundary between personal and professional roles blurs such that confusion, discomfort, and, at times, exploitation occur.
Exploitation	The mentor uses his or her position to manipulate or coerce something from the subordinate protégé (e.g., work, emotional support, sex).
Attraction	The experience of attraction toward the mentor provokes anxiety in the protégé and results in distancing, seductiveness, or some other mentorship-disruptive behavior.
Unethical or illegal behavior	The mentor engages in or encourages the protégé to engage in unethical or illegal behavior, such as fraud, theft, or plagiarism.
Abandonment	The mentor exits the mentorship prior to the natural phase of separation. This occurs as a result of death, illness, job change, or mentor-initiated termination of the mentorship. The effects are negative and disruptive for the protégé.
Dysfunctional protégé traits	Specific traits and behaviors on the part of the protégé stymie the relationship (e.g., dependency, procrastination, or impression management).

reer plans, research interests, and personal values or religious belief may portend disagreement, alienation, and, ultimately, termination of a mentorship (Eby et al., 2000; Feldman, 1999). The most common dimensions of bad matching include the following:

1. *Personality differences.* The mentor is intensely introverted and shy, preferring time alone, whereas the protégé is gregarious

and outgoing, preferring more time for interaction and socializing.

2. *Communication style differences.* The mentor is terse and direct, speaking in short sentences and getting right to the point even when discussing sensitive issues, whereas the protégé is verbally expansive and prone to lengthy narrative of his or her experience in each situation.

3. *Relationship preference differences.* The protégé envisions an emotionally bonded mentorship in which the mentor provides numerous psychosocial functions and becomes a long-term friend and colleague, whereas the mentor wants help with his or her research program and enjoys giving some career advice along the way.

4. *Work style differences.* The protégé is compulsive and well organized, preferring detailed planning of each stage in a research project and formally scheduled work meetings, whereas the mentor is casual and disorganized, preferring to work on projects the week before deadlines and telling the protégé to just "swing by" if something is needed.

5. *Career stage mismatch.* The mentor is fresh from graduate school and in the early-career phase, struggling to establish credibility and achieve tenure, whereas the protégé is older than the mentor, confident, successful in another field, and in need of little guidance.

6. *Career interest mismatch.* The mentor is a researcher and is only interested in mentoring protégés into the world of academia, whereas the protégé intends to be a practitioner and has little aptitude or interest in research.

PROBLEM 2: MENTOR INCOMPETENCE TYPE A—TECHNICAL INCOMPETENCE

Not all professors are competent mentors—either in the sense of knowing their specialty or in the sense knowing how to mentor graduate students (Eby et al., 2000; Goodyear, Crego, & Johnston, 1992; Johnson & Nelson, 1999). Your mentor may have a doctorate in the field, yet for a host of reasons may know relatively little about the area in which he or she teaches or supervises student research. Although hard to imagine, this happens. If it happens to you, you will be in the unenviable position of having to determine whether your mentor is competent enough to actually help you navigate the potentially hostile waters of a doctoral dissertation or whether the mentor's incompetence is public knowledge and this therefore diminishes the value of being mentored by him or her.

A second, and far more common, form of technical mentoring incompetence is incompetence with respect to mentoring itself. This form of incompetence is most common among very junior faculty with little experience at managing relationships with graduate students. This mentor may be young, naïve, and relationally inexperienced. He or she may be so preoccupied with issues of teaching and preparing for promotion that little thought is given to mentoring. This mentor will have little appreciation for the common stressors and developmental needs of graduate students, and he or she may be unaware of the normal phases of mentorship or the important functions of a mentor. Although this form of technical incompetence is typically a function of inexperience, it can also reflect disinterest in students or self-absorption, both of which bode poorly for effective mentorship.

PROBLEM 3: MENTOR INCOMPETENCE TYPE B—RELATIONAL INCOMPETENCE

Most graduate school faculty suffer a range of personal and relational imperfections. Some faculty members may be world-renowned researchers, and even highly engaging and popular teachers, yet may be quite unable to maintain healthy and productive mentorships with students. In the halls of academia, there are many unfortunate examples of the interpersonally unsophisticated (though often well-meaning) professor. This mentor may have trouble with all interpersonal relationships, may avoid them for the most part, and may be perpetually uncomfortable with students. Such faculty may lack emotional intelligence (see chapter 4) in that they have little insight about their own emotions and minimal interest in or accuracy reading the emotional states of others. Obviously, this will hamper the extent to which a mentorship will offer psychosocial functions (e.g., friendship, counseling, emotional support).

Beyond mere deficits in relational expertise, a mentor may possess personality characteristics and evidence relational patterns that are more malignant and destructive in nature. For example, a faculty mentor may be narcissistic (in love with himself or herself), tyrannical, bullying, critical, and rigid (Bruss & Kopala, 1993; Eby et al., 2000; Scandura, 1998). Being in relationship with this person will feel abusive, demeaning, or depressing. Such relationally malignant mentors may be intolerant of the insecure or dependent student and be rejecting and criticizing instead of encouraging and supporting. The mentor's arrogance may make it nearly impossible for him or her to carefully attend to the needs and concerns of graduate students.

Finally, a mentor may be relationally incompetent to the extent that he or she has significant emotional or mental health problems. These may be long-standing styles of relating or symptoms of distress (e.g., depression, anxiety, or anger) stemming from the mentor's own life circumstances (e.g., job and family stress) or developmental issues (e.g., midlife or midcareer struggles). Whatever the cause, mentor psychopathology is certain to make a mentorship more arduous and, at times, dysfunctional.

PROBLEM 4: MENTOR NEGLECT

In a group of several hundred recent psychology doctorates, the primary complaint among those who were mentored was that their mentor was less available than they would have preferred (Clark et al., 2000). Mentor neglect is among the most common sources of mentorship dysfunction. It comes as no surprise that faculty mentors are tremendously busy. They juggle teaching, research, grant writing, scholarly writing, advising, and sometimes professional practice with the demands of life and family. The more successful they are, the greater the competition for their time. We recommend that you avoid forming mentorships with faculty who are overextended or who have a track record of neglecting protégés. Although neglect is a strong word, we believe the adverse effects are powerful when a mentor offers inadequate time and resources to protégés they have committed to mentor. Inadequate supervision of protégés also raises ethical questions (Goodyear et al., 1992) about a faculty member's practice with students. In any case, a mentor who neglects or avoids you is unlikely to prove helpful as either a career guide or a source of support and encouragement. Keep in mind that neglect by a mentor may signal a range of problems from simple overcommitment to relational incompetence to dissatisfaction with your performance as a protégé.

PROBLEM 5: CONFLICT

Conflict is an inevitable part of any relationship. Most mentor–protégé dyads can recount one or more episodes of disagreement or a minor argument regarding things as varied as appropriate research procedures, deadlines for drafts of the dissertation, or whether or not an appointment had been scheduled. However, conflict in the graduate school mentorship can grow much more intense and, if not resolved expeditiously, can alienate one or both members to the extent that the relationship is no longer viable (Bruss & Kopala, 1993; Eby et al., 2000; Scandura, 1998). Being in conflict with a mentor can be particularly distressing for a protégé. As the power-down partner in the scenario, the protégé stands to lose the most from termination with a mentor, particularly if this occurs close to the end of a graduate program when research hurdles must be cleared and letters of recommendation are required.

Conflict in mentorships may stem from disagreements regarding the content or style of a research or writing project, authorship issues on a scholarly paper, or clashing expectations regarding what the mentorship should entail. Mentors may become hostile, resentful, or jealous when a protégé is successful or if the mentor perceives disloyalty in the protégé's behavior. Protégés may become hostile and vindictive if they perceive sabotage in their mentors' behavior (e.g., less-than-glowing letters of recommendation, discussions with other faculty about how the protégé has let them down). Without intervention or calm discussion, conflict can escalate to the point that both parties are placing the other in relational binds, such as when a mentor demands that a student choose "work or family." Although episodically normal and unlikely to be damaging if addressed rapidly and responsibly, unchecked conflict may seriously undermine your mentorship. (See Box 8.1.)

PROBLEM 6: BOUNDARY VIOLATIONS

Problems occur in mentor relationships when either the faculty mentor or protégé pushes for or allows violations in the boundary between professional and personal roles. Ethical and professional guidelines require mentors to vigorously avoid entering into relationships with students that may interfere with professional duties, impair objectivity, or lead to exploitation or harm of students (Blevins-Knabe, 1992; Johnson & Nelson, 1999). The graduate school mentorship is a fiduciary relationship,

---

BOX 8.1: HOW IT WORKED FOR US — JENNY'S PERSPECTIVE

As a graduate school protégé, I experienced conflict with Brad while outlining the time line for my dissertation defense. Anticipating a change in academic positions and a major relocation to another university, Brad requested that I complete and defend my dissertation on a time line that seemed unreasonable to me. Like many protégés faced with the need for their mentors' support and endorsement, I considered the option of passively fulfilling Brad's request despite the cost to my other personal and professional priorities. Ultimately, I decided to discuss this conflict openly with Brad. Because we valued principles of honesty and compromise in our mentorship, this discussion led to a resolution that we both agreed would meet our individual needs.

or a "special relationship in which one person [the mentor] accepts the trust and confidence of another [the protégé] to act in the latter's best interest" (Plaut, 1993, p. 213). Boundary violations nearly always compromise the integrity and effectiveness of the mentorship.

Although the most obvious and clearly inappropriate boundary violation involves the development of a romantic or sexual relationship between a mentor and protégé, there are other more subtle violations that also threaten mentorship integrity and usefulness. For example, a mentor who conducts personal therapy with a protégé or a mentor who develops a deep friendship and frequently socializes with a protégé may have difficulty objectively evaluating the student. Similarly, a married protégé who develops romantic interest in his or her mentor may engage in a great deal of impression management, perhaps preventing the mentor from discerning the protégé's fears and frustrations while simultaneously worsening his or her own marriage.

Of course, boundaries cannot be so rigid that good mentoring is inhibited. Research on mentoring shows that the strongest and most rewarding mentorships are relatively long term, are mutual, and involve multiple roles and contexts for interaction. For this to occur, mentor and protégé must naturally spend some time together in contexts external to the classroom. In addition, graduate school mentorships are inherently characterized by numerous overlapping roles such as teacher, evaluator, research supervisor, academic advisor, and even employer in the case of assistantships and fellowships (Biaggio, Paget, & Chenoweth, 1997). In other words, mentorships are inherently "multiple" relationships in the sense of requiring faculty and students to walk relational tightropes while juggling potentially conflicting roles. Although mentorships are somewhat multiple-roled by nature, blurring the boundaries between personal and professional roles will often result in some dysfunction.

PROBLEM 7: EXPLOITATION

Exploitation exists whenever a person in a position of power (a mentor) uses this position to manipulate or coerce something from a subordinate (a protégé) who exists in a dependent or power-down position. Exploitation can take the form of overt bullying and intimidation or more subtle innuendo and seduction (Eby et al., 2000; Scandura, 1998). Perhaps the most egregious and destructive form of exploitation is sexual harassment.

We have noted elsewhere in this book that sexual activity between a mentor and protégé is always inappropriate and destined to negatively alter the relationship. Nonetheless, research indicates that between 15% and 17% of female doctoral students in psychology have sexual contact with a faculty member at some point during their program (Glaser & Thorpe, 1986; Hammel, Olkin, & Taube, 1996). Most concerning is the finding that in approximately 30% of these cases, the faculty member was the academic advisor (the person most likely to serve as a mentor). When a protégé has been exploited sexually or otherwise, or when a mentorship is sexualized for any reason, the mentorship has been irrevocably altered and usually diminished to the point that it will no longer be effective.

Once again, it is important to remember that exploitation need not only be sexual in nature. Consider the following case of nonsexual protégé exploitation:

> A female graduate student in her fourth year of a School Psychology PhD program files a complaint with a university ethics committee complaining of exploitation on the part of her faculty mentor and dissertation chair. She angrily demands "reimbursement" for all the hours "wasted" helping him with research projects during the past four years. During that time the student complains that she also spent many hours listening to the faculty member's personal problems, and that she felt "obligated" to provide constant "emotional support" to help him remain intact. Though she made many requests for his assistance with her own dissertation research, he repeatedly put her off and asked her to continue with his research for "a little longer." When she finally refused to continue with his research to the exclusion of her own and insisted he stop calling her at home for "counseling and reassurance," she complains that he "abandoned" her as a protégé, and that she now lacks a mentor and must "start from scratch" on a dissertation. (Johnson & Nelson, 1999, p. 200)

It is clear that this mentor was exploitive both emotionally and academically. Using his position of power, he coerced personal/emotional gratification and research assistance from a graduate student who had few options but to comply. If the material in this section sounds at all familiar to you, it is essential that you read the final section of this chapter carefully.

PROBLEM 8: ATTRACTION

Considering that good graduate school mentorships involve a mentor and protégé who are well matched along important dimensions such as personality, career interest, scholarly interest, and commitment to the relationship, and considering that as mentorships develop, they may be characterized by increasing mutuality and friendship, it is not surprising that attraction may become an issue at some point. Attraction is most likely to become a concern for participants in cross-gender mentorships. For graduate students, the experience of being attracted to a mentor, be it emotionally, romantically, or sexually, can be alarming and can lead to dysfunction if not handled well.

Although some attraction to an opposite-sex mentor is relatively common among graduate students (Clark et al., 2000), protégés may still respond to awareness of this attraction with shame or anxiety, fearing it is indicative of an aberration. If you find yourself attracted to your mentor, it is important to normalize these feelings and recognize that they make sense in light of your match and enjoyment of interactions with your mentor. Keep in mind that any significant relationship can generate emotional or romantic attraction. For example, a full 87% of practicing psychologists admit to occasionally being sexually attracted to one of their therapy clients (Pope, Keith-Spiegel, & Tabachnick, 1986).

The essential point here is that you acknowledge the attraction, put it in context, normalize it, and use the experience to learn about yourself and perhaps about relationships more broadly. In most cases, discussing the attraction with your mentor is unnecessary, and in some cases it can negatively affect the mentorship, either because a mentor is uncomfortable with this information or because he or she may interpret this disclosure as seductive or overwhelming. If the experience of attraction begins to interfere with your role as student or protégé, then we recommend seeking consultation from a trusted peer or perhaps a trusted faculty member from a different department or institution before deciding how to proceed.

PROBLEM 9: UNETHICAL OR ILLEGAL MENTOR BEHAVIOR

In rare cases, a faculty mentor may engage in behavior that you determine to be unethical or, worse, illegal. Mentors may occasionally slip or err in a way that violates ethical principles or legal requirements. In most cases, the mentor will be inadvertently behaving badly, often due to ignorance or inattention to ethical guidelines. In other cases, the illegal or unethical act may be more deliberate.

Examples of unethical or illegal behavior include engaging in or encouraging a student to engage in fraud (e.g., fake research data, change statistical results); wrongly taking credit for the work of others (especially yourself or other students); exploiting students financially, emotionally, or sexually; theft from a university or funding source; plagiarism; and misrepresentation of one's self or one's work (Clark et al., 2000; Goodyear et al., 1992). If you are like most protégés, it will be difficult for you to respect a mentor who engages in inappropriate conduct, and we predict this will diminish the value of your mentorship.

PROBLEM 10: ABANDONMENT

A mentor may leave an academic position, may be fired by the university, or may even become sick or die during the course of a mentorship. Whatever the reason for a mentor's rapid exit, the effects on the protégé can be substantial. In addition to grief following the death of a mentor, protégés may also feel anger at the mentor (even in cases of death) for perceived abandonment. Realistically, a protégé must struggle to find a new dissertation chair and academic advisor, sometimes well after the dissertation is begun. The protégé may never form another close mentorship with other faculty members and may feel the loss of a powerful advocate when it comes time to request letters of recommendation for fellowships or jobs.

The death of a mentor is often experienced as a profound shock to those who depend on him or her, including protégés. Even when a mentor is elderly and infirm, students are commonly stunned when the mentor dies. In closely bonded mentorships, protégés may grieve the loss of a mentor for some time. Take, for example, the case of Navy Admirals who enjoyed an important mentor relationship during their early years in the Navy (Johnson, Huwe, et al., 1999). In most cases, these mentorships lasted until the death of the mentor, and the loss was often poignant and painful—even for these war-toughened admirals. Here are the reflections of three of these admirals:

> The mentor relationship lasted into retirement, and ended when he died a year ago. I was devastated. . . . It continued throughout my Navy career—even after my mentor retired—and our friendship was equally strong until his death. . . . The mentor relationship ended when he died, yet perhaps not, because I still tried to do things he would have done. (Johnson, Huwe, et al., 1999, p. 45)

In still other cases, a protégé may feel abandoned by his or her mentor even though the mentor remains in the graduate program (Clark et al., 2000; Goodyear et al., 1992). Here, the mentor may refuse to continue the relationship in light of poor performance by the protégé, as a result of anger or conflict with the protégé, or because excessive time commitments prevent adequate attention to the protégé. In many ways, this later variety of abandonment may be most insidious and destructive: The relationship lacks a clear termination, yet none of the mentor functions are available to the student.

PROBLEM 11: PROTÉGÉ TRAITS

Although we began this chapter emphasizing that protégés nearly always have at least some role in generating or exacerbating a dysfunctional mentoring relationship, we have included dysfunctional protégé traits as the final mentorship problem to emphasize this point again. In contrast to some portrayals of protégés as victims, we believe that protégés' personality traits, problem behaviors, and specific reactions and decisions often contribute to the decline or termination of a graduate school mentorship (Feldman, 1999). For example, a protégé who is extremely dependent and lacking in initiative is likely to ultimately exasperate even the most patient mentor (Bruss & Kopala, 1993). As another example, Feldman (1999) highlighted the problems that stem from protégé impression management. Here a graduate student may use impression management techniques such as truth-stretching, faked enthusiasm, and flattering of the mentor to secure a mentor relationship. Later, when a mentor discovers that the student does not know certain statistical procedures, is not especially interested in the mentor's research, or is critical of the mentor's interpersonal style, the mentor might legitimately feel duped—leading to distancing and perhaps termination of the mentorship. The point here is that you should evaluate your own characteristics, behaviors, and expectations before assuming that a mentorship problem is exclusively the fault of your mentor.

Responding to Problems: What Not to Do

Before recommending some principles for responding appropriately to problems in your mentorship, let us first recommend several responses to avoid. As human beings, graduate students are prone to two major errors in dealing with mentorship dysfunction. First, protégés may respond to conflict with a mentor or dissatisfaction with the relationship with *self-defeating passivity*. The passive protégé may be anxious, confused, or inhibited when it comes to addressing problems with a mentor. Such passivity may take three primary forms: *paralysis, distancing,* and *appeasing*. These responses may be overlapping and intertwined, but the net effect is always failure to address the primary problem, and ultimately, further dissatisfaction and perhaps early termination of the mentorship.

Alternatively, protégés may respond to conflict or dissatisfaction with *self-defeating provocation*. Here the student reacts to dysfunction by intentionally *provoking* or *sabotaging* the mentor as a means of seeking revenge or getting the mentor's attention. In nearly every case, such provocative behavior further escalates conflict or alienates the mentor, and termination under unpleasant circumstances can be anticipated. Next, we briefly describe each of these self-defeating strategies. We strongly encourage you to avoid each of them, even when the urge to respond with passivity or provocation is intense.

1. *Paralysis.* Doing nothing about a significant problem in your mentor relationship is unlikely to resolve it. When marital partners refuse to broach dissatisfactions or wounds caused by the other, the marriage begins to decay. Even when the couple stays together, satisfaction wanes and rewards are diminished. The same is true with mentorships. Graduate student protégés may choose to ignore mentor incompetence, boundary violations, unethical behavior, or neglect because the perceived risks and potential costs of alienating the mentor are too great. Several qualities of a mentorship increase the probability of protégé paralysis. These include (a) task interdependence—ongoing and important projects such as the dissertation require the student to maintain the relationship; (b) public commitment to the relationship—fear that ending the mentorship would produce public scrutiny and shame for self or the mentor; and (c) relationship phase—protégés experience greater incentive to remain in a mentorship early during graduate school when their own stress level and dependency needs are highest (Feldman, 1999).

2. *Distancing.* Another form of self-defeating passivity involves intentional avoidance and interpersonal distancing from the mentor. Feeling hurt, angry, or betrayed, a protégé may attempt to restore equilibrium to a mentorship by reducing contact with and assistance to the mentor. Of course, the mentor must guess at the reasons for the protégé's behavior, and may guess incorrectly. Not only is distancing unproductive in terms of the real problem at hand, but it may also lead to attributions by the mentor (and perhaps other faculty) that a protégé is sullen, irresponsible, and perhaps uncommitted to graduate school.

3. *Appeasement.* Yet another dysfunctional passive response to problems with a mentor is appeasement on the part of the protégé, even when the primary problem is the mentor's behavior. Many protégés admit to engaging in various forms of mentor appeasement (Kalbfleisch, 1997). To appease an angry mentor, avoid conflict, and maintain the mentorship at all costs, students may compliment or praise the mentor (ego stroking), provide personal favors, or take the blame for a misunderstanding, even though the mentor is primarily at fault. Although each of us engages in some appeasement in everyday relational life, our primary concern here is about appeasement that becomes characteristic of a mentorship and is viewed by the protégé as required to maintain the relationship.

4. *Provocation*. At times a protégé may vent anger and frustration in a highly emotional and accusing manner. Screaming, arguing, accusing the mentor, or abruptly "firing" the mentor is unlikely to facilitate problem resolution. Such provocative behaviors are more common in protégés who allow problems to fester, those who have difficulty modulating emotions, and perhaps those who are hypersensitive to rejection or betrayal because of earlier relationship experiences.

5. *Sabotage*. A final dysfunctional reaction to mentorship problems is intentional or unintentional sabotage or betrayal on the part of the student protégé (Feldman, 1999; Scandura, 1998). Common examples include the student who broadcasts his or her dissatisfactions or accusations about the mentor to other students or faculty in the department, the student who complains to the department chair or dean before confronting the mentor, or the student who fails to complete an important component of the mentor's research as a means of seeking revenge. In nearly every case, such behavior will lead to termination of a mentorship and will likely cast the protégé in a negative light within the academic community.

Responding to Mentorship Dysfunction: Recommended Strategies

It is a truth about relational life that some conflict and dissatisfaction are inevitable. However, it is equally true that many relational problems can actually promote growth in the relationship and be addressed to the reasonable satisfaction of both parties. This is true of mentorships. We predict that your own reaction to problems in the mentor relationship will significantly affect the ultimate fate and value of the relationship for your graduate school career.

In this final section of the chapter, we offer nine general principles or recommendations for responding effectively to problems in your mentorship. We summarize these in Exhibit 8.1. Although we believe they apply to most forms of dysfunction, keep in mind that these recommendations are necessarily general versus more concrete. Each graduate school mentorship will involve a unique mix of circumstances, contexts, personalities, and problems. In the end, only you can best decide how exactly to respond to problems with your mentor. Nonetheless, the

EXHIBIT 8.1

Strategies for Responding to Mentorship Dysfunction

1. Proceed slowly and carefully while avoiding impulsive and emotion-driven responses.
2. Honestly evaluate your own contribution to problems in the mentorship.
3. Consider your professional and ethical obligations as a student and protégé.
4. Assess and dispute irrational demands and evaluations of yourself, your mentor, and the current problem.
5. Seek consultation from a trusted peer, faculty member, or other professional.
6. Be direct and clear in communicating with your mentor about the problem. Offer concrete examples and tangible requests. If helpful, put concerns and requests in writing.
7. Be collegial and cordial in communicating with your mentor. When discussing concerns and frustrations, begin by highlighting aspects of the mentorship that are going well.
8. Have a backup plan when confronting your mentor and seeking change. If remaining in the mentorship will provide few benefits or will likely be distressing, collegially move toward termination and transfer to a new faculty mentor. Know departmental procedures for student grievances.
9. Document specific problematic mentor behaviors, steps you take to resolve problems informally, consultations you have received, and clear rationale for your decisions and actions in confronting a mentor or terminating a relationship.

guidelines that follow should offer a solid framework from which to plan your response.

1. *Slow down the process.* Perhaps the most important recommendation we can offer is that you avoid the temptation to respond quickly or impulsively to frustrations or perceived wrongs related to your mentor. Anger or anxiety may result in impulsive provocation or betrayal that may permanently damage the relationship. As a general rule, the best decisions about how to proceed in responding to problems will be made after a period of careful reflection, analysis, and consultation.

2. *Honestly assess your own contribution.* We have noted several times in this chapter that relationship problems often stem from some combination of personalities and behaviors. If you are distressed about what you are not getting from your mentor, or even something your mentor has done, we think it wise to first consider how you may have contributed to this state of affairs. For example, have you failed to clarify your expectations, been withholding regarding your feelings or preferences, or distanced yourself rather than confronted concerns? Although we are not suggesting that you own all the blame, we do recommend that you responsibly acknowledge any way in which you have at least exacerbated the problem(s) of concern. It is generally wise to

begin discussions with your mentor by highlighting your own contribution to the difficulties.

3. *Ethics are for students too.* Adherence to ethical and professional guidelines is not an issue solely for the faculty mentor. Mentorships are reciprocal, and junior professionals (graduate protégés) are typically obligated to abide by several general ethical requirements (R. D. Brown & Krager, 1985; Kitchener, 1992). R. D. Brown and Krager (1985) recommended that graduate student protégés remain faithful to the following ethical principles: (a) *autonomy*—listen to the mentor's advice, but take responsibility for your own decisions and promote reciprocity, mutuality, and sharing in the relationship; (b) *nonmalfeasance*—avoid placing unrealistic demands on the mentor, avoid entanglements in personal matters with your mentor, and do not abuse your influence with your mentor; (c) *beneficence*—be aware of your mentor as a person, and be open to both receiving and giving assistance; (d) *justice*—accept the mentor as human without projecting unrealistic expectations or behaving unfairly in the relationship; and (e) *fidelity*—act consistently with your values across time and situation, and be truthful in self-representation.

4. *Dispute crazy beliefs.* At times, even the most mature and rational mentors and protégés fall prey to irrational beliefs (Johnson, Huwe, & Lucas, 2000). Irrational beliefs typically take the form of rigid demands about self, the mentor, or the mentor relationship. Irrational beliefs may also be harshly evaluative or may involve catastrophic thinking and poor frustration tolerance. Irrational beliefs always lead to some form of emotional disturbance (e.g., anger, anxiety, depression), and they often worsen problems in a mentorship. Examples of protégé irrational beliefs include the following: "I *must* always please and thoroughly impress my mentor," "My mentor *must* love and approve of me at all times," "My mentor *should* always predict and perfectly meet my needs," and "My mentor *must* never leave or disappoint me." Some protégés also have difficulty articulating wants and desires in a mentorship. For example, when asked to do something they do not want to do, they scramble to show that they "can't" or "shouldn't" do it, believing erroneously that they are not entitled to simply state their wishes or preferences in the matter. We recommend not masking the truth.

5. *Seek consultation.* Once you have slowed down the process, considered your own culpability in the dysfunction, and addressed any of your own irrational responses, it is time to consider consulting a trusted friend or colleague. In many instances, minor problems will not require consultation, and you should proceed

directly to a meeting with your mentor for the purpose of addressing your needs and concerns. However, there are cases in which consultation with a trusted peer, a trusted faculty member in another institution, or even a professional counselor will help you develop a balanced and reasonable strategy prior to confronting your mentor. Examples of problems meriting consultation include instances of boundary violation, exploitation, illegal or unethical behavior, and incompetence. Although we advocate seeking counsel whenever you feel overwhelmed or threatened by the prospect of addressing a mentorship concern, it is imperative that you take responsibility to maintain confidentiality. Your mentor should hear about your concern from you, not a colleague or another student.

6. *When you confront, be direct.* After you have gathered your thoughts, sought any needed consultation, and determined exactly what you need your mentor to hear, as well as how you hope to see the relationship change, it is time to schedule a formal meeting to address the problem. We recommend that you plan the meeting carefully and that you deliver your concerns and requests directly and clearly. Mentors are busy. Furthermore, many are not skilled at interpreting subtleties or reading between the lines interpersonally. Be kind but concrete, even committing your main concerns and desired meeting outcomes to writing so that later, there can be no doubt regarding what you presented.

7. *When you confront, be collegial.* We believe it is possible to be both direct and collegial when confronting a mentor. As a budding professional, it is important for you to treat your mentor as a colleague. Be kind, polite, and professional while unambiguously delivering your message and directly asking for change. Nothing will be gained from angry accusations or disparagement of your mentor's skill or personality. It is always useful to begin such confrontations with some statement of appreciation for things the mentor has done well (e.g., "Although I have really appreciated your commitment to giving me lots of opportunities to publish, lately I have been feeling a bit pressured to take on new projects, and frankly, I'm feeling overwhelmed right now. I need a moratorium on new projects for the time being.").

8. *Have a backup plan: Know your options.* In some cases, a mentor will be unwilling or unable to remedy his or her contributions to mentorship dysfunction. For example, a mentor may simply become angry when confronted about ethically dubious behavior or may ridicule a protégé who discloses feeling neglected by the mentor. In spite of clear and collegial confrontation, it may become evident when the mentor is unwilling to modify his or her

behavior. When collaborative resolution of the problem is unlikely, consider your options. In some cases, termination of the relationship and a search for a new mentor is indicated. We think of this as cutting your losses. Whenever a faculty mentor becomes intractable, hostile, or disparaging, it is important to consider moving on. In other cases, termination of the mentorship may not be in your best interest—particularly when the problem develops during your final year in graduate school and when the dissertation is well under way. Or, even if you seek a new mentor, it may be imperative that you take steps to address unethical or grossly inappropriate behavior on the part of your mentor (e.g., the mentor is engaging in fraud or exploitation of students). In this case, we recommend proceeding to your department chair (who should clearly inform you of department policies and procedures for making complaints). If unsatisfied at this level, it may be necessary to proceed to the university or graduate school dean.

9. *Document.* Although the idea of documenting your concerns and strategies for responding to mentorship dysfunction may seem dramatic or excessive, we think it is good practice. During your own professional career, there will be multiple instances in which you find yourself in conflict with students, colleagues, or supervisors and employers. In nearly every case, clear and concise documentation of facts, events, and rationale for your actions will serve you well should the situation escalate (or deteriorate) to the point of a formal complaint or even legal action. Although the chances of such an awful outcome in your mentorship are miniscule, clear documentation of concerns will at least help you to focus your thinking, understand the process, and plan a responsible approach to addressing mentorship concerns efficiently and productively.

On Being an
Excellent Protégé

9

Case 9.1

Ling began to fully realize the benefits of having a mentor relationship with Dr. Match during her 4th year of doctoral studies in political science. The 4 demanding years of graduate school had passed quickly, in large part because of Dr. Match's excellent guidance and sponsorship. Although she counted herself fortunate to have a good mentor, others understood it was to her credit that she sought out and established a mentor relationship early in her graduate school career. Even as a neophyte protégé, Ling understood it was not enough to simply secure Dr. Match's agreement to provide mentoring. Instead, she immediately set out to be a stellar protégé. She was conscientious about keeping her commitments and meeting the deadlines she and Dr. Match established for projects. She made extra effort to do excellent work on these projects, consistently striving to exceed her mentor's high expectations. Although she was quick to defer to Dr. Match's experience and expertise, she also shared her own opinions and vision with him.

As Ling's skills developed, Dr. Match suggested that she take on increasing responsibility. Despite the fact that she was frequently intimidated by these tasks, she readily accepted them. Like most graduate students, Ling faced more challenging semesters when her workload was particularly daunting. During these times, Ling communicated her appreciation for opportunities Dr. Match presented and worked collaboratively with him to establish reasonable deadlines that protected her own personal health and need for balance. Ling also discovered that Dr. Match appreciated her sense of humor and willingness to accept her own limitations. Two years later, Ling's first faculty appointment at a prestigious university suggested to her that her dedication to becoming an excellent protégé was well worth the investment.

Case 9.2

Although initially delighted about being accepted into a well-regarded MBA program, Mark's enthusiasm rapidly dwindled as he encountered the demands of coursework. Several of his buddies mentioned the importance of developing professional contacts in graduate school to increase the odds of landing a good first job. Mark also discovered that his graduate program encouraged faculty and students to develop mentor relationships. Mark understood that extra attention from a professor would likely help his chances for employment success after graduate school.

Although pleased when Dr. Industry agreed to become his mentor, Mark was surprised when Dr. Industry quickly identified mutual projects for the two to work on, and shocked when Dr. Industry suggested that the two develop concrete time lines for completion. Mark was also dismayed when Dr. Industry asked him to redo work because of its poor quality. Although willing to admit that his writing skills were not the sharpest, Mark found these requests demeaning, and he sometimes responded with hostility. Over time, Mark noticed that he resented the additional work and Dr. Industry's high standards. As a result, he began to miss deadlines. Despite the fact that he provided Dr. Industry with what appeared to be reasonable excuses for mediocre work (e.g., lack of sleep, difficult class demands, marital problems), Dr. Industry gradually offered him fewer and fewer opportunities. Toward the end of Mark's graduate education, Dr. Industry consented to write a letter of reference; however, the letter lacked much enthusiasm. Mark was disappointed by this but attributed the mediocre endorsement to Dr. Industry's unreasonably high expectations.

Excellence has its rewards in graduate school. More times than not, hard working, diligent, and conscientious graduate students quickly rise to the top of the class, setting standards and reaping rewards associated with excellent work. These students stand apart from their peers and are often the first to come to the attention of graduate faculty (potential mentors) and future employers.

Stellar protégés know that a sound investment in a mentorship may provide a variety of rewards. In chapter 2, we highlighted the major *predoctoral* and *postdoctoral* benefits available to protégés. We showed that predoctoral benefits frequently include professional skill development, formation of one's professional identity and sense of confidence, networking with other professionals, productivity, dissertation success, securing important training opportunities, realizing one's dreams, and experiencing satisfaction with one's doctoral program. Following graduate school, postdoctoral benefits involve long-term rewards such as salaries, career promotions and mobility, career satisfaction and achievement, and the potential of achieving eminence in one's career.

Protégés who do not perform to their full potential in their mentorship risk developing a habit of mediocre performance. This pattern can be damaging to the protégé in two ways. First, protégé mediocrity leads to fewer relationship benefits. Because most graduate mentors derive more satisfaction and reward from working with dedicated and energetic protégés, these students receive more attention from mentors and benefits from the relationship (Green & Bauer, 1995). In fact, mediocre protégés, such as Mark in Case 9.2, may find their mentors quickly lose interest in the relationship. Second, mediocre protégés fail to appreciate the long-term impact of this approach. They are likely to experience greater difficulty competing for initial employment.

This chapter describes 10 strategies for becoming an excellent protégé (see Exhibit 9.1), thereby maximizing the probability that your mentorship will yield beneficial rewards. We propose that being an excellent protégé requires specific protégé strategies, including keeping commitments and meeting deadlines, doing excellent work, communi-

---

EXHIBIT 9.1

10 Strategies for Protégé Excellence

1. *Keep commitments and meet deadlines*: The protégé demonstrates that he or she is able to establish and meet consensual deadlines and commitments, thereby establishing a high degree of reliability.
2. *Do excellent work*: The protégé maintains high standards of excellence for his or her performance, which allows for the development of more challenging and creative goals.
3. *Communicate directly and honestly*: The protégé balances the need to be direct and honest with tact and sensitivity for the mentor's needs.
4. *Accept a subordinate role*: The protégé understands that the primary focus of the relationship is to learn from the mentor and subsequently places himself or herself under the mentor's guidance early in the relationship.
5. *Accept increasing responsibility by saying yes*: The protégé knows that improving his or her professional skills requires accepting increasingly challenging opportunities supplied by the mentor.
6. *Incorporate good self-care*: The protégé maintains an awareness of his or her personal limitations and takes proactive measures to prevent professional burnout.
7. *Remain mindful of the mentor's goals*: The protégé understands that the mentor has personal and professional goals that require time and energy and seeks to find appropriate ways to support the mentor's efforts.
8. *Communicate appreciation*: The protégé understands that even seasoned mentors enjoy receiving positive feedback, and, as a result, seeks to communicate sincere appreciation in the mentorship.
9. *Admit mistakes*: The protégé is open about mistakes and quick to develop a plan with the mentor to avoid similar problems in the future.
10. *Maintain a sense of humor*: The protégé understands that gentle humor can help to maintain a sense of light-heartedness, which helps to inoculate against catastrophizing the ups and downs of graduate education.

cating directly and honestly, accepting a subordinate role early on in the relationship, accepting increasing responsibility and independence by saying yes to most opportunities provided by the mentor, and maintaining good self-care. We also propose that truly excellent protégés maintain an awareness of the mentor's professional needs and goals, communicate appreciation to the mentor, admit mistakes and express concerns honestly, and maintain a sense of humor in the relationship. We suggest that protégés who adopt these strategies will quickly distinguish themselves as truly excellent and deserving of the many benefits that they receive.

Strategies for Protégé Excellence

STRATEGY 1: KEEP COMMITMENTS AND MEET DEADLINES

Good mentors love reliable protégés! Mentors are most attracted to protégés who possess a strong work ethic, initiative, motivation, energy, and dedication (Allen et al., 1997). As an excellent protégé, the surest way to communicate your dedication to the relationship is to keep commitments and meet those deadlines established in your mentorship. This is particularly important early on in the relationship as you and your mentor develop mutual trust and acceptance. Commitments in the mentorship may be many and varied. Mentors and protégés may commit to developing research projects, submitting scholarly work, or presenting research at conferences. In most cases, commitments involve deadlines. Although graduate protégés often experience these deadlines as stressful, remember that deadlines are also an opportunity to demonstrate competence to your mentor.

There are several important reasons that excellent protégés work tenaciously to meet deadlines and keep commitments to their mentors. First, they understand that protégé reliability heightens mentor trust and that trust and opportunity are closely connected. Clear follow-through on smaller tasks leads naturally to more challenging and increasingly rewarding assignments. Second, completing assignments on schedule helps to develop productive momentum in the relationship as the mentor and protégé begin to dream about and take on new projects. Finally, excellent protégés realize that consistent reliability fosters a reputation that will serve them well beyond the primary mentorship.

STRATEGY 2: DO EXCELLENT WORK

In addition to meeting deadlines and keeping commitments, excellent protégés do excellent work for their mentors. Though this may at first seem obvious, it is important to appreciate the myriad obstacles to consistently producing top-quality work in graduate school. Common obstacles include demanding coursework, clinical or research responsibilities, financial stress, physical and emotional fatigue, and, of course, the dreaded dissertation. A sense of being overwhelmed by these obstacles can rise to monumental proportions during the education process. Nevertheless, excellent protégés work to cope with or modify these demands to minimize compromises in the quality of their work, particularly work for the mentor.

The importance of doing excellent work cannot be overstated. Research consistently confirms that mentors are more attracted to and invest more of themselves in high-performing protégés (Allen et al., 2000; Fagenson, 1992; Kram, 1985; Mullen & Noe, 1999; Olian et al., 1993). Good mentors know there is a certain element of risk associated with how the protégé's performance may reflect on them. Protégés who do excellent work not only establish their own reputations as high performers but also reflect positively on their mentors. Protégés who are weak performers (e.g., low level of proficiency, inferior writing skills, procrastination proneness) may tarnish the mentor's reputation. At the very least, these protégés force the mentor to take on the roles of parent, remedial trainer, or micromanager. Ultimately, the protégé's failure to integrate new learning and work at increasing independence will likely slow progress toward more creative and challenging goals. In contrast, when protégés produce excellent work, both mentor and protégé are free to explore increasingly challenging and rewarding endeavors.

STRATEGY 3: COMMUNICATE DIRECTLY AND HONESTLY

It should come as no surprise that effective communication is essential for a healthy mentor relationship. Excellent protégés understand the significance of good communication and strive to establish a mentorship characterized by open and reciprocal interaction. They intuitively work to balance the need to be direct and honest with tact and sensitivity to the mentor's needs. As a result, they neither leave their mentors guessing about their intentions or goals nor overwhelm them with needless or inappropriate information. Good mentors are aware of the benefits of working with a protégé who is skilled in this area. When surveyed, mentors frequently acknowledge their preference for protégés who are effective communicators capable of offering reciprocal feedback (Allen et al., 1997, 2000). (See Box 9.1.)

Good communication offers several specific benefits to the mentor and protégé. It enhances the effectiveness of the relationship. Research suggests that increased communication in the relationship is related to provision of more psychosocial functions by the mentor (Burke, 1984; Kalbfleisch & Davies, 1993). Effective communication decreases the potential for misunderstandings, breaches of confidentiality, and boundary violations that can infiltrate the relationship. In most cases, both the mentor and protégé experience more enjoyment in the relationship as a result of healthy communication. Although no protégé is a perfect communicator, excellent protégés work hard at communication skills in the context of the mentorship.

STRATEGY 4: ACCEPT A SUBORDINATE ROLE

Excellent protégés accept a subordinate role in the mentorship early on. They understand that the primary purpose of the relationship is to learn from the mentor. As a result, they are quick to consider and accept their mentors' recommendations. The following vignette highlights the significance of this skill from a mentor's perspective.

> Dr. Guidance was excited about the opportunity to mentor two equally talented and promising young medical students. Mary and Brent were in their 2nd year of medical school. Both had reputations for stellar work and excellent clinical instinct. Despite

---

BOX 9.1: HOW IT WORKED FOR US—BRAD'S PERSPECTIVE

During my mentorship with Jenny, I was especially appreciative of her strong communication skills and her willingness to be assertive in communicating concerns, mentoring needs, and appreciation of my own contribution as mentor. I found it particularly helpful that Jenny would look me in the eye and tell me if proposed writing deadlines were unrealistic and that she would clearly articulate her concerns or misgivings about a forthcoming hurdle (e.g., the dissertation defense or a conference presentation). Such direct communication allowed me to rethink overzealous goals and to remember to offer support and encouragement. In addition, Jenny's communication clarity put me at ease in the mentorship; I trusted her to speak her mind and quickly confront problems in the relationship.

their equally impressive qualifications, Dr. Guidance experienced considerable difficulty mentoring Mary. Although extremely bright and energetic, Mary frequently discounted Dr. Guidance's opinions and suggestions. When Dr. Guidance felt it necessary to emphasize his concerns about her plans and ideas, Mary often appeared indignant and insulted. When he gently offered a clear rationale for the potential long-term problems associated with her goals, Mary became increasingly distant and uninvolved in the mentorship. On the other hand, Dr. Guidance noticed that Brent was quick to listen to his opinions. Brent appeared willing and eager to acknowledge his mentor's expertise and frequently stated his appreciation for the opportunity to learn more through the mentorship. Because Brent had a solid appreciation of his own limitations, Dr. Guidance was confident about offering him increasing responsibility and independence. Dr. Guidance experienced significant satisfaction watching Brent benefit from his direction and support.

As this vignette highlights, excellent protégés accept a subordinate role in the early phases of the relationship. Unfortunately, students such as Mary may become defensive or demonstrate signs of narcissism and arrogance when the mentor attempts to lead. Willingness to accept a subordinate position early in the relationship promotes a faster rate of learning and has been rated by mentors as an important protégé characteristic (Allen et al., 1997). This does not mean that protégés should mask or dumb-down their knowledge or competence. However, excellent protégés understand that receptivity to learning from the mentor is essential.

STRATEGY 5: ACCEPT INCREASING RESPONSIBILITY

Protégés are frequently intimidated by their mentors' encouragement to take on increasing responsibility in the relationship. For example, graduate school mentors often invite students to present papers at professional meetings, teach a section of their course, or take the lead role on a piece of research or writing. Although a sense of self-doubt and anxiety is quite normal, there are several important reasons for saying yes when your mentor offers you increased responsibility or a high-profile opportunity. First, good mentors know that their protégés need to develop confidence in their skills if they are to become full-fledged autonomous professionals. One way that mentors help their protégés along in this process is by gradually increasing the challenge of tasks offered to protégés. Protégés who say no to these opportunities may hamper their own development. In addition to promoting growth, saying yes increases the likelihood that you will receive more benefits from the relationship (Noe, 1988a). Finally, your willingness to say yes to new opportunities and responsibilities sends your mentor the message that you trust his or her judgment in the relationship. Good mentors hope to pass on the mantle of their own mission or purpose (Blackburn et al., 1981). This happens most often through collaborative interactions, often resulting in long-term collegial relationships. Excellent protégés understand this and, as a result, say yes to most of the opportunities mentors send their way.

STRATEGY 6: INCORPORATE GOOD SELF-CARE

Although excellent protégés do say yes to most challenges and opportunities that mentors offer, they do not have superhuman energy and enthusiasm. In fact, it is essential that they balance openness to challenge with personal self-care. Recognizing and honoring the (sometimes tenuous) balancing act between doing excellent work and attending to important needs for rest, recreation, and other relationships are critical. Excellent protégés maintain their stamina and energy levels by caring for themselves physically and psychologically. Our observations of these protégés suggest to us that they rely on several specific goals to manage their self-care. Excellent protégés are willing to acknowledge personal limits and to watch for the "red flags" of burnout (e.g., diminishing work quality, decreased enthusiasm, irritability, frequent day-dreaming about vacation). They use these warning signs to increase their self-care behaviors and set appropriate limits on school-related work. Excellent protégés also work assertively with their mentors to establish reasonable deadlines that prevent the likelihood of exhaustion and burnout. Rather than saying no to opportunities offered by the mentor, these protégés are honest about their reasons for engaging in good self-care and negotiate more realistic time lines. In sum, excellent protégés are quite skilled at monitoring and maintaining their needs for balance between personal and professional activities. Instead of seeing this as the mentor's responsibility, they clearly communicate these needs to their mentors, with the understanding that good self-care promotes long-term professional productivity.

STRATEGY 7: REMAIN MINDFUL OF THE MENTOR'S GOALS

Perhaps one of the most difficult challenges for new protégés is to realize that their mentors too have professional goals and dreams. This awareness is particularly difficult because neophyte protégés are naturally focused on discovering their own dreams and developing their own professional identities. Nevertheless, excellent protégés maintain an awareness of and appreciation for their mentors' goals and professional needs. Although the mentor's career agenda must not take precedence in the mentorship, excellent protégés consider ways of assisting their mentor with important projects and tasks—particularly when they are consistent with protégés' goals. You might consider helping your mentor prepare a grant proposal, a conference presentation, or even a new course. Whatever the project, your mentor will experience gratitude for your assistance, spend more time interacting with you, and (we hope) come to more fully appreciate your talents. The point here is to search for ways in which your collaboration can be mutually beneficial. This will pay important dividends. Finally, great protégés understand that from time to time, the mentor will have less energy to invest in the relationship because of his or her need to prioritize other goals and responsibilities. Most importantly, excellent protégés are also eager to celebrate their mentors' accomplishments when their goals and dreams are realized. (See Box 9.2.)

STRATEGY 8: COMMUNICATE APPRECIATION

In addition to remaining mindful of their mentor's goals, excellent protégés communicate consistent and genuine appreciation to their mentors. Feeling appreciated and valued is just as motivational for mentors as it is for other human beings. In fact, research demonstrates that both mentors and protégés believe that communicating care is an important characteristic of healthy mentorships (Allen et al., 2000). Excellent protégés are sincere in offering affirmation and feedback to their mentors. They integrate this feedback into everyday conversations with mentors (e.g., "I appreciated your willingness to offer me constructive feedback" and "It was very helpful to me to watch you field those difficult questions"). Additionally, excellent protégés take advantage of opportunities

---

BOX 9.2: HOW IT WORKED FOR US—BRAD'S PERSPECTIVE

There have been many occasions in my career when a graduate student protégé has significantly lightened my professional writing burden by consenting to work at a rough draft of the introduction or method section of a scholarly article. Not only have I been grateful for their efforts, I have inevitably spent more time with these protégés (discussing the project, reviewing drafts), offered more mentor functions, included them as coauthors, and generally gotten to know them better.

to offer formal feedback about their mentors. For example, a protégé may offer positive feedback when the mentor has a departmental review or is applying for tenure.

STRATEGY 9: ADMIT MISTAKES

Throughout this guide, we have consistently highlighted the importance of honest communication between the mentor and protégé. For most protégés, this is not a particularly demanding task, unless it involves admitting mistakes or communicating important concerns to the mentor. Even excellent protégés working with supportive and nonjudgmental mentors dislike drawing attention to their own human fallibility. The difficult nature of this task makes sense given the competitive nature of most graduate schools. Nevertheless, there are several important reasons for protégés to intentionally integrate this strategy into their mentorships. Protégés who "cover up" or hide their mistakes and weaknesses are less able to benefit from their mentors' advice, coaching, and support. These are important mentoring functions that promote growth and development. Additionally, by masking these mistakes or failing to express concerns, protégés rob themselves of the opportunity to have these experiences "normalized" by their mentors. Great mentors actively share about the ups and downs of their own learning experiences and admit their own mistakes.

When excellent protégés share mistakes or shortcomings with their mentors, they are eager to solicit their mentors' advice on the matter. They are also quick to develop a plan that remedies the dilemma and helps them to avoid similar situations in the future. Finally, excellent protégés sometimes request some form of ongoing accountability from their mentors—particularly if the issue is a perennial problem or if "blind spots" increase the likelihood that problems will recur. In sum, excellent protégés do not feign perfection to gain their mentors' respect.

STRATEGY 10: MAINTAIN A SENSE OF HUMOR

Our discussion of the strategies for being an excellent protégé would not be complete without mentioning the significance of maintaining a sense of humor in your mentorship. Capacity for humor has been identified as an important protégé characteristic (Allen et al., 1997). Although humor means different things to different people, we are specifically referring to a consistent pattern of not taking yourself too seriously and openly acknowledging your human side. Excellent protégés know that the temptation to "catastrophize" mistakes or difficulties rarely leads to healthy coping. Instead, they remind themselves that, in time, difficult situations and experiences tend to resolve. Having a sense of humor about the limits of human nature (your limits and your mentor's) is an important key to managing the many vicissitudes and stressors of graduate education. Although this does not diminish the necessity of offering constructive feedback or confronting perennial problems in the relationship, excellent protégés understand that the skillful use of humor often helps to positively manage stress and diffuse crises.

Mentoring for Women and Minorities

Case 10.1

When Miguel moved from Southern California to begin doctoral training in sociology at a large northwestern university, he knew that it was unlikely that he would find many Hispanic faculty or peers, given both local demographics and general underrepresentation of minorities in higher education. Nevertheless, Miguel believed that having a mentor was critical to successfully launching his academic career after graduate school. Miguel also understood that a culturally sensitive mentor could be instrumental in helping him to deal with subtle and overt forms of racism he might experience in the process of obtaining his degree. As a result, he intentionally initiated dialog with Dr. Majority, a well-respected White faculty member in the department, with whom Miguel had enjoyed positive interactions and who seemed genuinely interested in Miguel.

When Miguel approached Dr. Majority about mentorship, Miguel was instantly encouraged by the professor's honesty and sincerity regarding cultural differences. From the start, Miguel and Dr. Majority acknowledged that there would likely be times when cultural differences resulted in misunderstandings between the two. As a result, both committed to intentionally discuss these issues soon after they occurred. Initially anxious about following through with this commitment, Miguel did address several racial concerns in the doctoral program and kindly informed his mentor of how culture and race shaped his relational behavior in the mentorship. Both were pleased by the enrichment that developed from talking openly about their cultural differences. Although Miguel eventually returned home to accept a faculty position, the two continued to collaborate on projects, knowing that their unique cultural perspectives added an important depth and richness to their professional endeavors.

Case 10.2

Linda was in her late 20s when she was accepted into an MBA program at a local university. Although a bit nervous about the

challenge of integrating graduate education into her full life as a
mother and part-time employee, she had high hopes for graduate
school. In particular, Linda wanted to develop a mentorship with
a female professor who could offer her advice about successfully
managing multiple roles during graduate school. Linda was
thrilled on the first day of classes when she met Dr. Balance, the
department's only female professor. Dr. Balance was bright,
charismatic, and vocal about her personal priorities for balancing
work and family responsibilities. Linda found herself excited
about the ways she could grow, both professionally and
personally, from working closely with a mentor like Dr. Balance.
Unfortunately, Linda quickly learned that many students were
attracted to this energetic professor. Although encouraged by
several peers to assertively approach Dr. Balance about the
possibility of advising, Linda dismissed this encouragement,
stating "She is probably too busy mentoring other students and
would not be interested in me." Linda also dismissed thoughts of
approaching several male faculty to discuss the possibility of
mentoring, because she was concerned that her initiation may be
misconstrued by others as too bold or flirtatious. From time to
time, Linda did have meaningful conversations with various
faculty about her professional goals; however, she never found
the courage to initiate an intentional mentorship.

If you are a woman or minority student, you already know that
finding a good mentor who understands your unique needs in graduate
school can be extremely difficult. Although there is growing attention
to issues of gender and culture in education, women and minority students continue to face institutional and social barriers that make it difficult to firmly establish healthy and productive mentorships in graduate
school. As a result, this topic warrants intentional consideration for both
mentors and protégés.

Unfortunately, female or minority graduate students frequently encounter a variety of cultural barriers that inhibit their ability to find an
ideal mentor. Among the most significant barrier is the fact that fewer
female and minority educators reach the rank of full professor. Traditionally, this has meant that women and minorities have less access to
same-gender and same-race mentors (Blackwell, 1989; Brinson & Kottler, 1993; Gilbert & Rossman, 1992). When same-race or same-gender
mentors are not available, women and minorities may fear that they
will be compromised by prejudice or marginalization when working
closely with a male or majority mentor. Gender and racial stereotypes
may also contribute to the misperception that women and minorities
are less interested in pursuing successful, competitive careers, thereby
making them less attractive to mentors. Finally, the historical marginalization of these groups may leave women and minorities unsure about
their right to assertively pursue or compete for the best mentors in graduate school.

Despite the presence of these substantive barriers, female and minority graduate students who do establish mentorships experience a variety of intrinsic and extrinsic benefits. In the spirit of encouraging women and minority students to pursue these benefits, this chapter is dedicated to exploring important issues related to mentoring for women and minority graduate students. To this end we explore pertinent issues, including women's access to mentors, the benefits associated with having a graduate school mentor, and considerations for selecting a male or female mentor. We then turn our attention to minority students' access to mentors. Of particular importance in this section is a discussion of the difficulties and rewards of working with a mentor of a different cultural background.

Mentoring and Women

WOMEN'S ACCESS TO MENTORS

During the past 20 years, the field of mentoring has turned its attention to the barriers that prevent women from gaining access to and advancement in graduate school and the job market (Bogat & Redner, 1985; Ragins & Cotton, 1993). In an attempt to understand why women experience lower rates of career advancement, the question has surfaced regarding whether women have more limited access to mentors when compared with men. A recent survey of male and female managers indicated that women are more likely to report (a) restricted access to mentors, (b) unwillingness on the part of potential mentors to engage in mentor relationships, (c) disapproval of the mentor relationship by others in the organization, and (d) concern that the mentor or others in the organization would misinterpret attempts to initiate a mentorship as sexual advances (Ragins & Cotton, 1991). Nevertheless, most research indicates that there are no significant differences between men and women with regard to having a mentor, the duration of the relationship, the number of relationships experienced, and the reason for terminating the relationship (Baugh, Lankau, & Scandura, 1996; Dreher & Ash, 1990; Erkut & Mokros, 1984; Fagenson, 1988; Ragins & Cotton, 1991; Ragins & Scandura, 1997; Swerdlick & Bardon, 1988).

Although rates of mentoring do not appear to be different for women and men, a growing body of literature strongly suggests that having a graduate school mentor is important for women. Women face unique challenges as they progress in their academic careers. For example, female graduate students in psychology have traditionally received less financial aid and institutional support, fewer fellowships, and smaller financial awards (Solomon, 1978). Women without mentors in the business field report lower career expectations and perceive fewer employment alternatives when compared with male and female peers who receive mentoring (Baugh et al., 1996). Women may also face gender stereotypes and tokenism (Bolton, 1980; Noe, 1988b), lack of access to information and professional networks that would assist them in advancement (Noe, 1988b; Richey et al., 1988), and a "glass wall" that prevents access to institutional power and senior positions (Gilbert & Rossman, 1991, p. 234). Given these obstacles, it is not surprising that women are more likely than men to report the need for a good mentor (Ragins & Cotton, 1991).

BENEFITS OF MENTORING FOR WOMEN

Extrinsic Benefits

A good graduate school mentor can yield a variety of important benefits for women. Female protégés are more likely to experience extrinsic benefits in the form of higher levels of career success (Riley & Wrench, 1985) and more promotions (Noe, 1988b) when compared with women who are not mentored. The mentor's sponsorship on research and writing projects can dispel harmful stereotypes that women do not have serious career aspirations (Bolton, 1980). Additionally, a good mentor is sensitive to both overt and covert forms of discrimination or stereotypical perceptions of the female protégé that would likely interfere with success (Ragins, 1989). The mentor may offer suggestions that assist the protégé in successfully navigating departmental politics or prejudice, thereby increasing her opportunity for advancement through the program, her visibility as a legitimate candidate for honors and awards, and her utilization of professional networks previously available exclusively to male protégés.

Intrinsic Benefits

Although less tangible, a host of intrinsic benefits are also available to mentored women. These benefits include, but are certainly not limited to, increased self-confidence, development of professional identity, and career satisfaction (N. W. Collins, 1983). A mentor's sponsorship, encouragement, and honest feedback can promote a female protégé's growing sense of self-confidence. Another important mentoring function, role modeling, is particularly significant as a female protégé seeks to forge her professional identity (Noe, 1988b; Ragins, 1989). Professional identity development may be particularly challenging for women who balance multiple roles (e.g., student, mother, partner, and wife) while facing the gender stereotype that marriage or parenting is incompatible with their professional role (Olian et al., 1993). A mentor's role modeling can be invaluable when a female protégé is learning to integrate these complex and demanding roles.

Career satisfaction is yet another important intrinsic benefit that the female protégé may experience as a result of her relationship with a mentor. Research demonstrates that mentored women report more career satisfaction when compared with women who are not mentored (Burke & McKeen, 1997; Riley & Wrench, 1985). Female protégés who experience the range of career and psychosocial functions are likely to have greater access to career paths of their choosing and to experience fewer negative effects from gender stereotyping and discrimination. In sum, women who are mentored in graduate school can anticipate receiving a variety of long-lasting benefits.

SELECTION OF SAME-GENDER OR CROSS-GENDER MENTORSHIPS

Considerations for Same-Gender Mentorships

Female graduate students face an important decision regarding whether to seek out a male or female mentor. Although women in business settings do not appear to prefer women mentors (Olian, Carroll, Giannantonio, & Feren, 1988), graduate psychology students (men and women) appear to prefer same-gender role models (Gilbert, 1985; Huntley, Schneider, & Aronson, 2000). Women educators often view themselves as having less time and fewer resources to contribute to a mentorship, but they are as willing to enter mentorships as are their male counterparts (N. W. Collins, 1983; Ragins & Cotton, 1993). Furthermore, female mentors tend to offer more psychosocial support to their protégés (Burke & McKeen, 1996; Burke, McKeen, & McKenna, 1990; Ensher & Murphy, 1997). Nonetheless, male mentors may be in better positions to sponsor their protégés because men continue to hold the preponderance of powerful leadership positions in business and academia (Gilbert & Rossman, 1992). Considering that women have not historically held positions of sufficient power to offer themselves as mentors, it is remarkable that so few differences appear to exist between men and women serving in this role.

Although male and female mentors offer similar mentoring functions to their protégés, female mentors are often uniquely prepared to provide valuable role modeling for their female protégés (Gilbert, 1985; Gilbert & Rossman, 1992; Ragins & McFarlin, 1990). Research suggests that female students value the role-modeling aspect of their mentor relationship with female faculty more than do male students (Gilbert, 1985). Expanding on the unique characteristics of this relationship, Gilbert and Rossman (1992) proposed that female mentors offer two distinct and valuable benefits to female protégés. First, female mentors provide role modeling that demonstrates how to achieve professional success without sacrificing important and meaningful family relationships. Second, female mentors' communication patterns tend to be more egalitarian and less hierarchical, therefore providing the female protégé with a greater sense of empowerment, confirmation, and acceptance.

Considerations for Cross-Gender Mentorships

A growing body of research dispels the myth that cross-gender mentorships are doomed to failure (Burke & McKeen, 1996; Clark et al., 2000; Gaskill, 1991; Noe, 1988b). A recent study of graduate psychology protégés revealed that nearly 90% denied any gender-related problems (Clark et al., 2000). In fact, cross-gender relationships may actually be more effective and efficient in some settings (Noe, 1988b). Cross-gender mentorships often provide tangible benefits such as a sense of complimentarity that contributes to creative synergy and friendship (Kram, 1985). Noe (1988b) reported that protégés in cross-gender mentorships were rated as more effective in their use of the relationship, possibly as a result of good attention to issues of boundaries and expectations. Because more faculty are male, and increasing numbers of graduate students are women, cross-gender mentoring is inevitable.

Common Problems and Suggestions for Cross-Gender Mentorships

Although anecdotal experience and research findings confirm that cross-gender relationships can be productive and rewarding, it is important to acknowledge that mentorship dysfunction may stem directly from gender differences between mentor and protégé. Most of the literature bearing on this issue addresses the unique concerns of female graduate students mentored by male professors (Adler, 1976; Kram, 1985; Noe, 1988b; Ragins & Cotton, 1991). Potential problems for women in cross-gender mentorships include the following:

1. *Sexist stereotypes and attributions.* Male faculty members may consciously or unconsciously assume that women lack the attributes required for success in academia, that they lack the drive for achievement needed to succeed, or that they will have trouble grasping statistical or other research concepts (Adler, 1976; Noe, 1988b). In addition, research shows that when women are successful, their performance is often attributed to luck or extra effort rather than to ability (Deaux & Emswiller, 1974).

2. *Mentor discomfort with cross-gender relationships.* Some male mentors may fear public perceptions of their relationships with female graduate students. Specifically, they may fear the relationship will be construed in sexual terms—leading to gossip, jealousy, and resentment. Other male faculty, particularly older faculty, may simply be uncomfortable managing nonsexual intimate relationships.

3. *Socialization practices.* At times, socialized gender roles will interfere with cross-gender mentoring (Kram, 1985; Noe, 1988b). In this case, women protégés may use relational strategies such as dependency, nurturance, and accommodation to form and maintain a cross-gender mentorship. For their part, male mentors may use strategies such as overprotection and paternalism. These practices may prevent development of an egalitarian cross-gender relationship, and the protégé's independence and professional identity may be constrained.

4. *Sexual attraction.* Because of the close proximity and intensity of their work relationships, sexual attraction may develop between a mentor and a protégé. In other cases, mentors and protégés may not experience sexual attraction yet still be concerned about the risk of perceived intimacy (Fitt & Newton, 1981; Ragins & McFarlin, 1990). As a result, cross-gender mentorships may require increased attention to boundary setting compared with same-gender mentorships.

It is important to emphasize that cross-gender problems may also occur in mentorships between male protégés and female mentors or in same-gender mentorships between gay or lesbian individuals, although gender-based problems in these relationships are less frequently documented. In any of these constellations, emotional or sexual attraction, as well as any stereotyped attributions or behaviors that interfere with the relationship, must be addressed.

Careful attention to these issues, particularly during the initiation stage, can help the mentor and protégé to manage issues that could lead to mentorship dysfunction. Although potentially awkward, you should consider discussing gender concerns (and a strategy for managing these) with your mentor. For example, Clawson and Kram (1984) recommended that cross-gender dyads avoid frequent meetings, numerous spontaneous meetings, meeting after hours, frequently meeting behind closed doors, developing "pet" expressions or nicknames, or using inside jokes that signal to others the "specialness" of the relationship. We also suggest that you personally consider how you will deal with romantic feelings, should they arise in the relationship. Although it is unnecessary to broach this topic with your mentor in advance, a proactive plan can help you to avoid either romantic entanglement (always a bad idea) or unnecessary distancing from the mentor. Keep in mind that should attraction to your mentor become a concern, it is not necessary to disclose these feelings to him or her (Clawson & Kram, 1984). Your mentorship will likely be better served by discussing these feelings with an objective and supportive third person.

THE IMPORTANCE OF ASSERTIVENESS FOR WOMEN

We end this section with a word of encouragement for female graduate students seeking a mentor. Historically, women in academia and business environments have been less likely than men to assertively initiate mentorships. There are several reasons for this (Ragins & Cotton, 1991). First, women may fear that the mentor (if male) or others in the organization will misconstrue such an approach as a sexual advance. Second, traditional gender role expectations encourage men to take a dominant role and women a passive role in initiating relationships. Finally, women may have fewer informal interactions or opportunities for developing mentorships with male faculty. Because there are still significantly more men than women in the upper ranks of academia (Ragins & Scandura, 1994), female faculty members are often besieged by requests from female students and junior faculty for mentoring. As a result of these (and probably other) factors, women often report restricted access to female mentors, and some male mentors appear less willing to enter into mentor relationships with them (Ragins & Cotton, 1991).

If you are a female graduate student, we hope that you are not discouraged by these concerns. On the contrary, we hope they serve to motivate you and renew your commitment to assertively seek out the right mentor. Many women will be successfully mentored in graduate school. More often than not, mentored women will be diligent and intentional in their approach to finding a well-matched faculty mentor.

Mentoring and Minorities

ACCESS TO MENTORS

Although most academic environments are beginning to recognize the benefits of attracting and retaining minority scholars as faculty members, minority faculty are still grossly underrepresented in most academic fields (Blackwell, 1989; Brinson & Kottler, 1993). There is also evidence that minority group members have less access to mentors when compared with their White counterparts (Cox & Nkomo, 1991). One strategy frequently used by minorities to overcome barriers to mentoring has been to seek minority mentors outside business and academic departments (Thomas, 1990). This strategy has been successful for many minority group students; however, we believe it is also important to consider seeking a mentor within your academic department for a variety of reasons presented in the first section of this guide.

BENEFITS OF MENTORING FOR MINORITIES

Extrinsic Benefits

Limited research exists pertaining to the extrinsic benefits that minority protégés receive in comparison with unmentored minorities. The extant research points to the conclusion that minority protégés do benefit from having a mentor in graduate school. When asked about their graduate and early-career mentorships, ethnic minority psychologists reported that having a mentor significantly enhanced their academic and career development (Atkinson, Neville, & Casas, 1991). These same protégés indicated that their mentors helped them develop necessary clinical or research skills, establish professional networks, understand the political structure of the organization, and increase their professional visibility. Graduate mentors also provide critical assistance accessing internship and employment opportunities that launch the minority protégé into his or her career path (Obleton, 1984). Given the many social and institutional barriers to advancement faced by minority students and professionals (Ramey, 1995), we believe the guidance and coaching of a skilled mentor can be a critical factor assisting minority protégés to obtain the tangible outcomes they desire.

Intrinsic Benefits

Minority students seeking a mentor can be assured that, if matched with a good mentor, they are likely to experience a variety of intrinsic benefits. Among the most common benefits reported by minority protégés are advocacy, encouragement, emotional support and understanding, enhanced creativity and problem-solving skills, and development of personal ethics and professional values (Atkinson et al., 1991). Additionally, opportunities to discuss cultural, sociological, and historical topics related to racism are likely to be valued by minority graduate students who hope to integrate their racial heritage with their professional identity (Watts, 1987). Although minority mentors may be in the best position, because of their direct experience with racism, to offer encouragement and support, culturally sensitive majority mentors can also provide important mentor functions.

SELECTION OF ETHNICALLY SIMILAR OR ETHNICALLY DIFFERENT MENTORS

Importance of Similarity

Minority faculty are often well suited to transmit valuable experiences related to how they addressed racial discrimination and other social barriers. Because minority students frequently see minority faculty as more sensitive and supportive to their own struggles with racism, it is easy to understand why racial similarity is frequently a salient factor when seeking a mentor. Perceived similarity may foster deeper trust, mutual understanding, and bonding that may be difficult to achieve in a mentorship with a racially different mentor. When surveying African American employees in a business environment, Kalbfleisch and Davies (1991) found that the mentor's race was the most important factor in predicting whether a relationship would develop between a mentor and protégé. Thomas (1990) noted that racial similarity was so important to African American employees that they were willing to develop mentorships with same-race individuals outside of their departments, despite the potential inconvenience or less optimal impact on career success.

Although attraction certainly exists between same-race mentors and protégés, it is unclear if racial similarity actually leads to increased support by the mentor. A study by Ensher and Murphy (1997) assigned interns to same-race and different-race mentors. Results suggest that although racial similarity resulted in the protégés' report of greater career support, it did not predict satisfaction with the relationship or the likelihood of continuing the relationship at the end of the program. Instead, attitude and value similarity were the most important factors predicting satisfaction with the relationship. In another study, Atkinson et al. (1991) asked ethnic minority psychologists to describe their graduate school mentorships both in graduate school and early career. They concluded that there is no evidence that psychologists with ethnically similar mentors received more benefits or were more satisfied with their mentorship than psychologists with White mentors. These results suggest that minority students are wise to consider both race and similarity of attitudes and values in seeking a mentor.

Mentorships With Ethnically Different Mentors

Whether or not racially similar faculty are available, many minority students will be faced with the choice of whether to develop mentorships with faculty of a different racial heritage, most often a White mentor. The pairing of a minority protégé with a White mentor has been referred to as cross-cultural mentoring (Brinson & Kottler, 1993). Brinson and Kottler (1993) described the following key components to successful mentorships involving a minority protégé and a majority mentor: (a) mentors have a genuine concern for their protégés' personal welfare; (b) mentors have the inclination, expertise, and professional influence to assist in protégés' professional development; (c) mentors are culturally sensitive and have invested time to learn about protégés' cultural heritage; and (d) mentors are aware and appreciative of protégés' individual differences within their culture. Although racially different mentors do not share first-hand knowledge of challenges related to racial discrimination, a mentor who is genuine, humble, and willing to learn from the minority protégé can be a tremendous asset. We hope that by investing in this relationship and teaching your mentor about your cultural heritage, you can experience a range of important benefits, including greater empowerment.

Common Problems in Cross-Cultural Mentorships

Unfortunately, racial differences may pose obstacles for mentors and protégés. Although there are a variety of problems resulting from overt racism or ethnocentrism, we believe graduate students are much more likely to encounter more subtle challenges that require the attention of both the mentor and the protégé. Brinson and Kottler (1993) identified the following problems that may surface and require engagement when a minority protégé works with a White mentor:

1. *Mistrust.* Difficulty establishing trust is common in cross-cultural mentorships. Many minority protégés find themselves on guard for any sign that the mentor is repeating the historically damaging relationship dynamics present between minority and majority groups. Mistrust that results from the historical relationship must be acknowledged and discussed by the mentor and protégé to facilitate the trust and intimacy that is necessary for a fulfilling relationship.
2. *Dynamics of power.* Power in the mentorship is misused or abused when the mentor assumes greater power on the basis of his or her race. For example, power is subtly abused when the mentor assumes that he or she knows what is best and subsequently behaves in a paternalistic manner toward the protégé.
3. *Differences in interpersonal style.* Minority protégés often elect a more cautious interpersonal style when relating to majority mentors, particularly during the initial stages of the relationship. Uninformed mentors may mistake this "introspective" interpersonal style for aloofness or disinterest and subsequently fail to fully engage the protégé in the relationship (Brinson & Kottler, 1993, p. 245).

4. *Difficulty requesting help.* Many minority graduate students have succeeded because of their strong motivation to achieve, despite a lack of minority role models in academic settings. Because they are accustomed to succeeding solely as a result of their own merits, minority protégés may fear that asking for assistance or sharing weaknesses with their mentors will be interpreted as incompetence or failure.

Although we believe that directly addressing problems that stem from cultural difference can be very successful, racial differences themselves do not necessarily need to be discussed for the mentorship to be satisfying. Thomas (1993) found that cross-race mentor dyads generally used one of two strategies for dealing with racial differences. The first strategy was *denial and suppression,* meaning that the pair never discussed race except in a superficial way. The second strategy was what Thomas called *direct engagement.* Here, the mentorship dyad processed race-related information and racial differences carefully and at different times during the relationship. The key finding in Thomas's important study was that the most productive and functional mentorships were those in which mentor and protégé shared a preference for the same strategy—the strategy itself was secondary in importance. Although there is something inherently healthy and positive about freely discussing racial differences and their meaning for the mentorship, this research indicates that such discussion is not necessary for a functional cross-race mentorship—as long as you and your mentor match with respect to a preference for either avoiding or directly processing racial issues.

IMPORTANCE OF ASSERTIVENESS FOR MINORITIES

If you are a minority student planning to develop a mentorship with a racially different mentor, we want to highlight several important recommendations offered by Brinson and Kottler (1993). First, select your mentor with care. Not all mentors possess cultural sensitivity or have the desire to learn more about cultural differences. Second, teach your mentor about your cultural or racial heritage. Open sharing with your mentor can lead to greater intimacy and trust. Third, be diplomatic and assertive when educating your mentor about cultural differences. Fourth, find support from other minority protégés. Collaboration with minority peers—and hopefully your mentor too—can promote positive advancement of minority issues within the department and broader university setting. Although we recognize that not all problems associated with racial diversity can be addressed with these suggestions, we hope these recommendations will assist minority protégés in developing fruitful and satisfying mentorships.

We conclude this chapter by acknowledging once more that many women and minorities have limited opportunities to establish a primary mentorship with a same-gender or same-race mentor within their university department. As a result, in chapter 11, we propose a variety of alternative strategies for women and minorities seeking mentors.

Some Additional Ways to Get Mentored

11

Case 11.1

Even before gaining acceptance to a top-rated business management PhD program, Charlie was familiar with the writings of Dr. Fame—a widely published business consultant and an expert on corporate mergers. A long-time faculty member in Charlie's doctoral program, Dr. Fame was seldom on campus. He taught one seminar each semester and was otherwise busy writing best-selling business books and lecturing internationally. Although the notoriety was good for the university, Dr. Fame had few doctoral students, and these he afforded only Spartan attention. Charlie had been attracted to Dr. Fame's writings during the application process and had taken one of his courses during his first semester. The two hit it off immediately, and Charlie became even more intrigued with Dr. Fame's area of expertise. After a great deal of consideration, Charlie decided to pursue Dr. Fame as a program advisor and mentor. In Charlie's view, the potential career pay-offs outweighed the problem of less interaction. During an initial meeting with Dr. Fame to discuss expectations, Charlie wisely requested scheduled meetings each month to collaborate on projects, including some opportunities for Charlie to participate in writing and presenting with Dr. Fame.

Because Charlie was aware that Dr. Fame would not be a helpful mentor in the area of research design, and because Dr. Fame was often unavailable for psychosocial support, Charlie pursued a secondary mentorship with Dr. Stat, a professor of economics with expertise in statistics. Dr. Stat was kind, considerate, and ultimately an ideal dissertation committee member. Charlie also organized a peer-mentoring group with three other doctoral students. In this group, Charlie received social support, counseling, and solid friendships. Group members offered one another performance feedback and encouragement. When Charlie graduated, his association with Dr. Fame paid off in the form of numerous job offers.

Case 11.2

Noel was also a doctoral student in the business administration program attended by Charlie (Case 11.1). Despite some efforts to establish mentorships with three different program faculty members, Noel was without a mentor in his 3rd year of graduate school. As one of the few African American students in his cohort, Noel became bitter about the fact that the program had no African American faculty members, and he wondered if unintended racism factored into his difficulty finding a mentor. Although there were African American faculty in several other doctoral programs in his graduate school, and although his own program had several African American students in other year groups, Noel retreated from both faculty and peers and became increasingly detached and disenchanted with graduate school. Noel dropped out of graduate school at the start of his 4th year. Noel's case is particularly tragic in light of the fact that his own university had a well-developed planned mentoring program for minority group students (Noel had refused to participate), and a national organization of graduate students in business had a peer-mentoring network, which had been quite effective in offering support to African American students in graduate programs around the country.

Our oft-repeated theme in this book is that there is much you can do to ensure development of a rewarding and enduring graduate school mentorship. Even so, not all graduate students will enjoy a traditional mentor relationship with a core faculty member in their graduate department. In fact, various surveys indicate that as many as 50% of doctoral students go without such a mentor.

You may find yourself in a graduate program with too many students per faculty member, faculty who are stretched thin with research requirements, or a climate that disparages or ignores mentoring altogether. You may lose a primary mentor early in your graduate school career or may terminate your mentorship for a variety of reasons (see chapter 8). It is possible that you will not find a mentor who is sensitive to or interested in your racial, ethnic, gender, religious, or sexual orientation experience. Although the mentoring research is clear that primary graduate school mentorships are nearly always the preferred method of maximizing both career and psychosocial mentor functions (Kram, 1985), the simple fact is that, despite concerted effort and careful planning, for some students no primary mentorship develops.

In circumstances of mentoring adversity, it is essential that graduate students nurture ingenuity and creatively strategize alternatives to the traditional mentorship form. In this chapter, we encourage readers to carefully consider a range of additional or adjunctive ways to get mentored. This chapter is *not* exclusively for those students who have been unsuccessful finding a primary mentor. On the contrary, even those readers who are well mentored by a faculty member in their own graduate program may benefit from considering additional sources of mentoring. For example, you may have a mentor who is an exceptional researcher, yet minimally skilled in offering acceptance, emotional support, or encouragement. Alternatively, you may have a kind and caring mentor who is unable to competently show you the ropes of grant-getting and research design. You may long for the role modeling and friendship of a same-race mentor or wish for a colleague with whom you could more often disclose about your experience of being a graduate student.

In our view, each of these wishes is legitimate and would call for consideration of alternatives or additions to the primary mentorship (Cunic et al., 2000; Philip & Hendry, 1996; Russell & Adams, 1997). Alternatives covered in this chapter include (a) secondary (external) mentorships, (b) team mentoring, (c) peer mentoring, (d) peer-group mentoring, (e) famous mentors, and (f) planned mentor programs (see Table 11.1). Each of these approaches to getting some of the salient mentor functions offers significant potential benefits. We end this chapter by recommending that all graduate students construct what we call

TABLE 11.1

Additional Ways to Get Mentored

Alternative mentor form	Description
Secondary (external) mentors	Mentors within or outside a protégé's academic department or field whose mentoring role is generally shorter in duration, less emotionally bonded, and frequently focused on one task or function.
Team mentoring	A group of protégés who meet collectively and regularly to receive mentoring functions from a single mentor.
Peer mentoring	A lateral mentorship in which a fellow graduate student provides career-enhancing and psychosocial functions to another student.
Peer-group mentoring	A group of peers who agree to meet regularly for the purpose of providing role modeling, networking, and psychosocial support.
Famous mentors	Well-known and highly influential scholars who provide specific and focused mentoring functions in a time-limited manner.
Planned mentoring programs	Formalized programs in which a minority student is paired with a faculty mentor or peer advisor who is invested in providing career and psychosocial support.

a *personal mentoring network*, which will (ideally) include a primary mentorship and one or more of the alternatives discussed here.

Secondary (External) Mentors

Because no graduate school faculty member is perfect or capable of offering all of the mentor characteristics and functions you might desire, it is reasonable to consider pursuing one or more secondary mentorships. Secondary mentors may be faculty members in your own graduate program, faculty in other academic departments, faculty in external universities, or supervisors (clinical or research) from various training experiences you have in graduate school. Secondary mentorships are generally shorter in duration, less emotionally bonded, and often focused around one task or one set of mentor functions (e.g., helping you learn research, honing your applied practice skills, offering a place to "vent" about problems in your graduate program). Secondary mentors can be tremendously helpful when it comes to "filling in the gaps": They may offer the very mentor functions you are unable to obtain in your primary mentorship.

The term *secondary* mentor does not imply reduced value or importance but rather the shorter duration and less frequent interaction characterizing these connections. Secondary mentorships often form serendipitously with supervisors, faculty members whose courses you enjoy, or professors and professionals to whom you are introduced by your primary mentor. As in the primary mentorship, you will appreciate the support, encouragement, guidance, challenge, or role modeling this person offers. The difference is that the mentoring will be less frequent and intense, or it may be focused on a single dimension of your development (Burlew, 1991).

As in the case of the primary mentorship, we encourage you to be intentional (see chapter 5) about finding secondary mentors to meet your mentoring needs. After you have begun to firm up and enjoy the benefits of a primary mentorship, or, if a primary mentorship remains elusive for you, consider the various faculty and supervisors with whom you have regular contact and consider how one or more of them might become important sources of support for you if you take the time to arrange more interaction with them. In addition to your identified program mentor, which faculty are you drawn to? Which ones appear inherently interested in you or particularly concerned with how you are doing? Which professionals have unique or specific expertise or experience? Which are well connected in career areas of primary interest to you? Are there faculty who might have particular sensitivity to issues of race and culture? Is there a faculty member who might be a well-balanced model of blending family and career roles?

Secondary mentorships are often particularly helpful to women or graduate students from minority groups who may have few options for same-gender, same-race, or same-culture mentors in their graduate program (University of Michigan, 1999). If you are a female student interested in a same-gender model and secondary mentorship, consider female faculty in other departments, women in your discipline whom you admire (even if they are geographically distant), and professional organizations dedicated to women in your field. (See Box 11.1.)

The options available for secondary mentorships can also be obtained through well-established organizations. Division 35 of the American Psychological Association (Psychology of Women) offers a mentoring network for female graduate students, and more broadly, the Association for Women in Science encourages one-on-one mentoring between female scientists and female graduate students in the sciences. Similarly, gay and lesbian graduate students can often find organizations, support groups, and mentoring networks for students through their primary professional organization. Gay and lesbian students often have great difficulty finding faculty who can serve as overt role models, and further, may find themselves in graduate programs that are subtly (or openly) hostile toward gay and lesbian students.

Finally, ethnic and racial minority students are strongly encouraged

---

BOX 11.1: HOW IT WORKED FOR US—JENNY'S PERSPECTIVE

I enjoyed a secondary mentorship with a female professor in my graduate department. This relationship developed informally, initially through classroom contact and supervision, and later when I worked as her graduate assistant. Although the relationship was never formalized, we met regularly over cups of tea to discuss important topics such as how to balance personal and professional responsibilities and how to address gender stereotypes. As a more experienced role model, her coaching, encouragement, sponsorship, and protection were invaluable to me as I negotiated departmental politics and launched my career. Although I no longer have routine contact with this secondary mentor, we continue to meet occasionally to update each other on our personal and professional lives. We are both pleased to discover that our informal mentorship has transitioned into a collegial friendship.

to actively pursue secondary mentorships with same-race or same-culture mentors if this is an important value and if such models are not available in the primary graduate program. Various graduate student networks and professional groups can be tremendously helpful in this regard. As an example, the Association of Black Psychologists (ABPsi) is a professional organization dedicated to enhancing the well-being of African Americans and serving as a collective voice for Black psychologists. ABPsi offers mentoring of graduate students by professional members, as well as a student section of the organization designed to foster peer support. Through ABPsi, a Black graduate student in psychology might relatively easily develop a secondary mentorship with a Black psychologist in the profession, thereby meeting certain mentoring needs that the primary mentor cannot.

Keep in mind that secondary mentorships are more likely to develop if you are active as a student member in professional associations. Student membership and conference registration fees are typically quite reasonable and are excellent formats for making connections with potential mentors external to your graduate department. By keeping updated on cutting-edge issues in your field and attending meetings with scholars and practitioners in your area of interest, you significantly increase the probability of interacting with people who are well positioned to provide important (if not comprehensive) mentor functions. We encourage you to consider approaching interesting speakers after they present at professional meetings. Introduce yourself, ask questions, discuss your own interests and professional goals, and you may just open the door to some ongoing dialog with a potentially important secondary mentor. Be bold!

Team Mentoring

In certain circumstances, particularly in graduate programs with large student-to-faculty ratios, an alternative to traditional primary mentorships is the team mentoring design. Here, a single faculty mentor meets regularly (weekly or biweekly) with a small team of graduate students —typically integrating students of various seniority levels in the program—for the purpose of providing mentoring functions in a more economical manner. Some graduate programs intentionally foster research or clinical teams to ensure that all students are assigned an advisor and that they meet routinely with this person (usually in the hope that a mentorship will develop). In these programs, students are often given a year to attend and explore several existing research teams before arranging with one faculty member to commit to his or her team.

Team mentoring offers faculty the advantage of streamlining the volume of time devoted to meetings with students. Teams additionally help ensure that students have regular contact with an advisor—albeit in a group format—and frequency of contact is a strong predictor of the development of a mentorship. Although students may meet occasionally with their mentor outside the routine team gatherings, this may be discouraged. Research or advising teams allow faculty to offer mentoring functions such as coaching, direct training, advice-giving, research supervision, and career planning in a format designed to benefit multiple protégés simultaneously. In addition, team mentoring often provides *intrateam* mentoring (Eby, 1997) in that student members offer one another support, performance feedback, and affirmation. Faculty mentors may use the team to encourage goal-setting, project planning, and skill development for individual members.

The downside of team mentoring is that it may deny protégés the opportunity to experience many of the psychosocial functions and personal collegiality and friendship frequently associated with traditional mentorships. If you are socially inhibited, fiercely competitive, or work poorly in groups, teams may be a problem for you. Mentoring teams often help to maximize the number of students who are mentored in larger graduate programs, yet as a team member, you may need to work at having an adequate number of personal exchanges with your mentor.

Peer Mentoring

Although student colleagues can never fully substitute for a seasoned and powerful faculty mentor, peer relationships can serve several important mentoring functions. Peer, or *lateral*, mentoring occurs in graduate school when fellow students support one another through career-enhancing and psychosocial developmental functions (Eby, 1997; Kram & Isabella, 1985). Career-enhancing functions include information sharing, career strategizing, and offering performance-related feedback, whereas peer psychosocial functions include confirmation, emotional support, personal feedback, friendship, and mutuality (Kram & Isabella, 1985).

Even if you enjoy a strong faculty mentorship, why not maximize the value of your relationships with one or two graduate school peers? Well-selected and reliable colleagues can offer several important mentoring functions, they are much more available than faculty, and peer relationships lack the hierarchical dimension of formal mentorships, thus making it easier to communicate and achieve mutual support and collaboration. In a study of several peer-mentor pairs, Kram and Isabella

(1985) discovered that in contrast to traditional mentorships, peer relationships were characterized by greater equality and longevity; you are likely to stay connected to close graduate school friends for years.

Some graduate programs are intentional about peer mentoring and work to create solid student-to-student mentorships. For example, in one graduate program at Purdue University, each new student was matched with a senior graduate student for the purpose of providing guidance, support, and information (Bowman, Bowman, & Delucia, 1990). Student mentors made introductions, offered advice and informal information (e.g., "insider" information regarding coursework, faculty, and degree requirements), and provided emotional support when needed. If your graduate program does not have a formal peer-mentoring program, we recommend that you consider pressing your student colleagues and department chair to create one. Peer mentoring has been shown to ease adjustment to graduate school, help students avoid common pitfalls in training, and encourage active involvement in departmental activities (Bowman et al., 1990).

Keep in mind that peer mentors cannot replace or supplant the faculty–student mentorship. Student colleagues will never have the experience, wisdom, professional connection, and power needed to offer some of the most potent and effective mentor functions. Still, you should actively develop at least one strong peer mentor relationship. Nearly every graduate student we know can use a dependable and trusted friend with whom they can vent, request feedback, and seek advice.

Peer-Group Mentoring

Another potentially valuable version of peer mentoring is peer mentoring with multiple graduate student colleagues. Peer-group mentoring occurs when multiple students meet regularly for the purpose of supporting one another. Group members offer each other important mentoring functions such as role modeling, networking, psychosocial support, and a powerful sense of inclusion and belonging (Dansky, 1996). In a sometimes threatening and overwhelming graduate school landscape, a peer group can enhance professional identity and personal esteem; this is often particularly true in the first year or two of graduate training. (See Box 11.2.)

If your graduate program does not formally assist with the formation of peer-mentoring groups—and most do not—we recommend that you seriously consider forming such a support group on your own. In some cases, peer-mentoring groups develop informally over time. For maxi-

---

BOX 11.2: HOW IT WORKED FOR US—BRAD'S
PERSPECTIVE

When I was a first-semester doctoral student, six married couples
in the program—including my wife and I—began meeting weekly
for the purpose of support during that first trying year. These
weekly meetings typically included food, socializing, lots of laugh-
ter, and a great deal of "normalizing" our individual experiences as
graduate students. We discussed the ins-and-outs of courses, faculty, and future program hurdles. We offered advice, shared anxie-
ties, and provided much needed encouragement when the going
got tough. Although the group was initially envisioned as a year-
long support group, it continued for the full 5 years of the doctoral program. This peer mentoring/support group remains one of
the most memorable and meaningful facets of my entire graduate
school experience.

---

mal benefit, however, we recommend speeding this process by intentionally recruiting and organizing well-matched student peers, peers you
would enjoy supporting and being supported by. Mentoring groups can
include significant others or can be focused around students alone.

In some cases (particularly in very small doctoral programs), you
may not be able to identify students in your program with whom you
would like to engage in a long-term group friendship. In this case, you
might consider graduate students in other programs, other departments,
or even students outside your institution yet in your discipline. Many
professional organizations have student chapters that may offer valuable
assistance when it comes to finding other graduate students in your
area, or even creating opportunities for student interaction via e-mail
or at regional or national professional meetings.

Famous Mentors

One of the most overlooked sources of mentoring for graduate students
is the "famous" or high-profile scholar. In every discipline and within
each specialty in a discipline are the prolific, well-known, and highly
influential scholars who can be tremendously helpful and even career-
changing secondary mentors. Although often located at distant universities—even in other countries—and nearly always inundated with responsibilities and invitations, many famous writers and researchers in

your specialty will take particular interest in graduate students who show a well-informed and sincere interest in their work.

As you become settled in your graduate program, develop a primary mentorship, and begin to consider a dissertation topic and a career plan, why not think about the top scholars in your area of research interest? Beginning a correspondence with one of these individuals may lead to an important professional connection and even some mentoring functions. Graduate students have found famous mentors by asking them for input regarding dissertation plans, asking them to serve as a dissertation committee member (most universities will allow an external member), or even asking for input regarding career trajectory planning if they are interested in pursuing a career similar to the scholar's. Although famous scholars are busy and should not be bothered with minutiae, they are a potential source of tremendous power and influence. (See Box 11.3.)

Our message to you is this: You have nothing to lose when it comes to seeking out a famous or high-profile scholar in your field. The influence, guidance, and opportunity available through an informal and cordial relationship with a top-notch scholar in your specialty could offer career-altering mentoring functions and benefits. If opportunities to interact with famous scholars present themselves, take them! If such opportunities do not present themselves, create them!

Planned Mentoring Programs

In some university settings, graduate programs are instituting planned or formalized mentoring programs for minority group students (M. C. Brown, Davis, & McClendon, 1999; Redmond, 1990). Particularly on campuses with predominantly White enrollments or with predominantly White faculty, these programs offer minority group graduate students important opportunities for advancement and assistance with the transition to graduate school. Planned mentoring programs include components such as assignment of a faculty mentor, assignment of a peer advisor, a formally established student support network, and workshops to enhance preparedness for various courses.

In our view, the most exciting component of most planned mentoring programs is the intentional pairing of minority students with an individual faculty mentor. Faculty who participate in these programs have expressed specific interest in mentoring minority group students, and key matching variables are considered in pairing students with mentors (Redmond, 1990). Some examples of cutting-edge planned mentoring programs in the United States include the Peabody Mentor-

---

BOX 11.3: HOW IT WORKED FOR US—BRAD'S PERSPECTIVE

When I was a brand new doctorate in the field, I sent a letter to Dr. Albert Ellis (one of the most famous psychologists in the history of his profession) asking him to clarify some of his theoretical points for a paper I was writing. To my surprise, Dr. Ellis responded almost immediately with a lengthy and cordial letter addressing each of the questions. Over the next several years, my connection with Dr. Ellis continued, and he became an important promoter of my career, writing letters of recommendation on my behalf, participating in symposia with me at professional meetings, and offering praise and encouragement at important points in my development. Dr. Ellis's impact on my life and career have been substantial. He has kindly offered many of the functions of a mentor.

---

ing Program at Vanderbilt University; the Graduate Mentorship Program at the University of California, Berkeley; the Graduate Opportunities and Minority Achievement Program at the University of Washington; and the Coordinating Council for Minority Issues at the University of Chicago. Each of these university-wide programs offers intentional facilitation of mentoring relationships between minority students and well-established and effective graduate faculty mentors.

Although assignment to a mentor does not ensure the development of a productive mentorship, planned mentoring programs help to increase the odds of this happening for minority group students. If you are an ethnic or racial minority group member, we recommend that you (a) give preference to graduate programs that offer planned mentoring programs and (b) strongly consider participation in the program once admitted.

Your Personal Mentoring Network

When it comes to getting mentored in graduate school, we have consistently encouraged you to find a well-matched faculty member in your own graduate program. This primary mentorship is likely to afford you the most mentor functions and the greatest mentoring benefit. In addition, we believe all graduate students should seriously consider adding one or more of the alternative mentoring components discussed in this chapter to their primary mentorship. For those graduate students who are unable to find a primary mentor, these alternatives to traditional mentoring will be especially important.

Wise graduate students will consider constructing a mentoring team (University of Michigan, 1999), or what we refer to as a *personal mentoring network*. A mentoring network is a combination of relationships and resources aimed at maximizing both the volume and value of mentoring functions at your disposal. Although a long-term mentorship with a primary faculty mentor should serve as the centerpiece of your mentoring network, you may also benefit substantially from secondary mentorships with faculty members in your program and at other institutions; you may find the mutuality and encouragement available through peer mentoring or peer-group mentoring to be invaluable; you may be surprised by the receptivity and openness of a "famous" scholar to offering you some support and guidance; and you may be pleasantly surprised by the collegiality and affirmation-rich environment available in a planned mentoring network for minority students.

It is important to be both creative and realistic when considering the composition of your personal mentoring network. Consider all your options. Core faculty, adjunct faculty, faculty emeriti (retired faculty who maintain a connection with the graduate department), peers, advanced graduate students, departmental staff, external supervisors, faculty from external universities, and even friends from outside academe can all serve some mentoring function; each can help at specific times with specific career and psychosocial needs. As you consider your needs and interests, it is helpful to imagine how each network member might offer important mentor functions (University of Michigan, 1999). For example, a seasoned full professor might offer research guidance or coaching in the art of job interviewing, whereas a junior faculty member might be more sensitive and empathic regarding the stresses of graduate school. Faculty in another department might offer political insight regarding your own department, and an advanced graduate peer might provide coaching and friendship at precisely the right times during your first years in graduate school.

We end this chapter, and *Getting Mentored in Graduate School*, with three final cautions regarding your own mentoring network. First, keep in mind that your time in graduate school will be limited. It is quite unlikely that you will have either the time for or the need of all the mentoring options we describe in this chapter. Select those that fit your case most elegantly. Second, constructing a personal mentoring network is your personal responsibility. The majority of graduate programs will not work hard at making sure you are mentored. Do it yourself. During your graduate school career, some golden opportunities for additional mentoring from a team, a secondary mentor, or a peer group will present themselves. Be ready to quickly recognize and pursue them. Finally, we end by emphasizing one last time that a primary student–faculty mentorship should be your paramount focus. Mentoring signifies a strong, enduring, and well-matched relationship. It will be in the context of this relationship that most of the essential and gratifying mentoring functions will show themselves. Relationships take time and energy to develop. Use your resources well, intentionally select a mentor, and begin developing this relationship as early in your graduate school experience as you possibly can.

References

Adler, N. E. (1976). Women students. In J. Katz & R. T. Hartnett (Eds.), *Scholars in the making: The development of graduate and professional students* (pp. 197–225). Cambridge, MA: Ballinger.

Allen, T. D., Poteet, M. L., & Burroughs, S. M. (1997). The mentor's perspective: A qualitative inquiry and future research agenda. *Journal of Vocational Behavior, 51,* 70–89.

Allen, T. D., Poteet, M. L., & Russell, J. E. A. (2000). Protégé selection by mentors: What makes the difference? *Journal of Organizational Behavior, 21,* 271–282.

Aryee, S., Lo, S., & Kang, I. L. (1999). Antecedents of early career stage mentoring among Chinese employees. *Journal of Organizational Behavior, 20,* 563–576.

Atkinson, D. R., Casas, A., & Neville, H. (1994). Ethnic minority psychologists: Whom they mentor and benefits they derive from the process. *Journal of Multicultural Counseling and Development, 22,* 37–48.

Atkinson, D. R., Neville, H., & Casas, A. (1991). The mentorship of ethnic minorities in professional psychology. *Professional Psychology: Research and Practice, 22,* 336–338.

Baugh, S. G., Lankau, M. J., & Scandura, T. A. (1996). An investigation of the effects of protégé gender on responses to mentoring. *Journal of Vocational Behavior, 49,* 309–323.

Belar, C. D. (1998). Graduate education in clinical psychology: "We're not in Kansas anymore." *American Psychologist, 53,* 456–464.

Berger, S. S., & Buchholz, E. S. (1993). On becoming a supervisee: Preparation for learning in a supervisory relationship. *Psychotherapy, 30,* 86–92.

Biaggio, M., Paget, T. L., & Chenoweth, M. S. (1997). A model for ethical management of faculty–student dual relationships. *Professional Psychology: Research and Practice, 28,* 184–189.

Blackburn, R. T., Chapman, D. W., & Cameron, S. M. (1981). "Cloning" in academia: Mentorship and academic careers. *Research in Higher Education, 15,* 315–327.

Blackwell, J. E. (1989). Mentoring: An action strategy for increasing minority faculty. *Academe, 75,* 8–14.

Blevins-Knabe, B. (1992). The ethics of dual relationships in higher education. *Ethics and Behavior, 2,* 151–163.

Bogat, G. A., & Redner, R. L. (1985). How mentoring affects the professional development of women. *Professional Psychology: Research and Practice, 16,* 851–859.

Bolton, E. B. (1980). A conceptual analysis

of the mentor relationship in the career development of women. *Adult Education, 30*, 195–207.

Bowman, R. L., Bowman, V. E., & Delucia, J. L. (1990). Mentoring in a graduate counseling program: Students helping students. *Counselor Education and Supervision, 30*, 58–65.

Braswell, M. (2000). *Graduate study in psychology, 2000*. Washington, DC: American Psychological Association.

Brinson, J., & Kottler, J. (1993). Cross-cultural mentoring in counselor education: A strategy for retaining minority faculty. *Counselor Education and Supervision, 32*, 241–253.

Brown, M. C., Davis, G. L., & McClendon, S. A. (1999). Mentoring graduate students of color: Myths, models, and modes. *Peabody Journal of Education, 74*, 105–118.

Brown, R. D., & Krager, L. (1985). Ethical issues in graduate education: Faculty and student responsibilities. *Journal of Higher Education, 56*, 403–418.

Bruss, K. V., & Kopala, M. (1993). Graduate school training in psychology: Its impact upon the development of professional identity. *Psychotherapy, 30*, 685–691.

Burke, R. J. (1984). Mentors in organizations. *Group and Organizational Studies, 9*, 353–372.

Burke, R. J., & McKeen, C. A. (1996). Gender effects in mentoring relationships. *Journal of Social Behavior and Personality, 11*, 91–104.

Burke, R. J., & McKeen, C. A. (1997). Benefits of mentoring relationships among managerial and professional women: A cautionary tale. *Journal of Vocational Behavior, 51*, 43–57.

Burke, R. J., McKeen, C. A., & McKenna, C. A. (1990). Sex differences and cross-sex effects on mentoring: Some preliminary data. *Psychological Reports, 67*, 1011–1023.

Burke, R. J., McKeen, C. A., & McKenna, C. (1993). Correlates of mentoring in organizations: The mentor's perspective. *Psychological Reports, 72*, 883–896.

Burke, R. J., McKenna, C. S., & McKeen, C. A. (1991). How do mentorships differ from typical supervisory relationships? *Psychological Reports, 68*, 459–466.

Burlew, L. D. (1991). Multiple mentor model: A conceptual framework. *Journal of Career Development, 17*, 213–221.

Busch, J. W. (1985). Mentoring in graduate schools of education: Mentor's perception. *American Educational Research Journal, 22*, 257–265.

Byrne, D. (1969). Attitudes and attraction. In L. Berkowitz (Ed.), *Advances in experimental social psychology* (Vol. 4, pp. 35–89). New York: Academic Press.

Cameron, S. W., & Blackburn, R. T. (1981). Sponsorship and academic career success. *Journal of Higher Education, 52*, 369–377.

Cesa, I. L., & Fraser, S. C. (1989). A method for encouraging the development of good mentor–protégé relationships. *Teaching of Psychology, 16*, 125–128.

Chao, G. T. (1997). Mentoring phases and outcomes. *Journal of Vocational Behavior, 51*, 15–28.

Chao, G. T., Gardner, P. D., & Walz, P. M. (1992). Formal and informal mentorships: A comparison on mentoring functions and contrast with nonmentored counterparts. *Personnel Psychology, 45*, 619–636.

Chickering, A. W. (1969). *Education and identity*. San Francisco: Jossey-Bass.

Clark, R. A., Harden, S. L., & Johnson, W. B. (2000). Mentor relationships in clinical psychology doctoral training: Results of a national survey. *Teaching of Psychology, 27*, 262–268.

Clawson, J. G., & Kram, K. E. (1984). Managing cross-gender mentoring. *Business Horizons, 27*, 22–31.

Collins, N. W. (1983). *Professional women and their mentors*. Englewood Cliffs, NJ: Prentice Hall.

Collins, P. M. (1994). Does mentorship among social workers make a difference? An empirical investigation of career outcomes. *Social Work, 39*, 413–419.

Corbett, L. (1995). Supervision and the mentor archetype. In P. Kugler (Ed.), *Jungian perspectives on clinical supervision* (pp. 59–77). Switzerland: Daimon.

Cox, T. H., & Nkomo, S. M. (1991). A race and gender-group analysis of the early career experience of MBAs. *Work and Occupation, 18*, 431–446.

Cronan-Hillix, T., Gensheimer, L. K.,

Cronan-Hillix, W. A., & Davidson, W. S. (1986). Student's views of mentors in psychology graduate training. *Teaching of Psychology, 13*, 123–127.

Cunic, T. L., McLaughlin, M., Phipps, K., & Evans, B. (2000). Graduate research training: Single mentor versus informal mentor models. *The Behavior Therapist, 23*, 108–109.

Dansky, K. H. (1996). The effect of group mentoring on career outcomes. *Group and Organization Management, 21*, 5–21.

Davis, L. L., Litle, M. S., & Thornton, W. L. (1997). The art and angst of the mentoring relationship. *Academic Psychiatry, 21*, 61–71.

Deaux, K., & Emswiller, T. (1974). Explanation of successful performance on sex-linked tasks: What is skill for the male is luck for the female. *Journal of Personality and Social Psychology, 29*, 80–85.

Dickinson, S., & Johnson, W. B. (2000). Mentoring in clinical psychology doctoral programs: A national survey of directors of training. *The Clinical Supervisor, 19*, 137–152.

Dion, K., Berscheid, E., & Walster, E. (1972). What is beautiful is good. *Journal of Personality and Social Psychology, 24*, 285–290.

Dreher, G. F., & Ash, R. A. (1990). A comparative study of mentoring among men and women in managerial, professional, and technical positions. *Journal of Applied Psychology, 75*, 539–546.

Duck, S. (1994). Stratagems, spoils, and a serpent's tooth: On the delights and dilemmas of personal relationships. In W. R. Cupach & B. H. Spitzberg (Eds.), *The dark side of interpersonal communication* (pp. 3–24). Hillsdale, NJ: Erlbaum.

Eby, L. T. (1997). Alternative forms of mentoring in changing organizational environments: A conceptual extension of the mentoring literature. *Journal of Vocational Behavior, 51*, 125–144.

Eby, L. T., McManus, S. E., Simon, S. A., & Russell, J. E. A. (2000). The protégé's perspective regarding negative mentoring experiences: The development of a taxonomy. *Journal of Vocational Behavior, 57*, 1–21.

Ellis, H. C. (1992). Graduate education in psychology: Past, present, and future. *American Psychologist, 47*, 570–576.

Ensher, E. A., & Murphy, S. E. (1997). Effects of race, gender, perceived similarity, and contact on mentor relationships. *Journal of Vocational Behavior, 50*, 460–481.

Erikson, E. H. (1963). *Childhood and society* (2nd ed.). New York: Norton.

Erkut, S., & Mokros, J. R. (1984). Professors as models and mentors for college students. *American Educational Research Journal, 21*, 399–417.

Fagenson, E. A. (1988). The power of a mentor: Protégés' and nonprotégés' perceptions of their own power in organizations. *Group and Organizational Studies, 13*, 182–194.

Fagenson, E. A. (1989). The mentor advantage: Perceived career/job experiences of protégés versus non-protégés. *Journal of Organizational Behavior, 10*, 309–320.

Fagenson, E. A. (1992). Mentoring—Who needs it? A comparison of protégés and nonprotégés' need for power, achievement, affiliation, and autonomy. *Journal of Vocational Behavior, 41*, 48–60.

Feldman, D. C. (1999). Toxic mentors or toxic protégés? A critical reexamination of dysfunctional mentoring. *Human Resources Management Review, 9*, 247–278.

Festinger, L., Schacter, S., & Back, K. W. (1950). *Social pressure in informal groups.* New York: Harper.

Fitt, L. W., & Newton, D. A. (1981, March–April). When the mentor is a man and the protégé is a woman. *Harvard Business Review*, 56–60.

Gaskill, L. R. (1991). Same-sex and cross-sex mentoring of female protégés: A comparative analysis. *Career Development Quarterly, 40*, 48–63.

Gibb, S. (1999). The usefulness of theory: A case study in evaluating formal mentoring schemes. *Human Relations, 52*, 1055–1075.

Gilbert, L. A. (1985). Dimensions of same-gender student–faculty role-model relationships. *Sex Roles, 12*, 111–123.

Gilbert, L. A., & Rossman, K. M. (1992). Gender and the mentoring process for women: Implications for professional development. *Professional Psychology: Research and Practice, 23*, 233–238.

Glaser, R. D., & Thorpe, J. S. (1986). Unethical intimacy: A survey of sexual contact and advances between psychology educators and female graduate students. *American Psychologist, 41*, 43–51.

Goldstein, E. (1979). Effect of same-sex and cross-sex role models on the subsequent academic productivity of scholars. *American Psychologist, 34*, 407–410.

Goleman, D. P. (1997). *Emotional intelligence.* New York: Bantam Books.

Goodyear, R. K., Crego, C. A., & Johnston, M. W. (1992). Ethical issues in the supervision of student research: A study of critical incidents. *Professional Psychology: Research and Practice, 23*, 203–210.

Green, S. G., & Bauer, T. N. (1995). Supervisory mentoring by advisers: Relationships with doctoral student potential, productivity, and commitment. *Personnel Psychology, 48*, 537–561.

Haensley, P. A., & Parsons, J. L. (1993). Creative, intellectual, and psychosocial development through mentorship: Relationships and stages. *Youth & Society, 25*, 202–221.

Hammel, G. A., Olkin, R., & Taube, D. O. (1996). Student–educator sex in clinical and counseling psychology doctoral training. *Professional Psychology: Research and Practice, 27*, 93–97.

Hatfield, E., & Sprecher, S. (1986). *Mirror, mirror: The importance of looks in everyday life.* Albany: State University of New York Press.

Hirschberg, N., & Itkin, S. (1978). Graduate student success in psychology. *American Psychologist, 33*, 1083–1093.

Hite, L. M. (1985). Female doctoral students: Their perceptions and careers. *Journal of College Student Personnel, 26*, 18–22.

Huntley, D., Schneider, L., & Aronson, H. (2000). Clinical interns' perception of psychology and their place within it: The decade of the 1990s. *The Clinical Psychologist, 53*, 3–11.

Jennings, L., & Skovholt, T. M. (1999). The cognitive, emotional, and relational characteristics of master therapists. *Journal of Counseling Psychology, 46*, 3–11.

Johnson, W. B., DiGiuseppe, R., & Ulven, J. (1999). Albert Ellis as mentor: National survey results. *Psychotherapy, 36*, 305–312.

Johnson, W. B., & Huwe, J. M. (2002). Toward a typology of mentorship dysfunction in graduate school. *Psychotherapy, 39*, 44–55.

Johnson, W. B., Huwe, J. M., Fallow, A. M., Lall, R., Holmes, E. K., & Hall, W. (1999, December). Does mentoring foster success? *Proceedings of the U.S. Naval Institute, 44–46.*

Johnson, W. B., Huwe, J. M., & Lucas, J. L. (2000). Rational mentoring. *Journal of Rational–Emotive and Cognitve–Behavior Therapy, 18*, 39–54.

Johnson, W. B., Koch, C., Fallow, G. O., & Huwe, J. M. (2000). Prevalence of mentoring in clinical versus experimental doctoral programs: Survey findings, implications and recommendations. *Psychotherapy, 37*, 325–334.

Johnson, W. B., & Nelson, N. (1999). Mentor–protégé relationships in graduate training: some ethical concerns. *Ethics and Behavior, 9*, 189–210.

Kalbfleisch, P. J. (1997). Appeasing the mentor. *Aggressive Behavior, 23*, 389–403.

Kalbfleisch, P. J., & Davies, A. B. (1993). An interpersonal model for participation in mentoring relationships. *Western Journal of Communication, 57*, 399–415.

Kanter, R. M. (1977). *Men and women of the corporation.* New York: Basic Books.

Kaslow, N. J., & Rice, D. G. (1985). Developmental stresses of psychology internship training: What training staff can do to help. *Professional Psychology: Research and Practice, 16*, 253–261.

Kinnier, R. T., Metha, A. T., Buki, L. P., & Rawa, P. M. (1994). Manifest values of eminent psychologists: A content analysis of their obituaries. *Current Psychology: Developmental, Learning, Personality, and Social, 13*, 88–94.

Kirchner, E. P. (1969). Graduate education in psychology: Retrospective views of advanced degree recipients. *Journal of Clinical Psychology, 25*, 207–213.

Kitchener, K. S. (1992). Psychologist as teacher and mentor: Affirming ethical values throughout the curriculum. *Professional Psychology: Research and Practice, 23*, 190-195.

Kram, K. E. (1983). Phases of the mentor relationship. *Academy of Management Journal, 26,* 608–625.

Kram, K. E. (1985). *Mentoring at work: Developmental relationships in organizational life.* Glenview, IL: Scott Foresman.

Kram, K. E., & Isabella, L. A. (1985). Mentoring alternatives: The role of peer relationships in career development. *Academy of Management Journal, 28,* 110–132.

Laband, D. N., & Lentz, B. F. (1999). The impact of having a mentor on earnings and promotion: Evidence from a panel study of lawyers. *Applied Economic Letters, 6,* 785–787.

Lageman, A. G. (1986). Myths, metaphors, and mentors. *Journal of Religion and Health, 25,* 58–63.

Lamb, D. H., Baker, J. M., Jennings, M. L., & Yarris, E. (1982). Passages of an internship in professional psychology. *Professional Psychology, 13,* 661–669.

Levinson, D. J. (1996). *The seasons of a woman's life.* New York: Ballantine.

Levinson, D. J., Darrow, C. N., Klein, E. B., Levinson, M. H., & McKee, B. (1978). *The seasons of a man's life.* New York: Ballantine.

Mallinckrodt, B., Leong, F. T. L., & Kralj, M. M. (1989). Sex differences in graduate student life-change stress and stress symptoms. *Journal of College Student Development, 30,* 332–338.

McQuaide, S. (1998). Women at midlife. *Social Work, 43,* 21–31.

Mehlman, E., & Glickauf-Hughes, C. (1994). Understanding developmental needs of college students in mentoring relationships with professors. *Journal of College Student Psychotherapy, 8,* 39–53.

Mellott, R. N., Arden, I. A., & Cho, M. E. (1997). Preparing for internship: Tips for the prospective applicant. *Professional Psychology: Research and Practice, 28,* 190-196.

Merriam, S. (1983). Mentors and protégés: A critical review of the literature. *Adult Education Quarterly, 33,* 161–173.

Mintz, L. B., Bartels, K. M., & Rideout, C. A. (1995). Training in counseling ethnic minorities and race-based availability of graduate school resources. *Professional Psychology: Research and Practice, 26,* 316–321.

Mobley, G. M., Jaret, C., Marsh, K., & Lim, Y. Y. (1994). Mentoring, job satisfaction, gender and the legal profession. *Sex Roles, 31,* 79–85.

Mullen, E. J., & Noe, R. A. (1999). The mentoring information exchange: When do mentors seek information about their protégés? *Journal of Organizational Behavior, 20,* 233–242.

Murray, B. (1997, May). Unique mentor programs bolster students' careers. *APA Monitor, 50,* 50.

Newby, T. J., & Heide, A. (1992). The value of mentoring. *Performance Improvement Quarterly, 5,* 2–15.

Noe, R. A. (1988a). An investigation of the determinants of successful assigned mentoring relationships. *Personnel Psychology, 41,* 457–479.

Noe, R. A. (1988b). Women and mentoring: A review and research agenda. *Academy of Management Review, 13,* 65–78.

Obleton, N. B. (1984). Career counseling Black women in a predominantly White coeducational university. *Personnel and Guidance Journal, 62,* 365–368.

Olian, J. D., Carroll, S. J., & Giannantonio, C. M. (1993). Mentor reactions to protégés: An experiment with managers. *Journal of Vocational Behavior, 43,* 266–278.

Olian, J. D., Carroll, S. J., Giannantonio, C. M., & Feren, D. B. (1988). What do protégés look for in a mentor? Results of three experimental studies. *Journal of Vocational Behavior, 33,* 15–37.

O'Neil, J. M., & Wrighstman, L. S. (2001). The mentoring relationship in psychology training programs. In S. Walfish & A. Hess (Eds.), *Succeeding in graduate school: The complete career guide for the psychology student* (pp. 113–129). Hillsdale, NJ: Erlbaum.

Orpen, C. (1995). The effects of mentoring on employees' career success. *Journal of Social Psychology, 135,* 667–668.

Orzek, A. M. (1984). Mentor–mentee match in training programs based on Chickering's vectors of development. *Clinical Supervisor, 2*(1), 71–77.

Philip, K., & Hendry, L. B. (1996). Young people and mentoring: Towards a typology? *Journal of Adolescence, 19,* 189–201.

Phillips-Jones, L. (1982). *Mentors and protégés*. New York: Arbor House.

Plaut, S. M. (1993). Boundary issues in teacher–student relationships. *Journal of Sex and Marital Therapy, 19,* 210–219.

Pollock, R. (1995). A test of conceptual models depicting the developmental course of informal mentor–protégé relationships in the work place. *Journal of Vocational Behavior, 46,* 144–162.

Pope, K. S., Keith-Spiegel, P., & Tabachnick, B. G. (1986). Sexual attraction to clients: The human therapist and the (sometimes) inhuman training system. *American Psychologist, 41,* 147–158.

Ragins, B. R. (1989). Barriers to mentoring: The female manager's dilemma. *Human Relations, 42,* 1–22.

Ragins, B. R., & Cotton, J. L. (1991). Easier said than done: Gender differences in perceived barriers to gaining a mentor. *Academy of Management Journal, 34,* 939–951.

Ragins, B. R., & Cotton, J. L. (1993). Gender and willingness to mentor in organizations. *Journal of Management, 19,* 97–111.

Ragins, B. R., & Cotton, J. L. (1999). Mentor functions and outcomes: A comparison of men and women in formal and informal mentoring relationships. *Journal of Applied Psychology, 84,* 529–550.

Ragins, B. R., & McFarlin, D. B. (1990). Perceptions of mentor roles in cross-gender mentoring relationships. *Journal of Vocational Behavior, 37,* 321–339.

Ragins, B. R., & Scandura, T. A. (1994). Gender differences in expected outcomes of mentoring relationships. *Academy of Management Journal, 37,* 957–971.

Ragins, B. R., & Scandura, T. A. (1997). The way we were: Gender and the termination of mentoring relationships. *Journal of Applied Psychology, 82,* 945–953.

Ragins, B. R., & Scandura, T. A. (1999). Burden or blessing? Expected costs and benefits of being a mentor. *Journal of Organizational Behavior, 20,* 493–509.

Ramey, F. H. (1995). Obstacles faced by African American women administrators in higher education: How they cope. *Western Journal of Black Studies, 19,* 113–119.

Redmond, S. P. (1990). Mentoring and cultural diversity in academic settings. *American Behavioral Scientist, 34,* 188–200.

Reskin, B. F. (1979). Academic sponsorship and scientists' careers. *Sociology of Education, 52,* 129–146.

Richey, C. A., Gambrill, E. D., & Blythe, B. J. (1988). Mentor relationships among women in academe. *Affilia, 3,* 34–37.

Riley, S., & Wrench, D. (1985). Mentoring among women lawyers. *Journal of Applied Social Psychology, 15,* 374–386.

Roche, G. R. (1979). Much ado about mentors. *Harvard Business Review, 57,* 14–28.

Rose, G. L. (1999). *What do doctoral students want in a mentor? Development of the ideal mentor scale.* Unpublished doctoral dissertation, University of Iowa.

Russell, J. E. A., & Adams, D. M. (1997). The changing nature of mentoring in organizations: An introduction to the special issues on mentoring and organizations. *Journal of Vocational Behavior, 51,* 1–14.

Sanders, J. M., & Wong, H. Y. (1985). Graduate training and initial job placement. *Sociological Inquiry, 55,* 154–169.

Scandura, T. A. (1992). Mentorship and career mobility: An empirical investigation. *Journal of Organizational Behavior, 13,* 169–174.

Scandura, T. A. (1998). Dysfunctional mentoring relationships and outcomes. *Journal of Management, 24,* 449–467.

Solomon, L. C. (1978). Attracting women to psychology: Effects of university behavior and the labor market. *American Psychologist, 33,* 990–999.

Swerdlik, M. E., & Bardon, J. I. (1988). A survey of mentoring experiences in school psychology. *Journal of School Psychology, 26,* 213–224.

Thomas, D. A. (1990). The impact of race on managers' experiences of developmental relationships (mentoring and sponsorship): An intra-organizational study. *Journal or Organizational Behavior, 11,* 479–492.

Thomas, D. A. (1993). Racial dynamics in

cross-race developmental relationships. *Administrative Science Quarterly, 38,* 169–194.

Torrance, E. P. (1984). *Mentor relationships.* New York: Bearly.

Turban, D. B., & Dougherty, T. W. (1994). Role of protégé personality in receipt of mentoring and career success. *Academy of Management Journal, 37,* 688–702.

University of Michigan. (1999). *How to get the mentoring you want: A guide for graduate students at a diverse university.* Ann Arbor, MI: Author.

Vaillant, G. (1977). *Adaptation to life.* Little, Brown.

VanZandt, C. E. (1990). Professionalism: A matter of personal initiative. *Journal of Counseling and Development, 68,* 243–245.

Watts, R. J. (1987). Development of professional identity in Black clinical psychology students. *Professional Psychology: Research and Practice, 18,* 28–35.

Whitely, W. T., & Coetsier, P. (1993). The relationship of career mentoring to early career outcomes. *Organizational Studies, 14,* 419–441.

Wilde, J. B., & Schau, C. G. (1991). Mentoring in graduate schools of education: Mentees' perceptions. *Journal of Experimental Education,* 165–179.

Wright, C. A., & Wright, S. D. (1987). The role of mentors in the career development of young professionals. *Family Relations, 36,* 204–208.

Zajonc, R. B. (1968). The attitudinal effects of mere exposure. *Journal of Personality and Social Psychology, 9,* 1–27.

Zey, M. G. (1988). A mentor for all reasons. *Personnel Journal, 67,* 46–51.

Zey, M. G. (1991). *The mentor connection: Strategic alliances in corporate life.* New Brunswick, NJ: Transaction.

Zorich, L. L. (1999). *Mentoring across stages of graduate student development: A theoretical model.* Unpublished doctoral dissertation, George Fox University, Newberg, OR.

Zuckerman, H. (1977). *Scientific elite: Nobel laureates in the United States.* New York: Free Press.

Index

A

Abandonment, by mentor, 134, 142
Ability, demonstration of, 46
Acceptance, as psychosocial function, 19, 24
Access to mentors
  by minorities, 170–171
  by women, 165–166
Adams, D. M., 28
Admission guides, to graduate school, 80–81
Advisor, assignment of, 83, 84
Affirmation, of talent, 32–33
Alternative mentorship(s), 178–179
  famous, 185–186, 187
  peer, 183–184
  peer-group, 184–185
  planned, 186–187
  secondary, 180–182
  team, 182–183
Appeasement, as response to problem, 144
Appreciation, communication of, 159–160
Articulation of match, 41, 46
Assertiveness
  in mentor selection
    by minorities, 174–175
    by women, 170
Assistance, asking for, minorities and, 174
Attitudes
  of mentors, 67, 68–69, 73, 74
  similarity of, in ethnic mentors, 172

Attraction
  exposure and, 91–92
  in initiation, 118–119
  in intentional interaction, 91–92
  as issue, 134, 140–141
  liking and, 92
  romantic, in cross-gender mentorships, 140–141, 169–170
  sexual, in cross-gender mentorship, 169
  similarity and, 92
Attractiveness, physical, 92
Autonomy
  achievement of, 120
  protégé adherence to, 147
Availability, of mentor, 67, 71
  lack of, 73, 75

B

Behavioral characteristics
  of faculty, 88
  of mentors
    availability, 71, 73, 75
    communication skills, 71, 73, 75
    mentoring track record, 71–72, 73, 76
    productivity, 69–70, 74
    professional influence and power, 70
Behavior patterns
  of graduate students
    mentored, 41, 45–48
    unmentored, 51–52, 59
Beliefs, irrational, in mentorship, 147
Beneficence, protégé adherence to, 147

Boundaries
  inappropriate
    in friendship/mutuality, 25
    maintenance of confidentiality and, 102, 105–107
    in mentorship, 8–9, 49, 52, 102, 105–107, 129
    violations of, 134, 138–139

C
Career development, of minorities, 171
Career eminence, 34–35
Career function(s), 19
  challenging assignments, 23
  coaching, 22
  evaluation of, 108
  exposure and visibility, 21–22, 121–122
  protection, 22–23, 27, 122
  sponsorship, 20–21
Career interest mismatch, 134, 135
Career planning, in attraction of mentor, 41, 47
Career stage mismatch, 134, 135
Career success, mentorship and, 28–29
Career trajectory, investing in, 121
Case(s)
  compatibility, 63
  Dr. Able, protégé initiative and, 39
  Dr. Angst, emotional dependency of mentor, 129
  Dr. Arctic, procrastination in mentor selection and, 78
  Dr. Balance, women and, 163–164
  Dr. Capital, successful relationship, 97–98
  Dr. Chavez, good match, 77–78
  Dr. Fame, advantages and disadvantages of, 117, 177
  Dr. Frosty, bad match, 130
  Dr. Grant, demands on protégé, 63–64
  Dr. Guidance, and protégé subordination, 156–157
  Dr. Guide, for encouragement and coaching, 17
  Dr. Health, healthy relationship, 113
  Dr. Industry, protégé mediocrity and, 152
  Dr. Majority, ethnic minority and, 163
  Dr. Match, protégé excellence and, 151
  Dr. Mighty, unprofitable, unfulfilling relationship, 17–18
  Dr. Narcissus, dependency/arrogance of, 113–114
  Dr. Spontaneity, failed relationship, 98–99, 104
  Dr. Stat, as secondary mentor, 117, 177
  incompatibility, 63–64

Challenges
  in cultivation stage, 121
  for development, 19, 23, 121
  as mentor function, 23, 122
Coachability, of protégé, 42–43
Coaching, 19, 22
  by mentor, 17
Collaboration
  at conclusion of mentorship, 127
  in research and writing projects, 31–32
Collegiality, in confrontation, 148
Collegial relationship
  at end of mentorship, 126–127
  with mentor, 8
Commitment
  keeping, for protégé excellence, 153, 154
  of protégé, 44
Communication
  of appreciation, by protégé, 153, 159–160
  in attraction of mentor, 41, 47–48
  differences in, in bad matching, 134, 135
  by female mentor, 168
  by mentor, 67, 71
    ineffective, 73, 75, 78
  and protégé excellence, 153, 155–156
Competence, achievement of, in cultivation phase, 120–121
Conduct, unethical, of mentor, 73, 75
Confidence, development of professional, 30–31
Confidentiality, 97
  expectations of, 102, 105–107
Conflict
  in evaluation, 109
  handling of, 97
  interfaculty, 98–99
  unresolved, consequences of, 134, 137–138
Confrontation, of problems, 148
Consultation, for problems, 147–148
Contact, frequency of, 102, 103–104
Contracts
  benefits of, 109–110
  limitations of, 111
  in mentorship, 90, 93–94
  sample, 111
Control, internal locus of, mentoring and, 42
Core expectations
  in contracts, 109–111
  in mentorship
    balanced, 112
    boundaries, 105–107
    confidentiality, 105–107

cross-cultural issues in, 173–175
cross-gender issues in, 168–170
definition of, 99, 101
duration, 102–103
of duration, 103–104
goals, 105
separation, 107
Counseling, 19, 25, 27
Creative achievement, 35–36
Creative synergy, protégé and, 55
Creativity
fostering of, 35–36
sponsorship and, 28
Cross-cultural mentorships
discussion of racial differences in, 174
problems in, 173–175
strategies for, 174
successful, components in, 172–173
Cross-gender mentorships
discussion of, 98
protection in, 23
for women, 168
considerations in, 168
problems and suggestions in, 168–170
Cultivation
characterization of, 117
developmental tasks in, 117, 120–121
mentor functions in, 121–122
mutual trust in, 122
preparation for separation in, 122–123

D
Deadlines, meeting, for protégé excellence, 153, 154
Degree status, in attraction of mentor, 48
Denial, of racial differences, 174
Dependency
of mentor, 129
of protégé, 49, 50
Detachment/avoidance, mentorship and, 49, 50–51
Developmental needs, 114
Developmental tasks
during cultivation, 118, 120–121
identification with mentor, 28
during initiation, 118
mentor functions and, 27
of protégé, 27, 28
in redefinition, 117, 126–127
during separation, 117, 123–124
Disorganization, mentorship and, 49, 52
Dissertation, success of, 32
Distancing, as response to problem, 144
Doctoral programs
attention to mentoring, 82–83
guides to, 82
mentoring structure of, 84–85

responsiveness to direct inquiries, 83–84
satisfaction with, 33
Doctoral *versus* master's degree status, mentorship and, 48
Documentation, of mentorship dysfunction, 149
Dreams
definition of, 33
fostering of, 7, 8, 22, 32–33
Duck, S., 130
Duration, of mentorship, 102–103
Dysfunction. *See also* Problem(s)
criteria for, 132–133
definition of, 132
response to
self-defeating, 143–145
strategies for, 145–149
sources of, 133–143

E
Eminence, career, 34–35
Emotional instability
of mentor, 134, 136–137
mentorship and, 49, 51
Emotional intelligence
of mentor, 134, 136–137
of protégé, 41–43, 43
Emotional stability, of protégé, 40–42
Employment
early, 34
of minorities, 171
Erikson, E., 53
Ethical principles, protégé adherence to, 147
Ethics
development of
and mentoring of minorities, 171
of mentor, unprofessional, 73–75, 134, 141
Ethnicity
in cross-cultural mentorships, problems in, 173–175
difference of, in mentorships, 172–173
in precommitment stage, 87
similarity of, 77–78
importance of, 172
Evaluation
approaches to, 109
frequency of, 108
importance of, 102, 107–109
problems with, 109
scope of, 108
Excellent work, 153, 155
Expectations
in bad matching, 134, 135
clarification of, 99
definition of, 101

Expectations (*Continued*)
  differences in, 99
  shared, 99–101
  similarities and differences in, 100
  unrealistic, 118–119
Exploitation
  academic, 140
  emotional, 140
  sexual, 139–140
Exposure, 19, 21–22
  in mentorship initiation, 91–92

F
Faculty
  information about, 88
    from graduate students, 86, 88–89
  minority status and mentorship of, 89
  personal contact with, 86
  student ratings of, 86–87
Faculty interests
  postadmission, 85–86
  preadmission, 83
Famous mentors, 179, 185–186, 187
Feedback
  from faculty to protégé, 59–60
  from protégé to mentor, 109
Fidelity, protégé adherence to, 147
Fiduciary relationship, definition of, 138–139
First-semester reconnaissance, faculty information gathering in, 88
Flexibility, expectations and, 101
Friendship, 19, 25
  with protégé, 56
Function(s) of mentor, 19, 117
  career, 20–23
  during cultivation phase, 121–122
  factors shaping, 27
  during initiation of mentorship, 119
  psychosocial, 20, 23–28
    evaluation of, 108
  validation of, 20

G
Gender
  in mentorship. *See* Cross-gender mentorships; Same-gender mentorships
  in precommitment stage, 87
Gender role socialization, cross-gender mentoring and, 169
Generativity
  comparison with mentoring, 53
  versus stagnation, 55–56
Goals
  evaluation of, 108

of mentor, 153, 158–159
of protégé
  in mentorship relationship, 105
Graduate programs
  costs of, 4
  student ratings of faculty in, 86–87
Graduate school
  admission guides to, 80–81
  doctoral program guides to, 82
  faculty interests in, 82, 85–86
  first semester, 87–90
  initiation of mentorship in, 90–94
  mentoring in
    imperfect world of, 10–12
    prevalence of, 9–10
  postadmission reconnaissance, 84–87
  preapplication reconnaissance and, 80–84
Graduate students. *See also* Protégé
  faculty information from
    current, 86, 88–89
    former, 89
  mentored, 40–48
    articulation of match by, 46
    behavior patterns of, 41, 45–48
    career planning of, 47
    coachability of, 42–43
    commitment of, 44
    communication skills of, 47–48
    demonstration of ability and achievement by, 46
    emotional intelligence of, 43
    emotional stability of, 40–42
    initiation of mentorship by, 39, 45–46
    internal locus of control in, 42
    personality characteristics of, 40–45
    similarity to mentor, 45
  success of, factors in, 79
  unmentored, 49–52
    behavior patterns of, 49, 51–52
    characteristics of, 49–51
    dependent/needy, 41, 50
    detached/avoidant, 50–51
    emotional instability of, 51
    narcissistic/arrogant, 49, 50
    personality characteristics of, 49, 50–51
    procrastination of, 51
    underachievement of, 51–52

H
Halo effect, of mentor, 82
Hirschberg, N., 79
Humor, maintenance of, by protégé, 153, 160–161
Huwe, J. M., 142

I

Ideal mentor, 64–65
Illegal behavior, 134, 141
Imposter syndrome, 30–31
Income, mentoring and, 33–34
Incompetence of mentor
 relational, 134, 136–137
 technical
  mentoring, 136
  subject, 134, 135–136
Independence, sponsorship and, 28
Influence, professional, 67, 70
Information, protégé as source of, 54
Initiation
 attraction, potential, synergy in, 118–119
 characterization of, 117
 description of, 115
 first semester, 87–90
 formal, 189–190
 intentional interaction in, 90–93
 mentor functions in, 117, 119
 of mentorship, 41, 46, 77, 78–79
  failure to, 78
  gender concerns in, 169
 postadmission, 84–87
 preapplication, 80–84
Initiative
 mentoring and, 39
 of protégé, 39
Innovation, protégé promotion of, 35
Integrity, establishment of, 121
Intentional interaction, in mentorship
  formation, 90–92
Intentionality, in secondary mentor
  selection, 180–181
Internships, securing, 32
Interpersonal relationships, mentor
  incompetence in, 136
Interpersonal style, differences in, in
  cross-cultural mentorships, 173
Itkin, S., 79

J

Johnson, W. B., 106, 140, 142

K

Kram, K. E., 5–6, 114
 phasic model of mentorship
  development, 115–116

L

Lateral mentoring. *See* Peer mentoring
Levinson, D. J., 5, 25–26, 28, 33
Loyalty, of protégé, 54–55

M

Majority mentor
 culturally sensitive, 171
  for racial/ethnic minority student, 163
 problems with, 173–174
  strategies for, 174
Master's-degree status, mentorship in, 48
Match
 articulation of, 41, 46
 compatible, 63
 incompatible, 63–64, 130, 133–135
 mentor characteristics in, 14
Mediocrity, of protégé, 152–153
Mentee. *See* Protégé
Mentoring
 definitions of, 25–26
 description of, 3–16
 group/team approach to, 83
 guide to, rationale for, 3–5
 learning to, 36
 obstacles to
  cultural, 11–12
  department-specific, 11
  relational, 12
  structural, 11
Mentor mania, 4
Mentor(s)
 assignment of, 83, 84
 attitudes and values of, 68–69, 73, 74
 bad, 72–74
 benefits of, 17
 characteristics of, 14, 65–66
  behavioral, 67, 69–72
  ideal, 66
  personality, 66–69
 definitions of, 6
 female, 166–167
  advantages for female protégé, 167–168
 functions of, 7–8. *See* Functions(s) of
  mentor
 good, 65–72
 graduate vs. undergraduate school, 6
 historical perspective on, 5
 ideal, 64–65
 initiation of formal meeting with, 89–90
 male, discomfort with cross-gender
  mentorships, 169
 mentoring benefits to, 36, 53–56
  extrinsic, 53–55
  intrinsic, 55–56
 personality traits of, 66–68, 73
 selection of, 63–94
 work habits of, 68, 73, 74
Mentorship(s). *See also* Alternative
  mentorship(s)
 alternatives to traditional, 178

Mentorship(s) (*Continued*)
  benefits of, 28–29
    in informal vs. formal, 29
    for nontraditional students, 36–37
    postdoctoral, 33–36, 152
    predoctoral, 29–33, 152
  comparison of formal (assigned) and
    informal (nonassigned), 110
  core expectations in, 99, 102–109
  cross-gender, women and, 168–170
  cultivation of, 115, 117, 119–123
  dysfunction in, 132–133. *See also*
    Problem(s)
    sources of, 133–143
  evaluation of, 102, 107–112
  facilitation of, 83
  factors contributing to, 91–92
  formal, 84–85
  formalization of, 93–94. *See also*
    Contracting
  informal, 85
  initiation of, 115, 116, 117, 118–119
  "no fault" escape in, 100
  peer, 179, 183–184
  peer-group, 184–185
  phases of, 113–127
    examples of, 113–114
  primary, 6–7
  redefinition of, 115, 117, 1226–127
  same-gender
    advantages of, 167–168
    for women, 166–167
  secondary, 7, 177, 180–181
  separation in, 115, 117, 123–125
    problems in, 125–126
  shared expectations in
    definition of, 101
    importance of, 99–101
  strategies for securing. *See*
    Reconnaissance
  teaching, 30
  variables in, 7
Merriam, S., 5
Minorities
  access to mentors, 170–171
  assertiveness of, importance of, 174–
    175
  cross-cultural mentor and, 172–175
  mentoring of, 170–173
    benefits of, 171
  same-culture mentors for, 181–182
  same-race mentors for, 177, 181–182
  secondary mentors for, 181
Mistakes, admission of, by protégé, 153,
  160
Mistrust, in cross-cultural mentorships,
  173

Mobility, career, 34
Mutuality
  definition of, 19
  of mentor-protégé, 56
  in mentorship formation, 79
  of needs, 91
  in redefinition phase, 127
  of trust, establishment of, 122

N
Narcissism/arrogance, mentorship and, 49,
  50
Narcissism, of protégé, 157
Neediness, of protégé, 129
Needs
  of mentor, 91
  of protégé, 41, 50, 91
Neglect, by mentor, 134, 137
Nelson, N., 106, 140
Network
  mentoring
    definition of, 188
    of minorities, 171
    personal mentoring, 179, 187–189
Networking, mentor enhancement of, 31
Nobel laureates
  mentoring and, 4
  mentor selection and, 12–13
Nonmalfeasance, protégé adherence to,
  147
Nontraditional (second-career) students
  need for mentoring, 36–37
  obstacles for, 37

O
Obligation to society, mentorship as, 56
Obstacles
  to mentoring, 11–12
  for nontraditional students, 37
Overprotection, 23

P
Paralysis, as response to problem, 144
Peer-group mentoring, 179, 184–185
  cross-discipline, 185
  formation of, 184–185
Peer mentoring, 179, 183–184
  advantages of, 183–184
  importance of, 184
Peers
  as model for protégé, 58–59
Personality characteristics
  of graduate students
    mentored, 40–45
    unmentored, 49, 50–51
  of mentor, 66–69
    problematic, 136

Personality differences, in bad matching, 134–135
Personality traits, of mentors, 66–68, 73
Personal mentoring network, 179, 187–189
  as alternative to traditional mentoring, 187
  composition of, 188
  construction of, 188–189
Phillips-Jones, L., 24, 56, 100
Planned mentoring programs, 179, 186–187
Plaut, S. M., 140
Power
  dynamics of, in cross-cultural mentorships, 173
  professional, 67, 70
  reflective, 21
Power base, protégé in, 54–55
Primary mentor, 6–7, 177
Primary mentorship, alternatives/additions to, 179–189
Problem(s). *See also* Dysfunction
  abandonment, 142
  attraction, 140–141
  bad match, 133–135
  boundary violations, 138–139
  conflict, 137–138
  exploitation, 139–140
  mentor neglect, 137
  protégé traits, 142–143
  relational incompetence, 136–137
  response to
    self-defeating, 143–145
    strategies for, 145–149
  in separation, 125–126
  technical incompetence, 135–136
  unethical/illegal behavior, mentor, 141
Procrastination
  mentoring and, 39–40
  mentorship and, 49, 51
  strategies for eliminating, 59
Productivity
  of faculty, 83, 85–86
  of mentor, 69–70
    lack of, 74
  predoctoral, 31–32
  protégé and, 53–54
Professional activities, of faculty, 88
Professional associations, membership in, secondary mentorship and, 182
Professional identity
  development of, 30–31
    in cultivation phase, 120
    in women, 166
  peer-group mentoring and, 184

Professional identity crisis, mentorship and, 116, 118
Professional skill development, predoctoral, 29–30
Prominence, of mentor, 67, 70
Promotion, career, 34
Protection, 19
  in cross-gender mentorship, 23
  during cultivation phase, 122
  in cultivation stage, 122
  forms of, 22–23
Protégé
  action strategies for, 58–60
  behavior patterns of, 41, 45–48
    negative, 49, 51–52
    positive, 41, 45–48
  contribution to dysfunction, 146–147
  definition of, 6
  developmental tasks of, 28
  examples of
    excellent, 151
    mediocre, 151–152
  peer role modeling for, 58–59
  personality characteristics of, 40–45
    negative, 49, 50–51
    positive, 40–45
  prelude to being, 12–13
  problem traits of, 134, 142–143
  role of, 27–28, 156–157
  self-assessment inventory for, 56–58
Protégé excellence, strategies for, 153–161
Provocation
  as response to problem, 143, 145
  self-defeating, 145
Proximity, in mentorship initiation, 91
Psychological support, from protégé, 53
Psychology graduate students
  mentoring of, prevalence of, 9–10
  survey of functions in mentor relationship, 26, 27
Psychosocial function(s), 19, 20, 27–28
  acceptance and confirmation, 24
  counseling, 25–27
  friendship/mutuality, 25, 26, 27
  role modeling, 23–24
Publication record, mentor, 69–70

R
Race
  differences in, problems and strategies in, 173–174
  majority
    mentorship problems and, 173–174
    in precommitment stage, 87

Race (*Continued*)
  same
    in mentor relationship, 181–182
    in mentor selection, 172
    in secondary mentorship, 181–182
Redefinition
  characterization of, 117
  developmental tasks in, 117
Reflection, versus impulsive response, 146
Reflective power, through sponsorship, 21
Research
  collaboration in, 31–32
  in graduate school, 82
  mentor performance in, 69
  protégé in, 21
Responsibility, protégé acceptance of, 153, 157–158
Risk taking, as developmental task, 120
Role, protégé, subordination to mentor, 156–157
Role conflict, confidentiality and, 106–107
Role flexibility, of protégé, 27–28
Role modeling, 19, 23–24
  expectations of protégé, 102, 104–105
  by female mentor, 167–168
  by mentor, 8
  in teaching mentorships, 30
  for women, 166–167
Russell, J. E., 28

S
Sabotage, as response to problem, 143, 145
Same-culture mentors, for minority students, 181–182
Same-gender mentorships
  gay/lesbian
    gender-based problems in, 169
  for women, 167–168
Same-race
  in mentor relationship, 181–182
  in mentor selection, 172
  in secondary mentorship, 181–182
Satisfaction
  career, 35, 166
  with doctoral program
    mentorship and, 33
  in mentorship, 55
Scholars, as mentors, 179, 185–186
Secondary mentor, 7, 177
  characterization of, 180
  intentionality, in search of, 180–181
  same-race, same-culture, 181–182
  for women and minorities, 181

Second-career students. *See* Nontraditional (second-career) students
Self-assessment inventory, protégé, 56–58
Self-care, in protégé excellence, 153, 158
Self-esteem, mentor and, 17, 24
Separation
  acceptance of, 124
  characterization of, 117
  developmental tasks in, 117, 123
  mentor's function in, 125
  planning for, 102, 107
  preparation for, 122–123
  problems in, 125–126
  rites of passage in, 123
Sexual relationships
  as boundary violation, 139
  as exploitation, 140
Similarity
  in mentorship initiation, 92
  of protégé to mentor, 45
Sponsorship
  during cultivation phase, 122
  in graduate school, 19, 20–21
  for postdoctoral training and employment, 21
  for women, 166
Stereotypes, sexist, in cross-gender mentorships, 168
Stress
  mentorship and, 116, 118
  in separation phase, 124
Subordination, of protégé to mentor, 156–157
Support
  from mentor, lack of, 73, 75
  from protégé, 73, 75
Suppression, of racial differences, 174
Synergy, 28
  in mentorship initiation, 118–119
  protégé and, 55

T
Talent, affirmation of, 32–33
Team mentoring, 83, 85, 179, 182–183
  advantage to faculty, 182–183
  advantage to protégé, 182
  disadvantages to protégé, 183
Technical support, from protégé, 53
Termination
  in expected duration, 103
  of mentorship, 102, 107
  in mentorship dysfunction, 148–149
Time frame, in mentorship, 117
Tolerance, of self, 60
Torrance, E. P., 28
Track record, mentoring, 67, 71–72
Training opportunities, securing, 32

U

Underachievement, mentorship and, 49, 51–52
Unethical behavior, 73, 75
  of mentor, 134, 141

V

Vaillant, G., 5
Validation, 8
  of mentor functions, 20
Values
  development of
    in minorities, 171
  of mentors, 67, 68–69, 73–74
  similarity of, in ethnic mentors, 172
Visibility, protégé contribution to, 55

W

Weakness, target and develop areas of, 59

Women
  access to mentors, 165–166
  assertiveness and, importance of, 170
  cross-gender mentorships of, 168
    problems and suggestions for, 168–170
  mentoring of, 165–170
    benefits of, 166–167
  mentorship of, 163–164
    need for, 165–166
    same-gender, 167–168
  secondary mentors for, 181
Work habits
  of mentors, 67, 68, 73, 74
  of protégé, 39
Work style, in bad matching, 134, 135
Writing projects
  collaboration in, 31–32
  for women, 166

About the Authors

W. Brad Johnson is assistant professor of psychology in the Department of Leadership, Ethics, and Law at the U.S. Naval Academy and a faculty associate in the Graduate School of Business and Education at Johns Hopkins University. He is also an adjunct professor at the Naval Post-Graduate School in Monterey, CA. He earned a PhD in clinical psychology from Fuller Theological Seminary. A former Lieutenant Commander in the Navy's Medical Service Corps, Dr. Johnson served as a clinical psychologist at Bethesda Naval Hospital and at the Medical Clinic at Pearl Harbor, where he was the division head for psychology. He is a fellow and supervisor of the Institute for Rational Emotive Behavior Therapy in New York. Prior to joining the Naval Academy faculty, Dr. Johnson spent 4 years as a faculty member and director of research for the APA-approved clinical doctorate program at George Fox University in Oregon. He has been a member of Oregon's Board of Bar Examiners and an oral examiner for Oregon's Board of Psychologist Examiners.

Dr. Johnson has authored more than 50 scholarly articles and book chapters, as well as three books, in the areas of ethical behavior, mentor relationships, psychotherapy outcomes, and personality characteristics among distinct military populations. He is a contributing editor to several journals in the field of psychology. Dr. Johnson's primary research and training focus during the past 5 years has been on mentoring in higher education.

Jennifer M. Huwe is a psychologist resident at the Portland VA Medical Center. Dr. Huwe's clinical work currently focuses on the assessment and treatment of posttraumatic stress disorder in women veterans. She completed her APA-approved internship at the Portland VA Medical Center and her doctorate of clinical psychology at George Fox University. Dr. Huwe's dissertation explored the mentor relationships of highly distinguished naval admirals. Prior to completing her doctorate, she was an adjunct professor in the Department of Psychology at George Fox University. Dr. Huwe spent 4 years working in physiological research at Oregon Health and Sciences University prior to beginning graduate school. She has authored six scholarly articles and one book on the topic of mentor relationships.